Leading Teens to Freedom in Christ

Leading Teens to Freedom in Christ

Neil Anderson
and
Rich Miller

Regal

A Division of Gospel Light
Ventura, California, U.S.A.

Published by Regal Books
A Division of Gospel Light
Ventura, California, U.S.A.
Printed in U.S.A.

Scripture taken from the New American Standard Bible, © 1960, 1962, 1963, 1968, 1971, 1972, 1973, 1975, 1977 by The Lockman Foundation. Used by permission.

Other versions used are:
NIV—Scripture quotations are taken from the Holy Bible, New International Version®. NIV®. Copyright © 1973, 1978, 1984 by International Bible Society. Used by permission of Zondervan Publishing House. All rights reserved.
NKJV—Scripture taken from the New King James Version. Copyright © 1979, 1980, 1982 by Thomas Nelson, Inc. Publishers. Used by permission. All rights reserved.

Cover Design by Barbara LeVan Fisher
Interior Design by Britt Rocchio
Edited by Virginia Woodard

Library of Congress Cataloging-in-Publication Data
Anderson, Neil T., 1942-
    Helping young people find freedom in Christ / Neil Anderson and Rich Miller.
        p. cm.
    Includes bibliographical references.
    ISBN 0-8307-1840-0 (pbk.)
    1. Church work with teenagers. 2. Teenagers—Religious life.
    I. Miller, Rich, 1954- . II. Title.
    BV4447.A46 1997   97-8893
    259'.23—dc21   CIP

1 2 3 4 5 6 7 8 9 10 11 12 13 14 15 16 17 / 04 03 02 01 00 99 98 97

Rights for publishing this book in other languages are contracted by Gospel Literature International (GLINT). GLINT also provides technical help for the adaptation, translation and publishing of Bible study resources and books in scores of languages worldwide. For further information, contact GLINT, P.O. Box 4060, Ontario, CA 91761-1003, U.S.A., or the publisher.

··· Contents ···

Appendices

A Cry for Love

"The hardest thing was the wake. Seeing my brother lying there, and saying my last words to him. That's what they told me I should do."

Nine days before my (Rich's) conversation with Kevin, his younger brother, Marty, had ended his life—a fatal gunshot wound to the head.

This time Marty had wanted to make sure. Six months earlier he had survived his first suicide attempt—slashing his wrists. More than 80 stitches had been needed to put him back together that time. It was a cry for help, a cry for love. This time, though, all the king's horses and all the king's men...

> According to the National Youth Suicide Prevention Center in Washington, D.C., every hour of every day, approximately 228 teenagers in the United States attempt to take their lives. That is nearly 2 million a year.

He was only 18. A quiet, introverted young man, but by no means timid. In bondage to alcohol since he was 15, Marty got into fights a lot. Being more than six feet tall and weighing 200 pounds, he did not lose many battles; but he tragically lost the war for his life.

He always tried to measure up to his older, more extroverted brother, Kevin. Alcohol helped him to be outgoing and that was what hooked him. He just did not seem to be happy unless he was drunk or high on hash.

> According to the Encyclopedia of Youth Studies, 3.3 million 13- to 17-year-olds in the United States have serious alcohol problems.[1] An article published by the National Institute on Drug Abuse (NIDA) says that 41 percent of high school seniors have used marijuana.[2] A recent survey cosponsored by the NIDA shows that among illegal drugs, marijuana use is increasing the fastest among senior high school students.[3]

Marty had taken a Polaroid picture of himself and had written "I hate you! I hate you! I hate you!" all over it. A year before his suicide, he had drawn a picture of a head showing a gun pointed to it. Underneath was the caption "Life sucks."

His poem, entitled "A Good Day," is a story of grabbing for gratification without lasting satisfaction that Marty, like so many other teens, experienced:

> Icehouse, Lite, girls and hash
> Oh my god, what a bash!
> Trees, grass and the blue sunshine
> Look here now, the world is mine!
> Walking on water, standing on air,
> Do these things and people stare
> For this poem tells me so.
> Sometimes you feel like a "ho." [a prostitute]
> You always drive like a maniac
> When you get home you start to yack.
> You finally grab for the bed
> Then the pain reaches your head.
> When you wake up from your snooze
> Another day you've got to lose.

Several months before he took his life, Marty wrote in his journal:

I know that people care about me, so I don't want to hurt those people by killing myself. Hopefully God will make my life better. I don't know what I will do with myself if these people die.

Sadly, Marty never discovered the path to freedom God had planned for him. Our hope is that he has now found it in the arms of Jesus.

Like Marty, many teenagers today feel trapped in what could be called the "Less" Mess. They feel useless, worthless, helpless, purposeless and hopeless. Despair in many cases has robbed our teens of the idealism, energy and creativity of youth. "The thief comes only to steal, and kill, and destroy" (John 10:10).

Another sad incident exposes the sense of helplessness and hopelessness far too many young people feel today. A pastor friend of mine (Rich's) related to me the conversation he had with the mother of a young man who had just died of AIDS. She told of a heart-to-heart talk she had with her son just prior to his death.

"Mom, do you think I will go to hell for the things I've done?" The dying man looked up, hoping for reassurance. Another cry for love.

"I don't know, honey, but I bet a minister would know. A minister could answer that question. Do you want me to call one?"

The young man shook his head, discouraged. "No, mom, I'm sure a minister wouldn't want to talk to someone like me."

Two weeks too late my pastor friend found out about the young man's death. Tragically, I know that this minister (and most others, too) *would* have wanted to talk to him—to bring him good news of salvation and the hope of eternal life even in the face of death.

Not just "underachievers" like Marty, or AIDS victims are at risk. The "cream of the crop" of teens are locked in a life-and-death struggle for survival as well.

A survey of "Who's Who Among American High School Students" uncovered that 30 percent had considered suicide and 4 percent had actually made an attempt on their lives.

Why? Why would kids who seemingly had everything going for

them and a bright future ahead consider ending it all? Believe it or not, 86 percent felt worthless, 71 percent felt pressure to succeed and 65 percent were afraid to fail.[4]

Unfortunately, far too many teens have no clue about the real hope for life and freedom in Jesus and the Church. Sadly, the gospel remains one of the best-kept secrets in our nation.

A study by Josh McDowell Ministries discovered that in 1960 the greatest influences on 13- to 19-year-olds were, in order: the family, school, friends and peers, the Church. Twenty years later the changes were profound. The top four influences were, in order: friends and peers, family, the media, school. The Church had dropped out of the top four altogether.

Teenagers of today have largely been captured by the value system (or lack thereof) of the god of this world. It is the responsibility of Christian families and the Church to join the Lord Jesus Christ's mission to rescue this generation. There is no other hope.

In John 8:31,32, the words of Jesus rattled the souls of a group of Jewish believers. Those same words are meant to strip the scales from our eyes as well. Let's take a moment and eavesdrop on that eye-opening conversation:

> Jesus therefore was saying to those Jews who had believed Him, "If you abide in My word, then you are truly disciples of Mine; and you shall know the truth, and the truth shall make you free."

Did you catch it? The *truth* shall make you free. Not a program. Not a book. Not a counselor. The truth. From the context of Jesus' words, it is clear the truth He is referring to is the Word of God.

Some of those listening, however, took exception to what Jesus had to say, as John recorded for us:

> They answered Him, "We are Abraham's offspring, and have never yet been enslaved to anyone; how is it that You say, 'You shall become free'?" (v. 33).

Jesus' reply cut to their hearts and cuts to ours as well.

Jesus answered them, "Truly, truly, I say to you, everyone who commits sin is the slave of sin. And the slave
does not remain in the house forever; the son does
remain forever. If therefore the Son shall make you
free, you shall be free indeed" (vv. 34-36).

Jesus' message is simple and clear: Sin brings bondage. Truth lib-
erates. And the One who uses the truth of the Word of God to set us
free is the Son of God, Jesus. He is "the Truth" (John 14:6) and the
Word of God made flesh (see John 1:14). He is the "Wonderful
Counselor" (Isa. 9:6), not us.

What young people in bondage need is not a "what" at all; it is a
"Who." It is Jesus. He is the bondage breaker. A truth encounter—
really a Truth (Jesus) encounter—sets the captives free. The mission
of the Messiah, the Lord Jesus Christ, was spelled out with crystal
clarity by the prophet, Isaiah:

> The Spirit of the Sovereign Lord is on me, because the
> Lord has anointed me to preach good news to the poor.
> He has sent me to bind up the broken-hearted, to pro-
> claim freedom for the captives and release from dark-
> ness for the prisoners, to proclaim the year of the
> Lord's favor and the day of vengeance of our God, to
> comfort all who mourn, and provide for those who
> grieve in Zion—to bestow on them a crown of beauty
> instead of ashes, the oil of gladness instead of mourn-
> ing, and a garment of praise instead of a spirit of
> despair (Isa. 61:1-3, *NIV*).

Poor. Brokenhearted. Captives. Darkness. Prisoners. Mourning.
Grieving. Despair. Doesn't this describe the condition of many of our
young people today? Doesn't this describe the condition of many of
our *Christian* young people today? Sure, they may appear happy on
the outside, but what about deep down where only God sees?

I (Neil) wanted to find out what was happening in the lives of
young people, because the vast majority of adults' problems origi-
nated when they were children. So Steve Russo and I surveyed more

than 1,700 junior and senior high students for our book *The Seduction of Our Children*. We discovered that 71 percent of those professing Christian young people were hearing voices or struggling with bad thoughts.[5]

Do we believe that 7 out of 10 of our evangelical young people are paranoid schizophrenic or psychotic (as many counselors would diagnose them)? No, we don't! But we concur with 1 Timothy 4:1:

> But the Spirit explicitly says that in later times some will fall away from the faith, paying attention to deceitful spirits and doctrines of demons.

Is that happening? Yes, it is happening throughout the world! Much of what is being passed off as mental illness is nothing more than a battle for the mind.

Just as troubling to us is the 72 percent of teenagers surveyed who said they are different from other kids—that is: Christianity works for others, but not for them![6] Is that true? Of course not. Every one of God's children has been given everything needed for life and godliness (see 2 Pet. 1:3). If they believe they are different or hopeless or helpless or evil or dirty, however, will it affect the way they try to live their Christian lives? Absolutely!

So what is wrong with our Christian young people? What is wrong with our Christian families? What is wrong with our churches?

Doesn't the Bible say we are "more than conquerors through him who loved us" (Rom. 8:37, *NIV*) and we "can do all things through Him who strengthens" us (Phil. 4:13)? The pages of the New Testament sure seem to provide a lot more hope for victory than we see in the pews of the average church. Why is that?

Unfortunately, all too often the Christian faith has become a one-day-a-week spectator sport rather than a dynamic, intimate relationship with the living Lord and His Body. Too often Christian education involves merely imparting facts and information rather than developing loving character. Too often Christian counseling is dependent upon the latest technique instead of upon the guidance of the Holy Spirit.

In many cases, the good news of the gospel has been emasculated into a legalistic liturgy of "do's and don'ts," or simply an intellectual pursuit of head knowledge that fails to touch the heart.

Young people can sin and go down the wrong path in life a million and one ways, but the way home is always the same—"repentance toward God and faith in our Lord Jesus" (Acts 20:21). A teenager could have been abused in a variety of ways, but he or she would still have to forgive the abuser to be free in Christ (see Matt. 18:32-35).

Thousands of self-help groups, programs, counselors and psychological models are available to choose from, but the only answer is "Christ in you, the hope of glory" (Col. 1:27). Do we *really* believe that? Are we really convinced that apart from Christ we can do *nothing* (see John 15:5)?

Through my (Neil) study of the Scriptures and interaction with hurting people, I have been able to pinpoint seven major areas in which people typically struggle in their walk with Christ. Dave Park and Rich Miller then "high-schoolized" what have since been named the "Steps to Freedom in Christ." Those seven areas are as follows:

1. Counterfeit Versus Real
2. Deception Versus Truth
3. Bitterness Versus Forgiveness
4. Rebellion Versus Submission
5. Pride Versus Humility
6. Bondage Versus Freedom
7. Curses Versus Blessings

What we have discovered in walking people through this thorough spiritual inventory is that our "freedom appointments" are first and foremost an encounter with God. This ministry tool—the Steps to Freedom in Christ—simply provides the structure through which the Holy Spirit works. It is a *guide,* not a *god.*

Dependence upon the Holy Spirit on the part of the "encourager" (counselor) is critical to the success of the appointment. Of equal importance is the willingness of the counselee to honestly face and work through the issues in his or her life. Both of these factors will be discussed later on in this book.

We believe that the Steps to Freedom in Christ are simple enough that any spiritually minded, caring Christian can be trained to use them effectively. We recognize, however, that we dare not be simplistic in our approach. The human heart and human body are extremely complex.

We thank God for competent medical doctors, nutritionists and physical therapists who help us take care of our physical bodies. We live in a physical as well as a spiritual world and God created both. We need both the hospital and the Church because we are both physical and spiritual beings.

If we do not believe God's Word speaks authoritatively to the mental, emotional and spiritual needs of people, however, we are doomed to wallow in the mire of the latest counseling fad or technique. If we do not believe in the reality of the supernatural world and have a clear grasp of its interaction with us as believers, we are limited to helping people merely *cope* with the issues in their lives rather than *conquering* them in Christ.

Fortunately, we have a complete God and a complete gospel that interact with the complete person—body, soul and spirit.

What This Book Is About

In this book, we want to share with you—whether you are a parent of a teen, a youth leader or just a caring friend of a young person in need—what we have learned about helping young people find freedom in Christ. In the first part of the book we will focus on the following areas:

- Address some of the issues that make the teenage years so explosive;
- Talk about how we as adults can let young people know that we are on their team;
- Examine the role of the Holy Spirit and the power of intercessory prayer in watching teens find freedom in Christ;
- See what it takes to be used by God to help hurting teens;
- Discuss the difference between *freedom* and *maturity*.

Then, in the second part of the book we will walk you step by step through the process of taking a young person through the Steps to Freedom in Christ. We will look at how to set up and start the appointment, what to expect during each of the seven Steps, as well as how to finish your time together and provide encouragement for continued growth.

In the chapters that follow, we will also take a peek at some of the tough issues in counseling youth—abuse, occult bondage, eating disorders and rebellion.

If you desire a more comprehensive explanation of the theology, philosophy and methodology of discipleship counseling for adults, we recommend you read Neil's book *Helping Others Find Freedom in Christ.*

Our desire and prayer is that this book will be a resource of hope for you. Maybe you are a sincere Christian parent of a teenage son or daughter who is apathetic or rebellious toward God. Maybe you are a youth leader who yearns to help a depressed teen in your youth group. Maybe you hurt for a niece, nephew, grandson or granddaughter who is dabbling in the occult.

Whatever your reason for reading this book, be encouraged as you hurt for and seek to help the young people around you. Whatever your age, temperament, spiritual maturity level, experience (or lack of experience) with teens, God can use you to have a significant influence on young people.

You do not have to be a stand-up comic to get the attention of teenagers. You do not have to be a great athlete or be up on all the latest music, TV shows, movies or video games to gain an ear. You do not have to be a "wild and crazy guy" to have a profound influence on a young person's life.

What teens are looking for is adults who will be real with them and who will love and accept them and hang in there with them in spite of their mood swings, demands, failures, struggles and sins.

Poor. Brokenhearted. Captive. Darkness. Prisoners. Mourning. Grieving. Despair. Christian young people are hurting. *Who* they need is Christ. *What* they need is for us to be a light to point them to Christ, and to see that all their "acting out" is really expressing a deep-down, gut-level, desperate need for attention and affirmation.

Ultimately, it is a cry for God. It is a cry for love.

Christ will answer that cry by bringing good news to the poor, binding up the brokenhearted, proclaiming freedom to captives and releasing prisoners from darkness.

He will comfort those who mourn and bring a crown of beauty to the grieving and a garment of praise to those who are in despair.

What will be the result in the lives of those to whom the Messiah ministers in this way? Let's allow Isaiah to finish his prophecy:

> They will be called oaks of righteousness, a planting of the Lord for the display of his splendor. They will rebuild the ancient ruins and restore the places long devastated; they will renew the ruined cities that have been devastated for generations (Isa. 61:3,4, *NIV*).

Do you believe that your son or daughter, youth group member, friend, neighbor, niece, nephew, grandson or granddaughter could become an "oak of righteousness"? Could almighty God take the struggling teens you know and use them to *rebuild, restore* and *renew* this troubled land?

It all starts with freedom. It all starts with the truth. It all starts with Jesus Christ.

Part One

Understanding Our Teenagers

chapter one

Teenagers! What Makes Them Tick?

Mark Twain was quoted as saying, "When a child turns twelve you should put him in a barrel, nail the lid down, and feed him through a knot hole. When he turns sixteen, plug the hole."[1]

If you are a parent of a teen, you may be thinking, *Hmm, the old chap might be on to something there!* The days of being able to reasonably predict your child's behavior being long gone, you probably have resigned yourself to six or seven years of predictable unpredictability!

One day your kids think you hung the moon and the next day they are questioning whether you have the intelligence to hang your clothes! Time was when they wanted to be picked up, held and cuddled, and now suddenly they run from you, shouting, "Unclean! Unclean!"

Perhaps you have discovered the following three great truths of teenagers after naively trying to find out *anything* about what they have been up to:

Their favorite thing to do: *Nuthin'*.
Their favorite place to go: *Nowhere*.
Their favorite answer to any other question: *I dunno*.

You also may be able to relate to the following common and honest cries of frustration from parents of teens:

What in the world do I have to do to get through to this kid?
What happened to my little girl? She's never home anymore!
What did we do wrong? We tried our best! Why did he turn out this way?

Of course, our comments about teenagers are generalizations, but allow us to begin by stating the obvious. The teenage years are a time of explosive change—God-designed change, incidentally—to move a person from childhood to adulthood.

Physically, adolescents sprout hair and develop muscles (and fat!) where they had not been before. Voices change, bodies grow and hormones course through their veins like a flash flood. Endless hours are spent in front of the mirror doing major surgery on pimples that probably no one else will notice. Understandably, it is a time of great confusion, anticipation, anxiety and vulnerability for teens.

To that boiling cauldron of change, add a sex drive that has kicked in from neutral to overdrive. Toss in a growing desire for independence from parents. Throw in a developing cognitive ability to question, think, rethink and make decisions, and you have an emotional time bomb controlled by a hair trigger.

Try to tell your teenagers something, and you may be accused of *yelling* at them. Offer to help them through a problem, and you are likely to be chastised for *treating them like babies*. Should you be so bold and audacious as to ask questions about their friends or activities, you are quickly criticized for *invading their privacy*.

As anyone who has ever raised teens or worked with them for any length of time will tell you, however, they also have an incredible potential for good. Not just "when they grow up," either. Right now.

In my 20 years of youth ministry, I (Rich) have seen teens raise thousands of dollars to travel to foreign missions projects. I have seen them stand up in front of large groups of their schoolmates and boldly proclaim the gospel. I have seen them compassionately surround, embrace and pray for a hurting friend. I have seen Jesus shine through the lives of teenagers and as a result, glorified their Father in heaven.

In raising or working with teenagers, it is critical that we come to the point of being able to see life—at least in the core areas—from their vantage point. Take yourself back to those emotional roller-coaster days of your own adolescence for a moment.

Remember the intense longing to fit in when you felt as though you stuck out? Can you recall the frustration of being expected to act like an adult while being treated like a child? Remember the growing desire for independence while secretly hoping your parents loved you enough to still set (realistic!) boundaries?

Try to put yourself in the Nikes of today's youth as we talk about perhaps the most critical area for teenagers. It also happens to be the most critical area for finding freedom in Christ as well—*the search for identity.*

The Search for Identity

"Identity crisis." That phrase was coined by Erik Erikson during World War II. It was used to describe the confusion some shell-shocked soldiers in the heat of battle experienced. Many could not even remember their names.[2]

Looking back on what I (Rich) went through from about ages
▌ ▌ ▌ ▌ ▌ 12 to 14, I can only say that I was convinced puberty was a terminal illness!

Realizing that teenagers are going through an "identity crisis" all their own, Dr. Les Parrott devoted the first chapter of his book *Helping the Struggling Adolescent* to the topic of "A Struggle for Identity." Some of his opening comments are well worth quoting:

Achieving a sense of identity is the major developmental task of teenagers. Like a stunned soldier in a
state of confusion, sooner or later, young people are
hit with a bomb that is more powerful than dyna-
mite—puberty. Somewhere between childhood and
maturity their bodies kick into overdrive and fuel
changes at an alarming rate. With the acceleration of
physical and emotional growth, they become
strangers to themselves. Under attack by an arsenal of
fiery hormones, the bewildered young person begins
to ask, "Who am I?"[3]

We all know to what Dr. Parrott is referring. The junior-high years
are often the most traumatic of our lives. Looking back on what I
(Rich) went through from about ages 12 to 14, I can only say that I
was convinced puberty was a terminal illness! My search for an
identity through which I could find *self-respect, dignity, acceptance by
others, a sense of belonging and happiness* hit a brick wall.

In my junior high school, the monthly newspaper printed the
most incredibly insensitive column I have ever seen. It was called
"Perfect Boy, Perfect Girl." Every month someone would go around
and judge the student body in the following categories: hair, com-
plexion, smile, eyes, nose, physique/figure, athletic ability, personality and brains. It was awful.

Every month I longed to be on that list. Every month I angrily
closed the paper, convinced once again that I would never measure
up. Until one month I made it—for "Perfect Brains."

Now, I am in no way diminishing the importance of intelligence.
It is a precious gift of God for which I have since rejoiced many
times.

For a 13- or 14-year-old boy trying to make it in a sports-oriented
school, however, it was like a sentence of death. They might as well
have put my name under "Perfect *Nerd*" as far as I was concerned.

Nearly 30 years later, I can chuckle about it. At the time, though,
my skinniness, acne, braces and dandruff felt like a prison from
which I would never escape. The pain was nearly unbearable—I felt
like a misfit, wondering if anyone would ever accept me.

I remember one time crying out in my heart to whomever might be able to hear, "I just want to be normal!"

Translation? I just want to fit in and belong.

Maybe you can relate to the pain I lived through. Maybe not. Maybe you were like those in school whom I envied—good looking, athletic, popular and secure—at least on the outside. All teenagers, though, no matter whether they are "beating the system," "getting beat up by the system" or "telling the system to 'beat it!'" are going through a struggle for identity.

As adults, we need a large dose of compassion for teenagers. It is easy to forget the pain we experienced in adolescence and therefore to trivialize the struggles of the young people we know and love.

When I (Rich) went to a doctor to try to get some help in gaining weight, the balding, overweight physician leaned back and smugly commented, "Just be glad you're not fat!" I was not encouraged.

Remember what Dr. Parrott said: Teens are in a war. It is not, however, simply a battle with hormones. It is a desperate struggle against the world, the flesh and the devil. It is primarily a spiritual battle, and Christian teens are right in the thick of it.

Finding Acceptance, Security and Significance

All of us, including Christian teens, have an inherent need for *acceptance, security* and *significance*. In other words, we need to know we are loved and that we belong. We long to feel safe and have the sense that somehow we are being taken care of. We all desperately yearn to know that our lives mean something and are somehow important.

As a child, those three critical areas of need are predominantly to be fulfilled by the family. Tragically, that is too often simply not the case. So children are often forced to look elsewhere. How many children (and teenagers) run away hoping to find life and love they never found at home? Unfortunately, the grinning, inviting face of the "world out there" too often hides a vicious set of fangs ready to devour the naive or rebellious.

Satanists, looking for young recruits to join them in the dark world of the occult, will often target teens and preteens who are floundering in life, devoid of any meaningful identity. These "outer fringe" kids are often highly intelligent, creative individuals and have vivid imaginations. The right bait, such as playing a game of Dungeons & Dragons® with a group of peers/adults, can provide a counterfeit sense of belonging for these young people. In addition, an unhealthy curiosity and lust for evil knowledge and power can be awakened.

God's plan, however, is for teenagers to learn to find their acceptance, security and significance *in Christ*, as opposed to anything in the world or in the flesh. Sadly, this is a radical departure from the way most Christian teens live, and much of the blame has to fall on the shoulders of Christian adults.

How many times have you read (or written!) those annual family newsletters that get hidden inside Christmas cards? Usually they will say something like this:

> George is staying busy on the job and as a deacon in church while I stay busy with the home and chauffeuring the kids back and forth from games and practices. Jason made the All-Star soccer team this year and Rebecca is involved in gymnastics five days a week. Michael really likes to walk around the house swinging the tennis racket, just like his dad.

What is wrong with that picture? It sounds so normal, so healthy, so American. Certainly nothing is inherently wrong with jobs, church responsibilities, homes and sports. They are a part of life. What is the message we are subtly communicating to others, though? What is the message children of Christian families are picking up from adults? It goes something like this:

> You will be happy in life if you are good looking, perform well in school, sports or other activities, and get a nice job and go to church.

That is the basic philosophy of the baby boomer generation and is the way many Christian families live. However, an increasing number of baby busters—AKA "generation X"—are not buying it.

Of course, some teens really are baby boomers at heart and are finding their identity in things such as money, sports, preppie clothes and so on.

Maybe your teen is not like that. Maybe he wants to sit around all day wearing his headphones and playing his guitar. Maybe she does all her shopping at the thrift store and wears colors that make army fatigues look bright.

Teens today, we believe, are looking for a deeper reality in life rather than just activities and things. They can get excited about working together to clean up a beach or start a recycling campaign.

Why is knowing who you are as a child of God so important?

▮ ▮ ▮ ▮ ▮ *Because we always end up living according to the way we see ourselves.*

They can get pumped up about building a house for a poor family in the inner city. They are truly looking for a life that has meaning.

Unfortunately, many of today's teens see little hope for lasting meaning in life. Many have come from broken or dysfunctional homes so they have serious doubts about the value of marriage and family. Looking at the state of the economy and politics in our nation, they suspect they will never experience the American dream. Despair about the future can lead to a frenzied search for excitement and fulfillment today—in music, movies, video and computer games, alcohol, drugs, sex, crime and other risk-taking activities. An American nightmare.

It is all a cry for love. Teens may be unaware of it, but it is a cry for God. So more than ever, teenagers are responsive to the gospel. For only in Christ does life have any ultimate meaning.

That is why it is critical for Christian teenagers to be firmly rooted and grounded in their true identity as children of God. Their *true identity* (who they really are) must become their *perceived identity* (who they think they are). Without this biblical grounding, all other efforts to help teenagers find freedom in Christ will be only shallow and temporary.

Why is knowing who you are as a child of God so important? *Because we always end up living according to the way we see ourselves.*

How does God see a Christian teen? Take a long look at His Word:

> How great is the love the Father has lavished on us, that we should be called children of God! And that is what we are!...Dear friends, now we are children of God (1 John 3:1,2, *NIV*).

God wants Christian teenagers to find their acceptance, security and significance in Him and in His Body, the family of God. Why? Because everything else is ultimately a dead-end street.

Teenagers today are longing for relationships that are authentic and real. When they begin to connect with that Father-child relationship with God and those brother-sister relationships in the family of God, they experience faith, hope and love. You see, if you have felt like trash all your life and someone picks you up, cleans you off, accepts you just the way you are and then calls you "friend," you respond. God does exactly that and so should His Body, the Church.

It is simply not enough to be content that our Christian teens feel good about the way they look, or how they are performing academically, artistically or athletically. It is not enough that they have friends who like them and that they get along with the significant adults in their lives. It is not enough that they have bright and successful careers ahead of them. It is not even enough that they go to church regularly.

Those things are certainly not wrong. They are just not enough. For one day the body will begin to bag, sag and drag. (Been there, done that? Are there, doing that?) The performances will fail or pale in comparison with someone else.

Friends may come and go and even the best of relationships have rocky times. Money can sprout wings and job security is at best an oxymoron.

Finding Identity in Christ

I (Rich) was speaking at a conference in Georgia on the subject of our identity in Christ. After I finished, a young man came up to me. Your average youth leader would drool about this kind of kid. He was good looking, a straight-A student, a varsity football player and a spiritual leader at his high school. He came from a strong Christian home and his parents were godly, full-time Christian workers.

He shook my hand and said, "I have felt such pressure to excel in these things." Heaving a sigh of relief he added, "Thank you for telling me that there is finally Somebody who accepts me just the way I am in Christ."

Pure acceptance. Not because of his appearance or performance. Not an "I love you *if*..." or an "I love you *because*...," but an "I love you—*period*."

The next morning, the female version of that boy (minus the football part!) came up and gave a similar testimony. She handed me what she had written. Her comments are profound:

> I have been a Christian for 14 years. I prayed to receive Christ as a young child. I was raised in a Christian home and both of my parents are missionaries. I have always been considered a leader among my peers and a person with a very strong faith in God and love for him.
>
> I always have quiet times and I always try to put Christ first and others before myself. But it wasn't until recently [actually the night before] that I've really come to experience God's love for me.
>
> I was always told that God loves me and has a wonderful plan for my life, but I felt more like God loves everyone as a whole and...well...that includes me.
>
> God kept me up all night last night and I looked up Bible verses of who God says that I am and that I myself am significant, that God loves me for who I am and loves me just as much as he loves Jesus.
>
> All the talk of God's love was never really made evident to me. It was dry, until I realized how God sees

me, and that I am accepted and secure and I have great significance.

Now when I look at Scripture it's more than words. There's feeling and love behind them. They were written for me! Now Christianity is really more than rules. It's real. It's a relationship.

A rock-solid base of finding our acceptance, security and significance in our Father-child ▮▮▮▮▮ relationship with God through Jesus Christ is the only foundation that can survive the storms of life.

That is what God desires for every Christian teen to experience—an intimacy with Him that goes beyond head knowledge to heart experience. The apostle Paul put it this way:

> For you have not received a spirit of slavery leading to fear again, but you have received a spirit of adoption as sons by which we cry out, "Abba! Father!" The Spirit Himself bears witness with our spirit that we are children of God (Rom. 8:15,16).

A rock-solid base of finding our acceptance, security and significance in our Father-child relationship with God through Jesus Christ is the only foundation that can survive the storms of life. After all, Christ *is* our life (see Col. 3:4).

A principle that teens need to be taught is this: *Where you find your life is where you will find your identity.*

Does your teen think his life will be found in earning money and having nice things? Then that is where his identity (who he is) will be found also. He will be convinced that his value and meaning as a person comes from achieving those materialistic goals. He will also make all adjustments necessary to make that happen.

Does your teen think her life will be found in making friends and being popular? Then that is where her identity (who she is) will be found as well. She will be certain that her value and meaning as a person comes from being well liked. She will also do whatever is necessary to achieve that goal.

Jesus bluntly put it this way:

> For where your treasure is, there your heart will be also (Matt. 6:21, *NIV*).

Trying to find meaning, a sense of worth, happiness or security in anything other than God is like building a house upon sand. It is doomed to fall, and great indeed will be its fall.

We cannot overemphasize how important it is for Christian teenagers to know who they are in Christ and to live with Jesus as the center point of their lives. In reality, anything else is none other than *idolatry*.

Around what is your teenager's life centered? Is it in "having fun"? Is it in music? Is it in a boyfriend or girlfriend? Is it in sports? Those things were never intended to be the "hub of the wheel," so to speak. They were intended to be the "spokes," connected to the hub—Jesus—and under His wise control.

The first of the Ten Commandments puts it as clearly as can be:

> You shall have no other gods before Me (Exod. 20:3).

The spirit of that command was not that of an angry, demanding tyrant. Instead, it was the solemn warning of a loving God who had already liberated His people from the clutches of cruel slavery. He was simply showing them the way to *remain* free!

Understanding Who You Are in Christ

The following story illustrates the power of understanding one's identity in Christ in a very graphic way. Your teenager may not have as dramatic a transformation as the teenage boy in this story, but understanding who you are in Christ is a life-changing revelation to all who experience it.

Blair had come nearly 1,000 miles to a retreat where I (Rich) was speaking. At first, he thought he was just coming to have fun. He soon found out he had actually traveled 1,000 miles to find life and freedom in Jesus Christ.

On Saturday night of that four-day retreat, Blair gave his heart to Jesus. Then, typical of teens at a youth camp, he trashed one of the guys' rooms a couple of hours later. He actually did some damage with the shaving cream he had shot all over the place.

Feeling guilty for what he had done, Blair went to the camp director and confessed to the crime.

"I can't figure it out," Blair told the director. "I have done these kinds of pranks all my life, and I've never felt guilty before. What's wrong with me?"

It was obvious nothing was wrong with him at all. On the contrary, his conviction by God's Spirit was evidence something was very *right* with him!

On his own initiative, Blair decided he needed to confess his sin to the whole group. This is something that old, mature Christians are reluctant to do, yet Blair (just several hours old in the Lord) was willing to humble himself that way! God blessed his humility in a powerful way.

On Sunday night, he came to the front of the auditorium and first confessed Christ as his Lord and Savior. Then he confessed his role in the vandalism of the night before.

The atmosphere in the place was electric, and it was clear the Spirit of God was moving. The camp director gave an invitation for others to come forward and give their lives to Christ.

A young man, Jonathan, stood up and slowly shuffled his way forward. The whole place erupted in applause. Every eye was riveted on him as he began to speak.

"I have been living a lie. For two years I have been coming to youth group, but I haven't been a Christian at all. I want to give my life to Jesus." Jonathan practically bathed the front of that room with the sweet tears of repentance and surrender.

Then the floodgates opened. An 89-pound girl came forward because she wanted to be set free from anorexia. Larry Beckner, a Freedom in Christ Youth Ministries staff person, counseled her and prayed with her.

Then two girls came forward to confess their anger and bitterness toward God because of chronic illnesses He had not yet healed. Then two more girls suffering from anorexia came forward as well. This went on for several hours.

Overcoming Addictions

I went and sat next to Blair because I wanted to congratulate him for his courage and honesty. I could tell something was bothering him.

"What's wrong?" I asked him.

"The whole side of my face feels like it's going numb and it's hard to talk," Blair replied. Fear and confusion were written all over his face.

"Have you ever had this happen before?"

Blair nodded. "Just once. Last night when I opened my heart to Christ."

It did not take a genius to know that this young man was under spiritual attack. So I asked him to follow me upstairs where we could talk in private in the cafeteria area.

Not quite sure how to help him, I prayed for wisdom. I felt the Lord leading me to have him read through a list of Bible-based statements declaring his new identity in Christ (see the IN CHRIST list at the end of this chapter).

Blair began reading that list out loud and seemed to be getting stronger. Suddenly an awful pain gripped his shoulder, as if someone were wringing out the muscle like a dishrag. I prayed for him, exercising my authority in Christ, and the pain eased a bit.

Then he turned to me and asked carefully, "Rich, have you by any chance ever struggled with alcohol?"

"Yeah, drinking and partying were a big part of my life, even after I became a Christian my freshman year in college. Why do you ask?"

"Well, I haven't told many people this, but I'm an alcoholic." Blair kind of lowered his eyes in shame, as if ready for me to lower the boom on him.

I was hoping my answer would communicate the love and acceptance of him that I truly felt in my heart. "Blair, you are not an alcoholic. You are a child of God who has struggled with alcohol. There is a big difference."

He perked up a little and after some encouragement confessed and renounced his use and abuse of alcohol. Then he resumed his reading out loud of the IN CHRIST list. It was exciting to see the truth beginning to click deep inside him.

Then that excruciating pain grabbed his shoulder again. Wondering what in the world was going on, I prayed once more to bind the powers of darkness that still seemed to have a grip on Blair.

Then he turned to me once again and admitted, "Rich, I've never told anyone this before, but I'm a junkie, too."

Summoning all the love in me, I tried to encourage him again. Smiling, I said, "Blair, you are *not* a junkie. You are a child of God who has struggled with drugs. And you can be free from the enemy's bondage by confessing and renouncing your drug use— just like you did with the alcohol."

So he did. Blair had been involved with about five or six different drugs and he declared out loud that he was done with them all.

He finished reading through the IN CHRIST list, and I felt as though the forces of evil were getting it right between the eyes as Blair nearly shouted, "I am a child of God, and the evil one cannot touch me!"

As soon as he was finished, his eyes and face beamed with joy. The numbness in his face went away. The horrible pain in his shoulder was gone. The truth had indeed set Blair free.

What he said next startled me a little bit.

"Rich, you would not believe the high that I get from crack."

I was wondering why he told me that, when he continued:

"But this is so much better!"

To what was Blair referring? Obviously, he was overjoyed that the pain and numbness were gone. Certainly he was relieved that the demonic oppression and bondage were broken. I believe it went beyond that, though. I am convinced Blair was also rejoicing that the *labels* that had been pinned to his soul—*alcoholic, junkie*—had been torn off and replaced by God's label for him: *child of God.*

The beauty of God's label for Blair is that it is far more than a surface sticker, slapped onto his soul. It is who he really is. So it is for every teenage Christian as well.

Living with Labels

How many Christian young people live in bondage to another label they wrongly believe represents their true identity? Some common labels teens pin on one another are *jock, skater, prep, brain, nerd, skinhead, "cool," gay, stud, flirt, snob, clown* and *poser.*

Some labels the teen may like wearing, others may seem like a horrible stain that refuses to wash out.

Obviously, the label may change from group to group. The labels parents place on their children may be far different from those of peers. Parental labels can stick with their kids all their lives and function as either blessings or curses.

Psychiatrists, psychologists and counselors unwittingly may place a label on a Christian teenager in an effort to diagnose a condition—for example, manic depressive, schizophrenic, bulimic or sex addict.

Although the diagnosis may be accurate, the label (e.g., "I have A.D.D." [Attention Deficit Disorder]) can become the young person's main source of identity. He or she may attribute and excuse all behavior based on that label. He or she may view the condition as hopeless and unchangeable. That is tragic.

Sticks and Stones...but *Words* Will Never Hurt?

Proverbs 18:21 warns, "Death and life are in the power of the tongue, and those who love it will eat its fruit." We must be careful with the words we use around teenagers.

While going through the Steps to Freedom in Christ with Valery, she recalled an incident from her childhood that had a profound affect upon the way she viewed herself. She remembered one day she was eating a lot of food during a meal and her mom strongly disapproved.

"If you keep eating like that you are going to get fat like your grandmother!" Valery's mom scolded.

At that point Valery vowed that she would never get fat (and thus lose her mom's approval). The Spirit of God had brought that memory to mind as the beginning point of Valery's anorexia. Her mother's words had functioned as a curse, helping drive her into a lifestyle of obsession with food, counting fat calories, denial, overexercise and perfectionism.

Often during freedom appointments, counselees will make statements such as:

I can't do anything right.	I'm lazy.
I'm stupid.	I'm obnoxious.
I'm fat.	I've got a big mouth.
I'm ugly.	I'm no good.
I'll never amount to anything.	I'm just a victim.
I'm dirty and evil.	Nobody loves me.

Those are terrible labels to wear. From where do they come? They are all too often branded upon our souls in the critical years of our youth.

Angry, thoughtless words from parents, teachers, coaches, peers, brothers, sisters or others can help lock even Christian teens into identity perceptions far different from what God says is true. In addition, life experiences often confirm and reinforce in young peoples' minds that those labels are indeed correct. You can be sure the devil will add his "amen" to those words, pouring his fuel on the fire with a relentless barrage of accusing and tormenting thoughts.

Are you skeptical? Think about this: God says in His Word that we are new creations in Christ (see 2 Cor. 5:17), holy and dearly loved and chosen by Him (see Col. 3:12). We are saints (see Phil. 1:1) who can do all things through Him who strengthens us (see Phil. 4:13). Right?

Okay. If, however, you believed you were a miserable, wretched sinner, weak and helpless and failing a deeply disappointed God continually, would that perceived identity affect your life? Would it have any effect on the way you thought, felt or behaved? Of course!

The goal of raising or discipling young people is to provide an environment in which the Spirit of God can work to ground them in the truths of who God is and who they are in Christ.

No, teenagers ultimately cannot control the labels others put on them. Christian young people, however, can know they are God's dearly loved children and rest in the acceptance, security and significance that comes from Him. In a sense, God has put the ultimate label—the only one that is true and that truly matters—on the life of every Christian: *child of God.*

The teenager who knows Christ and understands and accepts an identity in Christ can then find the courage to project an image that reflects who he or she really is. That is, he can live out his faith boldly and humbly in a sin-sick world. Isn't that what Peter was writing about in his first letter?:

> But you are a chosen race, a royal priesthood, a holy nation, a people for God's own possession, that you may proclaim the excellencies of Him who has called you out of darkness into His marvelous light (1 Pet. 2:9).

Finding a Relationship with God

Many benefits are available to Christian teens who understand that their acceptance, security and significance come primarily through their relationship with God in Christ. Consider just the following three areas:

1. *True intimacy.* Teenagers want close, deep friendships. Until teens are secure in God's unconditional love for them, however, they are unable to consistently give love and affection to others. They are too insecure and self-centered to love, being more concerned about *getting* rather than *giving.* Once they learn to rest in the Father's care, however, they are free to develop godly friendships both with those of the same gender as well as with the opposite sex.

2. *Submission to authority.* Why do teenagers rebel? Generally, it is because they are convinced that the authorities in charge of them are robbing them of their fun and freedom. Teens who are walking in that day-by-day, hand-in-hand relationship with their all-wise

Father-God, however, will have the strength to trust Him to work through His lines of authority. The battles may still be there, but they will be far less likely to get out of control.

3. *Endurance in trial.* Everyone experiences tough times; but if security and significance are solidly based on an unchangeable relationship with God the Father, difficulties in life can become opportunities for growth. Disappointments will still be present, to be sure, but they need not devastate or disillusion the child of God who is secure in Christ.

Experiencing Freedom

So how can we help Christian teenagers experience the freedom that comes from knowing, believing and living according to their true identity? Nothing is guaranteed when trying to reach the complex human heart, but we believe the following six key principles will guide you:

1. Your influence will be an outflow of your walk with God, whether you are a parent raising a teenager or a youth leader or other adult seeking to have a godly influence in the life of a young person.

Ask God to speak to *you.* Yes, you! You might be saying, *Why do I need to do this? It's my kid who needs the help, not me!* Maybe so. Still, it is amazing how much spiritual junk can be present in our lives as adults without our being aware of it. Often the very issues God brings to the surface in us are affecting our families as well! So go ahead. Ask Him to open your eyes to any lies you have believed about God or yourself. Pray that the Holy Spirit would reveal to your mind the areas of bondage in your own life.

If you have not already read my (Neil's) books *Victory over the Darkness* and *The Bondage Breaker*, I strongly urge you to do so. Then go through the Steps to Freedom in Christ, which are located in the back of *The Bondage Breaker.*

Most Christian bookstores now carry an updated and comprehensive adult version of the Steps. The Steps to Freedom in Christ (Youth Edition) are found in the back of this book as well. Either one will provide a framework for God to minister to you. If you can't process the Steps on your own, ask a mature Christian of the same gender to walk you through them.

Neil has coauthored a book with Pete and Sue Vander Hook—*Spiritual Protection for Your Children*. Pete is an evangelical pastor who suddenly found his children under spiritual attack. Sue home schools their children and writes about their struggle to free their children. The book contains age-graded Steps for children under 12 years of age.

> 2. Cultivate an environment of grace and unconditional love and acceptance in your home and youth group. Let the teenagers around you know that God is on their side and so are you.

We will address this issue in detail in chapter two, so suffice it to say here that teenagers are masters at spotting hypocrisy. They will pick up almost immediately if you are talking about God's grace and acceptance in Christ while treating others with a legalistic, performance based acceptance.

> 3. Pray fervently and regularly for the teens in your home or youth group that the eyes of their hearts would be enlightened (see Eph. 1:18) to understand and live according to the truths of who they are in Christ.

This critical subject of "how to pray for youth" will be discussed later in this book.

> 4. Teach the *Busting Free* curriculum for youth (based on *Stomping Out the Darkness* and *The Bondage Breaker—Youth Edition*) in family devotions or youth group. Teens enjoy learning in groups. This material provides exciting learning activities to help teens grasp the

truths of their identity in Christ. Make sure to provide lots of time for discussion.

In a youth group, consider separating the guys and girls for part of the discussion time so they can feel the freedom to share deep, personal stuff. In a family, Dad could meet with the boy(s) and Mom with the girl(s).

Make sure you maintain an atmosphere of caring and acceptance in the group. In a church or youth-group setting, having leaders and peers gather around and pray for a hurting brother or sister in Christ gives youth a tangible picture of the love of God. The same kind of ministry can take place on a family level as well.

If the idea of having structured family devotions with your teens makes you laugh, you are not alone. Many families today would be happy to just have dinner together! No matter where you are spiritually as a family, do not be discouraged. Pray that God will begin to open up opportunities to talk openly and honestly with (not *to*) your teens. Share bits and pieces from what you are learning, including your failures. Family devotions or discussions can begin to emerge once you take the initiative to create an open forum for opinions and feelings to be aired. Do not give up!

5. If you are a youth leader, take your teenagers through the Steps to Freedom in Christ after completing the *Busting Free* curriculum. You can do that as a group while providing individual attention later for those who have deeper hurts. The second half of this book will provide principles in using the Steps effectively.

Parents often can lead their own younger children through the Steps to Freedom in Christ, but this becomes more difficult when they become teenagers. Teens need to feel the freedom to be completely open and honest while going through the Steps.

Young people have often done things they are deeply ashamed of, and will hesitate to share them in the presence of a parent for fear of being reprimanded or of causing pain to Mom or Dad. In addition, if teens have unresolved anger or a rebellious spirit toward their parents, they are much more likely to confront it thoroughly if neither one is present.

To be effective in this ministry to their own teenagers, parents have to first be free in Christ themselves and have a very open, trusting relationship with their kids. Certainly this can happen, though we feel it is unfortunately the exception rather than the rule. Let the Spirit of wisdom grant you the discernment to know what is best in your case. The bottom line is that you want to create the environment most conducive to your teen finding his or her freedom in Christ. How he or she reacts toward your being a part of that process should let you know loud and clear whether you should be involved directly or not.

In the majority of cases, having a youth leader or mature Christian friend of the family or caring church leader minister to a teen is a better option. As parents, assure your teens you will not violate the confidentiality of the ministry session. Let them know you are open to hearing what God did in their lives during the session, but that you will wait for them to take the initiative to talk if they wish. This will require a tremendous amount of self-control, but you will win major points with your teens if you follow through with your word.

> 6. In conjunction with or in addition to the Steps to Freedom in Christ, have the teens pray the following prayer (or something similar):
>
> Dear heavenly Father, would You please reveal to my mind any and all worldly, fleshly or demonic labels that have been pinned on me or that I have pinned on myself. I want to accept only that which comes from Your loving heart and Word of truth. In Jesus' name, amen.

Then, have the teen(s) write down those labels that come to his or her mind. If any other labels you know are applicable, feel free to suggest them after the youth has finished the list.

For each one the Lord brings to mind, have the teenager say the following declaration out loud:

> In the name and authority of the Lord Jesus Christ, I here and now reject the false label of _____. I confess that in the past I have believed that this label was my true identity. But now I choose to accept only the truth of God's Word. I am a child of the living God.

This exercise could be used as a youth group activity, or in the home if an atmosphere of openness and trust exists. It can be a great jump start for teens to begin seeing themselves the way God sees them.

We realize, of course, that it takes time to renew a mind, but that is how a life is transformed (see Rom. 12:2). Gently encourage the young people you love to take the IN CHRIST list (at the end of this chapter) and read through it out loud twice daily—once in the morning when they get up and once at night before they turn out the lights. This is particularly helpful advice if you start doing it first! Share the excitement of what God is showing you; that can act as a catalyst to others! It is also beneficial to look up the list's powerful verses in the Bible and study them in context.

The listings of the IN CHRIST list are actually the chapter headings in Neil's book *Living Free in Christ*, a book written to show how Christ meets our most critical needs of life, identity, acceptance, security and significance. Each of the 36 chapters is only five to seven pages long, and we encourage you to pray and work toward using it for family discussions or devotions. Read at your own pace, spending more time on the chapters most relevant to your teens.

Time and perseverance *will* pay off. Spiritual and emotional damage can be repaired. A wounded self-image can be healed. A broken heart can be made whole again. This is the work of that Greatest of all Surgeons and Healers, Jesus Christ. We have the incredible opportunity to assist Him in the operation.

IN CHRIST

I renounce the lie that I am rejected, unloved, dirty or shameful because IN CHRIST I am completely accepted. God says...

John 1:12	I am God's child.
John 15:15	I am Christ's friend.
Romans 5:1	I have been justified.
1 Corinthians 6:17	I am united with the Lord and I am one spirit with Him.
1 Corinthians 6:19,20	I have been bought with a price. I belong to God.
1 Corinthians 12:27	I am a member of Christ's Body.
Ephesians 1:1	I am a saint, a holy one.
Ephesians 1:5	I have been adopted as God's child.
Ephesians 2:18	I have direct access to God through the Holy Spirit.
Colossians 1:14	I have been redeemed and forgiven of all my sins.
Colossians 2:10	I am complete in Christ.

I renounce the lie that I am guilty, unprotected, alone or abandoned because IN CHRIST I am totally secure. God says...

Romans 8:1,2	I am free forever from condemnation.
Romans 8:28	I am assured that all things work together for good.
Romans 8:31-34	I am free from any condemning charges against me.
Romans 8:35-39	I cannot be separated from the love of God.
2 Corinthians 1:21,22	I have been established, anointed and sealed by God.
Colossians 3:3	I am hidden with Christ in God.
Philippians 1:6	I am confident that the good work God has begun in me will be perfected.
Philippians 3:20	I am a citizen of heaven.
2 Timothy 1:7	I have not been given a spirit of fear, but of power, love and a sound mind.
Hebrews 4:16	I can find grace and mercy to help in time of need.
1 John 5:18	I am born of God and the evil one cannot touch me.

I renounce the lie that I am worthless, inadequate, helpless or hopeless because IN CHRIST I am deeply significant. God says...

Matthew 5:13,14	I am the salt of the earth and the light of the world.
John 15:1,5	I am a branch of the true vine, Jesus, a channel of His life.
John 15:16	I have been chosen and appointed by God to bear fruit.
Acts 1:8	I am a personal Spirit-empowered witness of Christ.
1 Corinthians 3:16	I am a temple of God.
2 Corinthians 5:17-21	I am a minister of reconciliation for God.
2 Corinthians 6:1	I am God's coworker.
Ephesians 2:6	I am seated with Christ in the heavenly realm.
Ephesians 2:10	I am God's workmanship, created for good works.
Ephesians 3:12	I may approach God with freedom and confidence.
Philippians 4:13	I CAN DO ALL THINGS THROUGH CHRIST WHO STRENGTHENS ME!

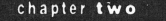

Help! My Kids Are Teenagers!

A mother once asked me (Neil), "Why won't my teenager talk to me? I know she's struggling at school."

I asked her, "Do you really want to know?"

"Of course," she said.

I knew her well enough to say, "She probably thinks she can't trust you."

She was surprised by my answer and said, "What do you mean she can't trust me? Of course she can trust me. I'm her mother."

I said, "Let me illustrate. Suppose your teenager came home from school and said, 'Mom, my best friend is smoking pot.' What would you do?"

She had to think long and hard about her response.

Let us ask you the same question. How would you as a parent respond if your son or daughter asked you that question? How would you as a youth leader who deeply cares about your young people react? We are sure you would fight to keep from overreacting, but you would probably offer some pretty strong advice.

Finally, this mother said, yes, she would tell her daughter to stop hanging around with that friend.

I said, "Exactly! That's why she won't share it with you."

"Well, what would you do?" she asked.

We never know how we would respond at any moment of crisis, but I do not think I would respond that way. At least I hope I wouldn't. Why not?

First of all, I would have no idea what the real problem is because I would not have heard the whole story. Did her friend try drugs once, or has she been taking drugs for months or years? Does she plan to continue, or was it a one-time bad experience?

Wise King Solomon wrote, "He who gives an answer before he hears, it is folly and shame to him" (Prov. 18:13).

Wouldn't it be better to say something like, "Honey, I'm really sorry to hear that. Can we talk about it?"

You need to realize that it is possible the one smoking pot is sitting right in front of you! If she finds out your reaction is harsh and condemning, that is the end of the story. She won't share any more with you unless she is absolutely desperate. Every parent and youth leader needs to realize this.

Four Levels of Parental Response

Lawrence Richards provides a helpful explanation of parent-child communication styles. Drawing from Ross Snyder's work, Richards describes four levels of parental response to their kids.

Picture a teen in a boat in big trouble as he nears the falls because of a wrong decision he made upstream. The following are the four parental responses:

The *advice-giver* distances himself from the emotional crisis. He shouts to his kid, "C'mon! What's the matter with you? Row harder! You got yourself into this mess in the first place, so get yourself out! If you weren't such an idiot you wouldn't be in this mess! Didn't I tell you this would happen?"

The *reassurer* tries to make the kid feel better about his situation. He calmly says, "Hang in there, bud. Your mom and I love you and believe in you. Besides, of the last three people who went over the falls, two survived. We hope you make it, too. Good luck!"

The *understander* gets even closer to the situation, trying to feel what the kid is feeling. He wades into the water and says, "Boy, this current sure is moving fast. You really are in trouble, aren't you? I can see now why you are so concerned. I'll try and get some help for you."

The *self-revealer* gets into the boat with his teen and immediately starts paddling to safety.

To illustrate, suppose your son comes home from school dejected. He loves to play basketball, but he just got cut from the squad. All his friends, however, made the team. How would you respond?

If you were an *advice-giver*, you might say something like, "Didn't I tell you to practice harder? Listen, there's a community team you can play for this season and if you work hard you can probably up your skill level to the point where you can make the team next year. Here's the coach's phone number."

If you are a *reassurer*, you will probably give your son a big hug and say, "Hey, it's okay. Your mom and I love you. Don't worry, you're a tough kid. You'll find something else to do and you'll show them what a good athlete you really are!"

If you are an *understander*, you might respond by saying, "You're really bummed out about this, aren't you? It must really hurt to be rejected like that and to be separated from your friends. Can you tell me what happened?"

A *self-revealer*, however, would hug the kid, listen to his story and then thoughtfully share something like this: "When I was 15 years old I got cut from the baseball team. I wanted to be part of that team more than anything else. When the coach told me to hit the showers, I thought my life was over. It sounds like you're going through something like that."

We have talked to hundreds of teenagers, asking them to identify how their parents respond to them in similar situations. Sadly, 95 percent identified their parents as *advice-givers*. Only 5 percent said their parents were *reassurers*. None of the teens identified their parents as *understanders* or *self-revealers*.

Now, we are not saying that giving advice or reassurance is wrong. Nor is any one response appropriate in every situation. Something is seriously wrong, though, in the way parents are communicating with teens if advice giving and reassurance are the only things being offered.

Alarming Surveys

As parents and youth leaders, we like to believe we are on top of what is happening in our teenagers' lives. Are we? Have we cultivated an atmosphere in which the young people in our homes or youth groups feel the freedom to share what is *really* going on? A study reported in *Parents & Teenagers* seems to indicate otherwise. The results in the following chart ought to send off an alarm into every Christian parent's heart:

Questions	Teens' Response	Parents' Response
1. Have you had one or more alcoholic drinks?	66% say yes	34% think they have
2. Have you considered suicide?	43% say yes	15% think they have
3. Have you ever smoked?	41% say yes	14% think they have
4. Do you tell your mom about boyfriends and sex?	36% say yes	80% think they do
5. Have you ever used drugs?	17% say yes	5% think they have
6. Have you lost your virginity?	70% say yes	14% think they have
7. Have you thought about running away from home?[1]	35% say yes	19% think they have

In his excellent book *Understanding Today's Youth Culture,* Walt Mueller cites a survey by Dr. Bob Laurent. In the survey, Dr. Laurent sought to understand the influence negative peer pressure has on believing adolescents. He studied 400 teens from Christian homes for three years and wrote of his findings in his book *Keeping Your Teen in Touch with God*.[2]

The teens surveyed were asked to say whether they agreed or disagreed with the following statements. How those Christian young people responded should bring us to our knees.

Statement	Christian Teens' Response
I am more likely to act like a Christian when I'm with my Christian friends and to act like a non-Christian when I'm with my non-Christian friends.	Agree
I get upset when my non-Christian friends leave me out of their activities.	Agree
I'd rather be with my friends than with my family.	Agree
I try to keep up with the latest fads.	Strongly Agree
My non-Christian friends' opinions are important to me.	Strongly Agree
If I needed advice, I'd ask my friends before I asked my parents.	Agree
It bothers me when my non-Christian friends think I'm too religious.	Agree[3]

Although Dr. Laurent's findings are likely an accurate reflection of Christian teens' struggles, we have found refreshing exceptions. We all know (and perhaps have had the joy of raising or discipling) Christian young people who are standing firm in the faith. They are not acting like "dead fish" being swept downstream with the current of peer pressure and public opinion. Instead, they are vigorously swimming upstream against the flow. In some cases, they have become the *new, positive peer pressure* in their home, neighborhood, school or youth group.

What can parents do to increase the chances their kids will do well in their teenage years, walking closely with God? The answer to that question is different for each person, but certain dynamics will certainly "up the ante" in that direction.

Art Imitates Life

In the movie *Dead Poets Society*, Robin Williams plays the part of a new teacher at an elite boys' boarding school. He challenges his students to celebrate life and *carpe diem* (seize the day) by discovering their own identity and purpose.

One young man attends the school because his dad wants him to be a doctor. The boy's heart, however, beats to be an actor on stage.

Against his dad's wishes, the teen secures the lead part in a Shakespearean play and becomes an instant success. His opening-night performance is greeted by a thunderous ovation from the audience.

His dad, however, who witnesses his son's performance, becomes furious with his son's disobedience, pulls him out of the play and the school.

The young man, feeling trapped and disillusioned, takes his life with his father's gun.

I (Neil) was involved in a similar parent-child conflict, which, fortunately, had a much happier ending.

Life Imitates Art

Jill's mom and dad were nominal Christians working in high-tech professions. Since the age of three, Jill had always been expected to excel. Driven to perfectionism by her parents, her grades were top-notch. During her high school years, however, Jill's and her parents' desires conflicted.

Jill wanted to attend a Christian college, but her parents wanted her to attend their alma mater and join her mother's sorority.

Together they went to see *Dead Poets Society*, and afterwards Jill's parents argued with her for hours that the father of the suicide victim had been right!

By the time Jill came to my office, she was anorexic and was struggling because of hearing voices in her head. She had also been cutting herself with a knife. In making a list of people she needed to forgive, mom and dad were at the top.

Although she had not shed a tear in years, the emotional floodgates opened as she prayed, "Lord, I forgive my father for never asking me what I wanted, for never even considering what I would like to do with my life."

Because Jill confronted the many complex issues in her life, many personal and spiritual issues were resolved. The voices stopped. She stopped cutting herself, and she experienced a peace of mind she had never known before.

The parent-child component, though, still had to be resolved. That came quickly as well. Her counselor's guidance helped Jill reach a compromise with her parents. She attended their alma mater for a year and then went on to the Christian school of her choice, after receiving her parents' blessing.

Training "Of the Lord"

Are we saying that overcontrolling parents are the cause of all their children's problems? Of course not. Scripture clearly warns, though, "Fathers, do not exasperate your children; instead, bring them up in the training and instruction of the Lord" (Eph. 6:4, *NIV*).

Those last three words are key: *of the Lord*. How many times do well-meaning but misguided Christian parents impose their *own* standards for life and conduct upon their kids while neglecting the training and instruction of the Lord?

Parents who do not know how to speak the truth in love but instead are angry controllers will give the "devil an opportunity" in their families (Eph. 4:26,27). A lack of forgiveness in the home will surely give Satan an advantage (see 2 Cor. 2:10,11). We must remember that the fruit of the Spirit is *self-control* (see Gal. 5:22,23), not spouse control or child control!

We are convinced that most Christian parents would do the right thing in raising their kids if they were sure what the right thing was. What does a good parent do, though? Is it ever right to try to control your teens? Is loving them the same thing as controlling them? Is controlling them the same thing as disciplining them?

Let's face it, when it comes to parenting, these are scary times. Teens *are* killed in drunk-driving accidents. Kids *are* abducted on the way to or from school. For many young people, the threat of violence is an everyday reality; and a lot of teens are scared.

Parental Control or Love?

George Gallup Jr., the pollster, discovered and reported in *Growing Up Scared in America*, "The sad fact is that many young people across the land, in homes of both the privileged and underprivileged, worry daily about their physical well-being."[4]

Where do parents need to draw the line in warning and protecting their teens? How do we know if our fears are creating unhealthy fears in our kids?

Vanessa Ochs in her book *Safe & Sound: Protecting Your Child in an Unpredictable World* suggests, "When protection turns to overprotection, regardless of how we rationalize, regardless of how and why it was motivated...it has serious, long-term consequences for a child's self-esteem and sense of well-being."[5]

The most insidious factor in situations in which parents overcontrol their kids is that their initial motivation is love. Too often, however, it is love that has stepped over the line, tainted by a controlling fear in the parent's own heart.

Vanessa Ochs offers some guidelines to help parents diagnose the times when pure parental love has slipped into impure parental control.

The Overprotected Teen:
1. Turns to parents for decisions he can make himself; he has little self-confidence.
2. Has unhealthy fears that restrict facing normal life challenges.

3. Perceives herself as frail or bound to fail.
4. Consistently complains of parental intrusion.
5. Lies to participate in (nonharmful) activities peers are permitted to do.

Signs of Overprotection as a Parent:
1. You cause your teen to question his abilities and to remain dependent on you.
2. You discourage your teen from taking (healthy) risks.
3. You teach your teen that no outsider can be trusted.
4. You treat your teen as you would a younger child.
5. You hide sad, disturbing or unpleasant news from your teen.

How You Can Let Go:
1. Let him make mistakes; let her experience the consequences of decisions whenever possible.
2. Support her in her efforts to develop in new (healthy) areas and discover who she really is.
3. Remind yourself how you resented parental intrusion when you were a teen.
4. Wait for him to express the need for comfort before leaping to offer it.
5. Search for healthy ways to reduce your own anxiety or fear level.[6]

Parenting Styles

A significant study was conducted several years ago to try to determine what kinds of kids were produced by various parenting styles. The study was conducted among hundreds of high school juniors and seniors throughout the United States. The questions were designed to reveal what kind of parents produced the following traits in their children:

1. Children who have a good self-image and are happy being who they are.

2. Children who submit to the authority of others and who are able to get along with their teachers and other authority figures.
3. Children who follow the religious beliefs of their parents, attend their parents' house of worship and are likely to continue doing so.
4. Children who identify with the counterculture, rebelling against the norms of society.

What was the result of the research? The survey showed that the two most powerful influences in parenting were *control* and *support*. *Control* by parents was defined as the ability to manage a child's behavior. *Support* by parents was defined as the ability to make a child feel loved.

Naturally, controlling the behavior of a child can be accomplished in various ways: guilt manipulation, intimidation tactics, cruel punishment, enticing rewards, or by establishing boundaries and providing choices.

On the other hand, what *truly* makes a child feel loved versus what we *think* communicates love may differ from the other. Merely providing "things" will not do the trick, nor will simply saying "I love you."

A parent has to be both physically and emotionally available to the child. Children have to know you are there for them when they need you. Consistent attention—including listening—and consistent affection (hugs and kisses) communicate love.

Based on various combinations of parental control and parental support, consider four distinct parenting styles:

The *permissive* parent provides high support but low control. The child feels loved and accepted by the parents, but little effort is exerted to manage his behavior. The child grows up believing he can get his own way. The result? A spoiled child.

The *neglectful* parent provides low levels of support and low levels of control. The child is basically left to fend for and raise himself while the parents live their own lives, ignoring their family responsibilities. This child grows up believing that something is wrong with him, that he is unlovable or worthless. He also quickly learns he can get away with whatever he wants to do. The result? The most dangerous of all conditions, a psychopathic child.

The *authoritarian* parent provides low support but high control. The child feels trapped because he is overcontrolled and underloved. Oftentimes he experiences high levels of guilt and shame and may strongly rebel against the system.

The *authoritative* parent provides both high support and high control. The child knows he is loved while being aware he cannot get away with wrong behavior. This situation provides the best soil for positive parent-child relationships as well as fruitful, productive lives.

The following chart shows how each parenting style ranks in the four categories targeted in the survey: strong sense of self-worth (SW), conform to authority (CTA), accept parents' religion (APR), rebel against society (REB).

High Support

	Permissive Parent	Authoritative Parent	
	SW 2	SW 1	
	CTA 2	CTA 1	
	APR 2	APR 1	
Low Control	REB 2	REB 3	High Control
	Neglectful Parent	Authoritarian Parent	
	SW 4	SW 3	
	CTA 3	CTA 4	
	APR 3	APR 4	
	REB 1	REB 1	

Low Support

Figure 1 Parenting style effectiveness.[7]

As the chart depicts, children raised by *authoritative* parents ranked first in self-worth, conforming (submission) to authority, and accepting parents' religion. They ranked last in rebellion against society.

In second place, to many people's surprise, came the *permissive* parent. This clearly indicates that loving your children (teenagers included) is more important than controlling their behavior. The tragedy is that most parents revert to an authoritarian style of leadership when the going gets tough.

Providing Love and Godly Counsel

Sometimes this need to control our kids comes from a false belief that our parental identity and self-worth is dependent upon how well our children behave. If we believe that way, we will automatically seek to control any person or circumstance that threatens our sense of well-being—our children included!

If, however, our identity is firmly rooted and grounded in Christ and we are set on being and becoming the people God created us to be, we will be far more concerned about controlling ourselves than controlling others.

> Only God can give us the capacity through His Spirit to ⦁ ⦁ ⦁ ⦁ ⦁ consistently and unconditionally love our teens, even in the face of their unloveliness.

Can anyone or anything keep us from developing Christlike characters demonstrated by the fruit of the Spirit? Can anyone or anything stop us from loving others? Being joyful? Full of peace, patience and kindness? No. The only person that can prevent that from happening is we ourselves.

But what if my teen rebels? we may ask. Our kids cannot stop us from being and becoming the men, husbands or fathers God wants us to be. Our kids cannot stop us from being and becoming the women, wives or mothers God wants us to be. Only we can do that.

During those times of family crisis our families need us more than ever to be the men or women of God He created us to be. You see, we may not always be able to control our teens' behavior, especially as they grow older. Because of who we are in Christ, however, we can always love them. That is the way God treats us, and that is the way we need to treat others.

God loves us because His character is love. He loves us even when we are not too lovable. When our resources of love run out, God's reservoir of love remains inexhaustible. Therefore, only God can give us the capacity through His Spirit to consistently and unconditionally love our teens, even in the face of their unloveliness.

Our identity, security and joy in Christ are not dependent upon other people (including our teens!) or circumstances we have no right or ability to control.

Once we grab hold of that truth, it will wonderfully liberate us as we seek to provide unconditional love and acceptance along with godly counsel and discipline to the teenagers in our homes or youth groups.

So, you may be asking, *how do I provide godly counsel and discipline to teenagers? How can I shape their wills without breaking their spirits?* Great questions. Before we get to some practical "how-to's," we have to make sure we are on the same page, talking about the same things.

To begin with, discipline is different from punishment. Punishment focuses on past behavior and involves paying someone back for what they did. Its motive is really revenge, as if to say, You did _____ to me (or someone else) and so I am going to do _____ to you in return!

As Christian parents, we have no right to punish our teens. When Jesus died on the cross, He cried out, "It is finished!" or "Paid in full!" (John 19:30). Christ took upon Himself the full payment for our sins—and our teenagers. When we punish our teens in anger and revengeful spirits, we violate Romans 12:19:

> Never take your own revenge, beloved, but leave room for the wrath of God, for it is written, 'Vengeance is mine, I will repay,' says the Lord.

Do you want to create anger and fear in your teens? Then punish them. If you want them to be conformed to the image of Christ, however, discipline them in love. The apostle John's words apply not only to our relationship with God, but also to teenagers' relationships with their parents:

> There is no fear in love; but perfect love casts out fear, because fear involves punishment, and the one who fears is not perfected in love (1 John 4:18).

Discipline, on the other hand, is future oriented. Discipline says, "I love you and don't want you to hurt yourself or others. Therefore, in order to protect you and help you to mature, this is what is going to happen..." Discipline in love superintends future choices.

The writer of the book of Hebrews reminds us that God does not punish His children in anger, but rather disciplines them in love:

> "My son, do not regard lightly the discipline of the Lord, nor faint when you are reproved by Him; for those whom the Lord loves He disciplines, and He scourges every son whom He receives" (12:5,6).

Though discipline is an act of love and not angry revenge, that does not mean it is a pleasant process. Again, the book of Hebrews explains:

> All discipline for the moment seems not to be joyful, but sorrowful; yet to those who have been trained by it, afterwards it yields the peaceful fruit of righteousness (v. 11).

An important distinction exists between *discipline* and *judgment* as well. Discipline is directed toward behavior, while judgment is related to character.

For example, suppose your teenage son drives the family car to the mall without permission. On the way home, he rear-ends another car and smashes the front of your car. How would you respond?

If you said, "Son, what you did was wrong. You had no right to take out the car without permission. You will be responsible for paying for the repairs," would you be judging him? Of course not. You are simply making a correct observation of his behavior and determining a healthy discipline as a result.

If, however, you said, "You idiot! How many times have I told you to ask before taking the car? You never listen! You are completely irresponsible!" then you would be judging him. You are attacking his character.

When we discipline our children in love based on observed behavior, they can own up to what they have done and receive God's forgiveness. The conflict has ended. They can learn from their mistakes and commit themselves to do better by God's grace. They will still have to live with any consequences of their sins, but that is part of the learning process for all of us.

On the other hand, if we attack the teen's character, what can he do about it? He can choose to change his behavior (what he does), but he can't immediately change his character (who he is).

Discipline never involves character assassination. When we attack a teenager's character, we can count on his becoming defensive. Who wouldn't? Then if we try to overpower his defensiveness by calling him names (such as "stupid," "jerk" or "no good"), we may crush his spirit. At the least, we will seriously damage our relationship with him. We need to ask our children to forgive us if we have verbally judged their character.

How much pain and damage to teenagers would be avoided if authority figures (especially parents) simply obeyed one command of Scripture:

> Let no unwholesome word proceed from your mouth, but only such a word as is good for edification [building up] according to the need of the moment, that it may give grace to those who hear (Eph. 4:29).

The next verse tells us that the Spirit of God is grieved when we use our tongues to tear down. Let's commit ourselves to become part of God's building crew rather than Satan's wrecking crew. Remember, reckless words do not wreck less, they wreck more.

As we begin to discuss the area of setting effective rules and handing out appropriate discipline for breaking them, let Galatians 6:1,2 be a foundational Scripture to protect your attitude as a parent or youth leader.

> Brethren, even if a man is caught in any trespass, you who are spiritual, restore such a one in a spirit of gentleness, each one looking to yourself, lest you too be tempted. Bear one another's burdens, and thus fulfill the law of Christ.

Restoration to Christ of the one caught sinning must be our desire. If we are walking in the fullness of the Spirit, demonstrating the Spirit's fruit of gentleness, and humbly admitting our own capacity

Wise, godly discipline must be based on prior clear communication of rules, rewards and consequences.

to react in the flesh, we can bear (not add to!) the burdens of another. In so doing, we will fulfill the law of Christ—we will love.

Wise, godly discipline must first of all be based on prior clear communication of rules, rewards and consequences. One sure way to exasperate a teen is to discipline him for something he did not know was wrong. As you are creating the ground rules, make sure you have your teen repeat back to you what you are saying. For teens who are in the habit of forgetting what was agreed upon, you will need to write down the rules.

Consider preparing a contract signed by the teenager and the parent(s). It certainly will remove all future doubt and can be a fun thing to do together if written in the right spirit. We encourage you to discuss with your teen what he feels are reasonable rewards and consequences for keeping his end of the bargain. If his ideas are good, go with them. If not, try to come to a consensus together. It will communicate to him that you care about his feelings and value his opinions. That gesture of trust may make all the difference in the world in his deciding to follow through on the commitment. The contract for a 15-year-old daughter might look something like the example on the following page.

Rules Must Be Effective

For rules to be effective, they must be *defensible, definable and enforceable.*

Defensible rules must have a legitimate basis for existence for both teen and parent. In the contract between parents and teenager, the parents' motivation was to allow their daughter more time to have fun in a healthy environment, but making reasonable provision for her safety.

Some rules are legitimate simply because parents want their teens to develop a sense of responsibility. For example, the rule "Your room must be clean before you are permitted to go out with your friends" may be met with the question, "Why?" If so, be prepared to give a calm, reasonable answer such as, "Because as your parents we believe it's important that you learn to be a good steward of your possessions."

In some cases, your teen's question may be a challenge to your authority, questioning whether you have the right to give an order and testing to see if he really has to obey it. You better ask the Lord for the strength and wisdom to stand firm and win these battles of the will, and you better be prepared for all manner of excuses, such as:

> It's my room. I should be able to keep it any way I want.
>
> None of my friends' parents make them keep their rooms clean.
>
> Can I do it later? I promise I'll do it before I go to bed.
>
> I know exactly where everything is. If I clean it I'll be lost.

You will also need to seek the Lord's wisdom and as parents agree ahead of time which issues are worth being firm about and which can be compromised.

Contract for Extended Curfew on Saturday Night

I, (name of parent), hereby grant our daughter, (name of daughter), permission to stay up until 12 midnight or out until 11:00 P.M. on Saturday nights, on the following conditions:

1. That we know where she is and have given our prior approval of her being there.

2. That we know who she is with and have given our prior approval of her being with them.

3. That she is up, dressed and ready for church Sunday mornings by 8:45 A.M.

Faithful obedience to the above conditions during a six-month time period will result in a similar extension of curfew for Friday nights. In addition, the option of hosting/participating in an all-night slumber party once every six weeks on a Friday night will be added.

Failure to fulfill any of the three conditions once will result in one month of 10:00 P.M. Friday- and Saturday-night curfews. Failure to fulfill any of the three conditions more than once will result in being grounded for a period of time to be determined later, should the necessity arise.

Signed _____

       (parent)   (date)

_____

     (daughter)   (date)

For example, how will you handle it when your teen decides he or she should no longer be required to do the following:

Go on family vacations with the rest of you?
Join you in visiting relatives for holidays and family reunions?
Eat dinner with the family?
Go to church, Sunday School or youth group?[8]

Do you set firm limits or do you compromise and allow for flexibility in the following areas?

What music they will listen to and how loud it
  can be in the house.
What friends they will have.
How they will wear their hair.
What part(s) of their bodies they will pierce.
What clothes they will wear (or won't wear).
What movies and TV shows they will watch.
How they will spend their free time.
What classes they will take in school.
What hobbies or extracurricular activities they will
  participate in.
How they will spend (or save) their money.
Who they will date and what time they will be home.
When (or if!) they will do homework.
Whether they will attend college.
What kind of car they will drive.
How much time they will devote to playing
  computer or video games.[9]

The list of possible areas of conflict seems never ending. Therefore, it is critical for parents to seek the Lord's wisdom in how to respond. He promises to give it generously as we ask in faith (see Jas. 1:5).

Some rules are not defensible because they represent a double standard. You can be sure your teen will pick up on any hypocrisy immediately. Rules such as "No music will be allowed in our home except Christian music, so get rid of that trash you're listening to" may be hypocritical.

Do you allow, for example, listening to and watching non-Christian music on TV in your house? Do you listen to country music yourself? To what radio station is the car stereo tuned?

Do your rules expose a naiveté about life (and teenagers)—a simplistic, uninformed approach that your kids will sniff out in an instant? Do you believe, for instance, that all secular music is evil and all Christian music is good? What about classical music, for example?

Rather than forcing some legalistic standard on your teens that is not biblically defensible, maybe you would be better off listening to some of your teenagers' favorite music together with them and discussing it in view of Philippians 4:8:

> Finally, brethren, whatever is true, whatever is honorable, whatever is right, whatever is pure, whatever is lovely, whatever is of good repute, if there is any excellence and if anything worthy of praise, let your mind dwell on these things.

Teach your teens how to make wise decisions on their own based on Scripture. Then you can win some points with your teens by doing the same exercise with the music (or TV shows, movies or books) *you* listen to, watch or read!

As you implement defensible rules in your home, you can help your teenagers develop strong moral convictions and principles that will instruct them all through life. They will learn to ask critical questions such as:

> Would Jesus do this? What would He do in this situation?
>
> Can I do this and not violate Philippians 4:8?
>
> Will doing this produce a deed of the flesh or the fruit of the Spirit?
>
> Would I want someone to be treating my sister, brother or me this way?

Can I glorify God in my body doing this and will I be
a positive witness for Christ?

Second, *definable* rules have meanings that are clear to everyone
involved. Rather than saying something like, "Clean your room or
you can't go out," be more specific. What is clean to your son or
daughter may look like a place needing federal disaster relief funds
to you. Make it clear that you want the bed made, dirty clothes
thrown in the hamper and so on.

◗◗◗◗◗ Remember: *Rules without relationship lead to rebellion.*

Again, do everything possible to maintain peace between yourself
and your teens (see Rom. 12:18). Sit down with them and talk through
the difficult rules. Make sure everyone agrees on the meaning of
words and the rationale for the rules themselves. Listen to what your
teens are saying. They may have some good ideas. You communicate
respect by talking with them rather than just laying down the law.

When tension is increasing in the home and teens seem to be
bristling because of your household rules and regulations, it is time
to strengthen your relationship with your kids. Remember: *Rules
without relationship lead to rebellion.*

Third, rules must be *enforceable.* Do not set any rules you will be
unwilling to enforce, and thus hinder the process of rendering the
rewards of obedience or consequences of disobedience.

Teens will push you to the limits of your patience and perseverance at times, but stick to your guns. That is the only way to maintain your authority and dignity as a parent.

Fred Green, in his article entitled "What Parents Could Have
Done," relates the words of juvenile offenders. Let them be a
reminder to you when you are tempted to cave in on the rules God
has led you to set up in your home:

SHAKE ME UP. Punish me when I first go wrong. Tell

me why. Convince me that more severe measures will come if I transgress again in the same manner. CALL MY BLUFF. Stand firm on what is right, even when your kid threatens to run away or becomes a delinquent or drops out of school. Stay in there with him and the bluffing will cease in 98 percent of the cases.[10]

Consistency is without a doubt the most difficult task in disciplining. Teens are masters at wearing down parents. You will probably have an easier time standing firm, however, if you work with a few strong rules rather than trying to keep track of a long list of family regulations. Pick your "battle fronts" carefully. Through diligently seeking the Lord's guidance and discernment through prayer, studying God's Word and consulting with other godly parents, you will know which limits to set and which to let go.

Finally, make sure the discipline you administer relates to the behavior you are trying to correct. Grounding, for example, is not a cure-all for every problem. It should be used as a discipline only when teens show that they are incapable of making wise decisions about where they go, what they do and who they are with outside the home. It is for the teen's protection as well as correction.

Deprivation (for a reasonable period of time) of an activity the teen enjoys can be an effective discipline. Again, however, make sure the consequences fit the "crime." For instance, forbidding a young person to be involved in an extracurricular activity at school would probably not be the best discipline for missing a curfew. It might be a legitimate discipline, however, if the teen is consistently tired and unable to stay awake to do homework.

Strong-willed and stubborn teens may balk every step of the way, refusing to bow their hearts to any correction you try to impose upon them. God, however, is bigger than the obstinate teen and is not mocked. Whatever someone sows, this the person will also reap. Teenagers who sow to their own flesh shall from the flesh reap corruption; but teens who sow to the Spirit shall from the Spirit reap eternal life (see Gal. 6:7,8).

Many acts of disobedience have natural consequences that accompany them. Young people who steal may get caught. Teenagers who lie could lose close friends. Sexually active teens might get pregnant or suffer a Pandora's box of sexually transmitted diseases (STDs).

It is an unfortunate fact of life that certain people simply have to learn the hard way. Those children born with a predisposition toward confrontational or oppositional behavior often fall into this category.

Be assured that God is fully able to bring the prodigal to his senses. The harsh reality of life is that not all will find their way back home again. Our role is to be ready to throw open our hearts and arms if he does.

If you are unsure about what kind of discipline is appropriate, ask God!

Like anything else, the Lord promises us wisdom when we lack it (see Jas. 1:5). Ask the Lord what discipline He wants you to give your teens, and for how long. He may have an idea you had never thought of.

For example, what kind of effect might it have upon your teenager to spend three months of Saturday nights working at a downtown rescue mission as a discipline for underage drinking? It could be life changing.

At the very least, God will enable you to be merciful and gracious even as you are being tough in your love. So bring Him into the discipline process. He is far more concerned about the character of your teens than you are!

An Effective Parenting Example

When my (Neil's) daughter, Heidi, was approaching her twelfth birthday, I took her out for a special talk over lunch. We discussed freedom and responsibility. I took out my Bible and read Luke 2:52: "Jesus kept increasing in wisdom and stature, and in favor with God and men." Then I drew a simple diagram on a piece of paper. See figure 2 on next page.

After drawing the diagram, I said to her, "Honey, Jesus wants you to be like Him and grow up spiritually, physically, socially and mentally. Right now you probably feel kind of boxed in, like my picture. I'm sure you want the freedom to be all that God wants you to be, and your mother and I want that for you as well.

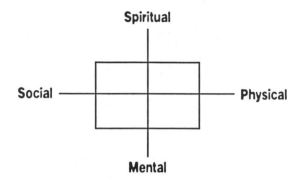

Figure 2 Four areas of growth.[11]

"Look at these four areas of growth. Spiritually, God wants you to have a great relationship with Him and grow up to be like Him. To do that you have to know the Word of God. You also need to learn how to pray and walk by faith in the power of the Holy Spirit. You have to put some effort into your relationship with God, just like you do with any other relationship.

"Your mom and I pray with you every night, take you to Sunday School, pay your way to Christian camps and encourage you to read your Bible. But someday, Honey, we won't be there to do that for you. You will go off to college or get a job and you'll need to pursue God on your own.

"Physically, we have helped you to develop good habits of eating, sleeping, exercising and taking care of your body. We hope that you will continue to develop these habits when you're on your own.

"Socially, we take you places and encourage you to have your friends over. We have attempted to teach you how to get along with others and to resolve conflicts when they arise. At times we have even had to step in between you and your brother when you were quarreling or fighting. But someday we won't be around to do that. It is our prayer that you will know how to get along with people and choose friends who will help you in your walk with God.

"Mentally, you are doing well in school. Right now we are here to remind you to do your homework and turn it in on time. When you go to college you will have to rely on your own study habits, not our reminders.

"You see, Honey, the outer lines on this square show where you are right now. They represent the boundaries we have set for you to live within. But we want to keep expanding those boundaries so that year by year you will have more freedom to make your own choices.

"We will increase your freedom as you demonstrate that you are becoming more responsible. For example, we still have to tell you to clean your room. But if you keep your room clean consistently, we will eventually let you decorate it the way you want.

"In a few years you can start dating when you show that you are ready. The first year you'll be allowed to stay out until about 10:00 P.M., depending on where you go. If you do well with that rule, we will give you more time to stay out. That will be true for every area of your life. When you show that you are responsible and can be trusted, we will give you more freedom.

"That's the way Jesus deals with all of us. He said, "'Well done, good and faithful servant! You have been faithful with a few things; I will put you in charge of many things'" (Matt. 25:21, NIV).

"Your mother and I will not decide how much freedom you have. That will be your decision, determined by how faithful and responsible you are. By the time you are 18, hopefully there will no longer be a box around you. You will be on your own and free to do whatever God wants you to do."

Parenting is, in reality, an 18-year process of letting go. God has ordained for the husband and wife to cleave together, but for the children to one day leave their parents (see Matt. 19:5).

During the years your children are in your care, the greatest gift you can give them is yourself. Your loving attention is the most effective tool at your disposal. Spend time with your kids. Put their special events on your calendar and consider them unbreakable appointments. Let them see the love and truth of Jesus Christ radiate in your actions and attitudes, not just in your words.

One day you will stand before God and give an account of the stewardship of the lives He entrusted to you. Will that moment be a time of celebration or mourning? Your faithfulness to unconditionally accept and lovingly discipline your kids will be what He looks for in you as a parent. What will the judgment seat of Christ reveal?

The following list, adapted from a Young Life parenting workshop, "Raising Healthy Teenagers," is sobering and challenging food for thought:

20 Ways to Encourage Your Children to Use Drugs

1. Never eat together as a family.
2. Never have family outings that occur weekly, monthly or annually—outings they can look forward to as a family unit.
3. Always talk to your teens, never with them. And never listen.
4. Punish your kids in public, and never praise them or reinforce their positive behavior.
5. Always solve their problems, and make their decisions for them.
6. Leave the responsibility of teaching morality and spirituality to the schools and church.
7. Never let your teens experience cold, fatigue, adventure, injury, risk, challenge, experimentation, failure, frustration or disappointment.
8. Threaten them. ("If you ever try drugs or alcohol, so help me, I'll...")
9. Expect your kids to get A's in school in all subjects.
10. Always pick up after them, and don't encourage them to accept responsibility.
11. Discourage your teens from talking about or expressing their feelings (anger, sadness, fear, anxiety, etc.). Instead, just tell them to "trust God."
12. Be overprotective; don't teach your kids the meaning of the word "consequence."
13. Make them feel as though all their mistakes are sins.
14. Always put your teens off when they ask "Why?" by answering, "Because I said so."
15. Do all you can to appear perfect and infallible. And never, ever admit to your kids when you are wrong.

16. Keep your home environment in a state of worry, hurry and chaos.
17. Never let your teens know how much you love them; never discuss your feelings with them.
18. Never hug them or display any affection for your spouse in front of them.
19. Always expect the worst and make sure you point out something wrong with everything they do, no matter how good a job they did.
20. Never trust them.[12]

In the mid-seventies, Harry and Sandy Chapin wrote a haunting song, "Cat's in the Cradle." It is the story of a man too busy to be home and play with his boy as he grows up. He misses his son's first steps and passes up those precious, once-in-a-lifetime moments of being involved in the boy's life. Before the dad realizes what he has missed, his son is off to college and busy with his own life.

Now retired, the dad tries to recapture those lost years, longing to get involved again in his son's life. The dad calls him on the phone, hoping to get together. His boy, however, now fully grown, has a hectic life of his own and all the responsibilities of a job and family. He puts off his dad's attempts of getting together, much like his dad had once done with him.

Some of the final words, spoken by the dad after that disappointing phone call, are still a wake-up call 23 years after they were written:

"And as I hung up the phone it occurred to me: My boy was just like me. He's turned out just like me."

We are not able to turn back the clock and change what has already happened. The ways in which we have neglected, abused or in some way violated our sacred responsibility as parents dare not be denied or continued. Yet, though much damage may have been done, there is always hope in the grace of our Lord Jesus Christ and in the God whose mercies are new every morning (see Lam. 3:22,23).

It is not wishful thinking nor is it trite sentimentalism, but the truth of God that He indeed "causes *all things* to work together for good to those who love God, to those who are called according to

His purpose" (Rom. 8:28, emphasis added). Do you know that? Do you *believe* that? If so, then why not join us in prayer:

> Dear heavenly Father,
>
> You are the perfect Parent, completely loving, perfectly just and unswervingly faithful. I stand before You to admit my imperfection and even sin as a father/mother. (Be specific in confession as the Lord directs). But I also stand before You washed in the blood of Jesus who cleanses me from all sin (1 John 1:7). Thank You for Your wonderful forgiveness.
>
> Lord, please turn even the mistakes and iniquities of my past dealings with my children into good. I do indeed love You and know I am called according to Your purpose of becoming like Your Son, the Lord Jesus (Rom. 8:28,29). Please heal the hurts I have caused my children.
>
> I now declare my complete dependence on You, Father, for all my needs. I am Your child; I need You to be my Parent. And I need You to give me Your power, wisdom and love today to be the father/mother You want me to be. In Jesus' forgiving and healing name I pray. Amen.

Let Freedom Ring!

It is tough enough being a parent when you are the primary influence in a child's life. Life at best, though, is not so simple. A battle is raging for the heart and soul of every teenager, and the influences from the world, the flesh and the devil are a constant threat.

To help our young people find and maintain their freedom in Christ, it is crucial that parents and youth leaders are able to say they are not ignorant of Satan's schemes. If we ignore or deny the reality of the supernatural world, the devil will surely take advantage of us (see 2 Cor. 2:11).

The following letter is a true story. Names and places have been altered, but the chilling reality is that the spiritual battle that took place in the life of this young man is not unique. It is being repeated in thousands of ways in thousands of homes—Christian homes—across our nation. Fortunately, this story ends in victory. Tragically, that too often is not the case.

Dear Dr. Anderson,

My husband pastors a church in the Midwest and a large portion of our congregation went through your books Victory Over the Darkness *and* The Bondage Breaker *last year with wonderful results. We appreciate your ministry very much, but this week it hit especially close to home.*

On Monday morning we were getting ready to leave for an area pastors' meeting when we received a phone call from the mother of a close friend of my 14-year-old son (we have five other children). She shared with us that our son, Nathan, had had a phone conversation with her daughter the night before. He had expressed to her great fears he had, and thoughts of suicide which included how he thought of carrying out his plan.

We knew Nathan had been troubled recently but he hadn't been able to open up to us. He had been at a youth retreat recently as well as a youth conference that had been a very powerful time. He shared with his friend that while at those events he would be bombarded with thoughts such as— You don't belong here. This isn't for you, etc.

Nathan made a commitment to Christ as a young boy, but I feel through various choices as he grew older, opened up doors to the enemy. Probably one of the most significant was poor choices in music which had lyrics which filled his mind with many suggestions of violence, etc.

When we received this call Monday we were of course shocked, concerned and upset. Nathan was already at school and so we went on to our meeting after crying out for God's help.

Our meeting began with a time for worship. At the end of the worship, a man shared a "vision" he felt the Lord gave him during that time. He had seen someone hanging from a craggy cliff by a thread. He saw the thread become a rope, then a rope ladder, then a stairway, then an escalator. God had a plan of rescue for this person. I broke down and wept. This was God's encouragement to us that He was at work. Our friends gathered around and supported us in prayer.

What I have seen this week is God's orchestrated plan for Nathan unfolding before my eyes. It has been awesome to see things fitting together. My husband has been taking the senior high students at my son's Christian school through the youth editions of your books. They are scheduled to pray through the Steps to Freedom in Christ next week. We didn't feel God wanted Nathan to have to wait that long.

We asked many people to pray for us. Along with a close friend, we spent some time with Nathan. Thankfully he was able to share some of his fears and thoughts with us. We prayed and encouraged him to go through the Steps to Freedom with our friend and Nathan's youth pastor. We praise God! He was willing to do that. They met that evening and Nathan did business with God. We know he now walks in new freedom in Christ.

Since the end of October we have been experiencing an amazing awakening in our fellowship with some of the most powerful things happening among our youth. We know this is just a taste of what God has ahead, but we are rejoicing and being refreshed by His Spirit.

We know that when God moves like this, the enemy also steps up his attacks. We thank God for your materials which are helping us to train ourselves and our congregation to stand in victory.

And we thank God for the difference this made in our son's life this week.

Elisha's Supernatural Protection

The king of Syria was upset. No, he was *furious*. Each time he made battle plans against Israel, they were foiled. Israel somehow always managed to escape from his cleverly calculated schemes. The king's *natural* conclusion? A traitor must be involved!

His servants, however, assured him that something else was going on, something *supernatural*. Their answer is recorded in 2 Kings 6:12:

> And one of his servants said, "No, my lord, O king; but Elisha, the prophet who is in Israel, tells the king of Israel the words that you speak in your bedroom."

What an unnerving thought! It certainly was to the king because he made immediate plans to go to Dothan and capture the eavesdropping prophet. To make sure he got his man he sent "horses and chariots and a great army there, and they came by night and surrounded the city" (v. 14).

Early the next morning, Elisha's servant—no doubt yawning and stretching and rubbing his eyes—went outside and almost choked on his morning cup of coffee. Panic stricken about seeing the attacking Syrian army surrounding the city, he cried out to his master, Elisha, for help.

Was Elisha worried? Did he immediately start formulating an escape plan? Was he caught up in his servant's fear? Absolutely not! Instead, Elisha encouraged his servant and prayed for him. Elisha's words and God's response to his prayer are critical for us to understand:

So he [Elisha] answered, "Do not fear, for those who are with us are more than those who are with them." Then Elisha prayed and said, "O Lord, I pray, open his eyes that he may see." And the Lord opened the servant's eyes, and he saw; and behold, the mountain was full of horses and chariots of fire all around Elisha (vv. 16,17).

You see, both the king of Syria and Elisha's servant had the same basic problem: they did not understand the reality of the supernatural world. They relied solely on what their five senses and rational minds could teach them. They needed to have their eyes opened. Perhaps you do, too.

The fascinating thing about Elisha's answer to his servant is how discerning he is into the spiritual realm. Notice he said, "Those who are *with us* are more than those who are *with them*." Who were the ones *with us*? Clearly it was the angelic host of God pictured as horses and chariots of fire surrounding Elisha with a protective shield! Then who was *with them*? The evil powers of darkness—unseen yet clearly motivating the attack against the man of God!

What an encouraging word to us when we feel as though all hell is arrayed against us or our teens! Truly "greater is He who is in you than he who is in the world" (1 John 4:4)!

An Eye-Opening Process

During the course of my Christian life, I (Rich) have gone through a process of having my eyes opened. At first, I thought the reality of spiritual powers was something prevalent only in the first century. Jesus had to confront the demonic because "those people back then" were primitive and unsophisticated. So I thought, certainly in twentieth-century America we are beyond that superstitious nonsense.

Then I began to hear of incidents of demonic encounters in remote tribal areas around the world today. So not wanting to label all these missionaries as liars or fools, I admitted the possibility that demon activity could still be around today—over there.

After a while, I was willing to believe some pretty weird stuff was going on in some parts of our country—groups of satanists in isolated rural areas and maybe in the ghettos of the deep, inner city. That kind of thing.

Then I began to see that the spiritual battle was much closer than I had first thought. I started meeting with wonderful Christian people—teenagers included—who were struggling with unexplainable blackouts, depressions, fears, voices and frightening compulsions to do evil and inflict harm. My eyes were opened to the reality of the spiritual realm *in the Church!*

The last stage of this eye-opening process was the most humbling. Seeing areas of bondage in my own life broken by submitting to God and resisting the devil brought me to the stark reality that spiritual battle is not *out there*. It is *here!* It is primarily a battle for our minds.

The Battle for the Mind

A common question at this point goes something like this: *How do we know that a problem is spiritual and not just psychological?* Or maybe you are wondering, *How can I tell if my teen is suffering from some form of demonic influence or whether it is a mental illness?*

The motivation behind these concerns, we believe, is a legitimate desire to get to the root of a person's problem and not cause unnecessary trauma. That should always be our desire. The problem, though, is that our lives are not divided into neat little compartments—body, soul and spirit—that have no interaction between them.

A physical illness can result in depression. Depression can cause physical illnesses. The physical affects the mental and emotional and vice versa. The medical profession claims that more than 50 percent of physical illnesses are psychosomatic in origin.

Psychologists or psychiatrists define "mental health" as being in touch with reality and relatively free from anxiety. That is a fair measure, but people under spiritual attack would fail on both counts.

For example, we have counseled many people who claim to "hear" voices in their heads or have nagging, obsessive thoughts. Is this just a chemical imbalance in the brain causing the misfiring of neurotransmitters? Does it not seem remarkable that random chemical reactions create intelligible thoughts that run counter to the truth of the Word of God? Could that possibly happen? Could another explanation be that people are "paying attention to deceitful spirits" (1 Tim. 4:1)?

The average secular counselor, however, would say this person is hallucinating or "out of touch with reality." Who, though, is *really* the one "out of touch"—the one struggling with a battle for his or her mind or the counselor who denies the possibility that a spiritual problem exists?

It is imperative that we create an environment in our homes, youth ▪ ▪ ▪ ▪ ▪ groups and churches in which teens feel the freedom to be themselves and speak openly.

The rise of New Age philosophies prompts some counselors to identify these voices as helpful "spirit guides." Is that true? Not having a biblical grid through which to take their experience, these counselors will be unable to help their patients resolve their conflicts.

If what is being diagnosed as mental illness is in reality nothing more than a battle for the mind, how can it be discovered? That is what we hope to clarify in this book.

When visiting a doctor and complaining of a physical ailment, we expect to have our blood, urine, vital signs and so on checked. If the tests all indicated we were in good physical health, would we be upset? Of course not. We would simply move on to investigate some other possible cause for our problems.

If your teen is struggling with obsessive thoughts, chronic depression or anxiety attacks, wouldn't you want a safe way to check the source of those problems? Beyond that, wouldn't you want some answers to help resolve the conflicts if indeed the root problems were spiritual?

If churches followed the procedure described in this book, the teens you love would not be labeled, judged, rejected or charged! If the conflicts are not resolved by the end of the appointment, go see a doctor! You have nothing to lose.

It is imperative that we create an environment in our homes, youth groups and churches in which teens feel the freedom to be themselves, speak openly and "walk in the light" (1 John 1:7). God operates in the light of truth, sincerity and honesty. The devil loves the darkness and tries to keep young people from sharing what they are really thinking and feeling.

Creating the Right Atmosphere

What does it take to produce an atmosphere in which teens feel the freedom to share what is *really* going on inside?

First and foremost, it takes the prayers of God's people to pull down the fleshly defense mechanisms that keep young people (and adults) closed off from others.

Second, it takes grace-filled parents or church leaders who communicate verbally and nonverbally that home, church, youth group and so on are safe places where acceptance is "in" and rejection is "out."

Third, it usually takes someone breaking the ice and sharing something personal and painful in his or her life—maybe confessing a sin or struggle or failure.

It is crucial that parents and youth leaders set the pace in letting down their guard and admitting they have feet of clay just like the rest of the world.

Being Vulnerable

A few years ago I (Rich) had dinner alone with my parents. I took the opportunity in that restaurant to ask my mom and dad what they wish I had done differently when I was a teenager. My mom did not hesitate to answer.

"We wish you had cooperated more. You were so disagreeable. If we said 'black,' you said 'white.' If we said 'yes,' you'd say 'no.'"

My dad nodded in hearty agreement between bites of his prime rib.

Hoping that my vulnerability would be reciprocated by my parents, I waited for them to ask me what I wished *they* had done differently. The silence was loud. Finally I just decided to plunge in and ask the question.

"Mom, Dad, do you mind if I tell you what I wish you had done differently when I was a teenager?"

My mom seemed eager for my answer. My dad did not seem quite as confident.

I decided to jump in anyway. "I wish that you had admitted to me when you were wrong and apologized to me when you had hurt me. I knew when you were wrong and I lost respect for you when you refused to own up to it."

My dad's response was classic. "Parents are not supposed to admit to their kids when they're wrong!"

I was glad my mom jumped in. "Oh, they are so, John!"

My parents never really knew what was going on inside my brain during those volatile teenage years. Had they taken a few steps back then to tear down the façades and yank off the masks, maybe I would have felt the freedom to be more real myself.

The Mystery of a Teenager's Mind

Usually we do not know what teenagers are thinking for two obvious reasons. One reason is that we can't read minds. The other reason is that too often they are afraid to tell us what they are thinking for fear of being laughed at, embarrassed, rejected or labeled "mentally ill" or "crazy."

We need to talk frankly and lovingly about the battle going on for our minds so that teenagers can know they are *not* alone in their struggles and that they are not losing their minds. They are being victimized by a cruel enemy, but they have great hope in Christ because He came to "destroy the works of the devil" (1 John 3:8).

Freedom from Anxiety

If being in touch with reality is the first criterion for mental health, the second is being relatively free from anxiety. In our book *Know Light, No Fear*, which is the youth version of Neil's book *Walking in the Light*, we analyze and offer a lengthy biblical response to both fear and anxiety. Let us touch on some key points here as they relate to our discussion.

Anxiety is a troubling, unsettling fear of the unknown. It comes from a lack of trust in God and results in feelings of uncertainty. We worry about whether our needs will be met and what tomorrow may bring (see Matt. 6:25-34).

What is the solution? Seek first the kingdom of God and His righteousness and all the things we need will be provided for us (see v. 33). We are warned not to worry about what the future holds, but to just concern ourselves with today and trust God for tomorrow (see v. 34).

We can cast all our anxieties on the Lord because He cares for us. He is looking after us (see 1 Pet. 5:7). Therefore, when anxious thoughts threaten to derail our faith, we are told to let our requests be made known to God with thanksgiving. Why thanksgiving? Because giving thanks demonstrates faith in God. The result? God promises His supernatural peace will keep us from going crazy or losing heart (see Phil. 4:6,7).

Freedom from Fear

Unlike anxiety, fear has a specific object. Fear *of heights*, fear *of open spaces*, fear *of death* are just some examples. For a fear object to have control over us, we must perceive it to be both *present* and *powerful*. That is, we feel it is nearby and able to hurt us.

To strip that fear of its control we need merely to remove one of those two attributes. For example, normally I (Rich) have a healthy fear of great white sharks. But am I afraid right now? No, because I am high and dry in my upstairs office. No sharks are *present* in my office. However, put a wet suit on me and drop me into San Francisco Bay, and watch my emotions of fear soar!

Fear of the Darkness

Larry had been afraid of the dark for more than 40 years, and he never understood why. Dark water, dark houses and unknown situations posed a very real threat to him.

After going through the Steps to Freedom in Christ, he still sensed that fear was there. So he asked the Lord to reveal to his mind the root cause of it. The Lord immediately answered!

When Larry was four or five years old, he was riding in the family car in the middle of a stormy night. His dad fell asleep at the wheel and the car almost went off a cliff into a rain-swollen river. Providentially, a small tree blocked their path and saved their lives.

So taking his authority in Christ, Larry, as an adult, renounced any stronghold of fear that had taken root in his life as a result of that accident. He affirmed in Christ that the fear could no longer control him.

About a week later he was teaching a Bible study with his family and he mentioned how he had handled that fear. His mom added further insight into how traumatic that event had been for Larry.

"You would not believe how terrified you were that night," she said. "You were hysterically crying and nothing would calm you down. When your dad wanted to go for help, you refused to stay in the car. You had to go with him."

Because of the authority Larry exercised in Christ, the back of that fear has been broken. He is now able to get up at night and walk through the house without turning on every light. He has gone outside in the dark and even hunted at night without that terrorizing fear gripping him.

At times the thought comes back to his mind, *Larry, you need to be afraid.* When he recognizes where that thought is coming from and takes it "captive to the obedience of Christ" (2 Cor. 10:5), it leaves. When he forgets to do that, the fear can take over again.

Obviously, it is impossible for Larry to avoid darkness completely. That will only happen in heaven. So how has he been able to overcome his fear? By breaking its power over him, recognizing that fear is not from God and that the Lord Himself will guard and protect him.

Overcoming the Fear of Death

So how can you help a teen recover from the fear of death? I (Rich) was recently speaking at a youth ski retreat where a young man,

Patrick, approached me with that very problem. He was confused about whether he should believe the Bible or scientific research on life—or no life—after death.

I told him I did not know of any scientist who had been dead for three days and then came back to life, so I was inclined to believe what Jesus said about death and life.

Jesus taught, "Truly, truly, I say to you, he who hears My word, and believes Him who sent Me, has eternal life, and does not come into judgment, but has passed out of death into life" (John 5:24).

After some more questioning and probing, I was able to discern that Patrick had never really trusted Jesus as his Savior and Lord. Was he ever ready, though! Several minutes later he bowed his head and prayed one of the most sincere prayers of repentance and faith I have ever heard.

Then I had him renounce the devil and all his works and all his ways, including the fear of death. Why? Because Scripture says:

> Since then the children share in flesh and blood, He Himself likewise also partook of the same, that through death He might render powerless him who had the power of death, that is, the devil; and might deliver those who through fear of death were subject to slavery all their lives (Heb. 2:14,15).

An incredible change came over Patrick's face once he knew he was a child of God! The Spirit bore witness with his spirit that he was God's child (see Rom. 8:16) and the fear of death was instantly gone.

Why? Had Patrick's faith in Christ eliminated the *presence* of death? No. It is appointed for men to die once, Hebrews 9:27 tells us, and the possibility of physical death is a constant reality. In Christ, however, the *power* of death was defeated in Patrick's life just as the apostle Paul cried out triumphantly in 1 Corinthians 15:55-57:

> "O death, where is your victory? O death, where is your sting?" The sting of death is sin, and the power of sin is the law; but thanks be to God, who gives us the victory through our Lord Jesus Christ.

Every believer in Christ has the same opportunity to overcome the fear of death that Patrick had. The truth sets us free.

Physical life is not the ultimate value anyway. Spiritual life is. We will experience heaven when our souls separate from our bodies, unless we reject Christ. Then it will be hell—literally. Scripture warns, "And do not fear those who kill the body, but are unable to kill the soul; but rather fear Him who is able to destroy both soul and body in hell" (Matt. 10:28).

We dare not assume that the teens in our homes or churches know Christ just because they are "nice kids" who go to church and attend youth-group activities. Patrick had done those things, but did not know Christ. Jesus warned about people who would get really excited about the gospel and show signs of growth. Their true colors, though, eventually would be revealed when the heat was on (see Matt. 13:20,21).

Do not assume that a church-going teen's problems are all a matter of *freedom*; they could be a matter of *salvation*!

Why is the "fear of the Lord" the "beginning of wisdom" (Prov. 9:10)? Because living life wisely begins with a deep reverence for God, humbling oneself under the authority of the source of life, Jesus Christ, and trusting in Him. The "fear of the Lord" is the one fear that expels all other (unhealthy) fears. Consider the words spoken by the Lord to Isaiah:

"You are not to fear what they fear or be in dread of it.
It is the Lord of hosts whom you should regard as holy.
And He shall be your fear, and He shall be your dread.
Then He shall become a sanctuary" (8:12-14).

That is an incredible promise! Do you want your teens to find security, safety and freedom from the fears that plague people of the world? Then teach them a healthy, holy fear of God, and He will become their sanctuary!

Perhaps no other truth needs more desperately to be taught to today's youth culture than a healthy fear of God. The "fear of the Lord is to hate evil" (Prov. 8:13) and to avoid evil (see 16:6).

Why do teenagers experience so much rampant sin in their lives today? Why do *Christian* teenagers experience so much rampant sin in their lives today? Could it be because "there is no fear of God before their eyes" (Rom. 3:18)?

What two attributes of God make Him the ultimate fear object? He is omnipotent (all-powerful) and omnipresent (always present). It is impossible to eliminate either one of those qualities of God.

Unfortunately, too many Christians have missed the fear of God and are instead bound by a fear of Satan. In essence, they have reversed James 4:7, which says, "Submit therefore to God. Resist the devil and he will flee from you." Rather than submitting to God and resisting the devil, they are resisting God and submitting to the devil. No wonder struggles are prevalent!

Fearful Encounters

When I (Neil) have asked Christian audiences around the world if they have had a fearful encounter with some spiritual force, at least 50 percent have said yes. The percentages are even higher among Christian leaders, which is not surprising. If Christians are Satan's target—and they are—then Christian leaders are the "bull's-eye"!

At least 35 percent of the audiences I have surveyed say they have awakened at night, feeling terrified. They probably were half asleep, and perhaps felt pressure on their chests or something grabbing for their throats.

When they tried to speak, they could not say a word. Why not? Because they needed to submit to God first, then resist the devil. God knows our hearts, so we can always turn to Him in our minds. Then we can verbally call on the name of the Lord and be saved. That is how we resist the devil in the case of panic (anxiety) attacks.

We are never told in the Bible to fear the devil. We are warned to "be on the alert" (1 Pet. 5:8), but not to fear. His intimidation tactics are designed to bully us into submission. Satan, however, is a defeated foe because he was disarmed at the Cross (Col. 2:15). He must flee when resisted by a child of God living under submission to the Lord's authority.

Experiencing True Mental Health

A major difference exists, however, between these kinds of attacks and fears that develop over time. Irrational fears (phobias) learned over time must be unlearned, and that takes time. Phobias (as opposed to healthy fears) either compel us to do something irresponsible or prevent us from doing something responsible.

Teenagers who are controlled by phobias need to renounce verbally the fears that have mastered them and affirm out loud, "God

> **True mental health is a by-product of spiritual health, and is built upon the foundation of a true, experiential knowledge of God and a clear understanding of who we are in Christ.**

has not given us a spirit of fear, but of power and of love and of a sound mind" (2 Tim. 1:7, *NKJV*).

Teenagers need to be encouraged to make a commitment to not let that fear (e.g., of people) control them. Have them ask the Lord to give them a plan of action to overcome the fear. Pray with and for them. The plan (if no danger to the teen is involved) may involve facing that fear head-on. A wise man once said, "Do the thing you fear the most, and the death of that fear is certain."

Most fears are like mirages. They dissipate when you move ahead and face them. Avoid them, however, and they can grow to become giants!

Clearly, then, the standard definition of mental health is inadequate. Clearly what is needed, then, is a *biblical* perspective about mental health. In reality, true mental health is a by-product of spiritual health, and is built upon the foundation of a true, experiential knowledge of God and a clear understanding of who we are in Christ.

Mentally healthy teens know that God loves them. They are growing in their ability to trust Him, knowing He is willing and able to meet their needs. They are learning that they can do all things through Him who strengthens them.

They know that He will never leave them nor forsake them and that their sins have been forgiven in Christ. They have grasped the truth that they are children of God and that there is therefore now no condemnation for them in Christ Jesus.

Again, true mental health comes from knowing God and understanding our identity in Christ. Will a teenager's walk with God affect his or her physical, mental and emotional state? Definitely. Consider the following Scripture references:

> When I kept silent [about my sin], my bones wasted away through my groaning all day long. For day and night your hand was heavy upon me; my strength was sapped as in the heat of summer (Ps. 32:3,4, *NIV*).

> Do not be wise in your own eyes; fear the LORD and turn away from evil. It will be healing to your body, and refreshment to your bones (Prov. 3:7,8).

> Why are you in despair, O my soul? And why are you disturbed within me? Hope in God, for I shall again praise Him, the help of my countenance, and my God (Ps. 43:5).

The Interrelationship of Body, Soul and Spirit

Many other passages in the Bible clearly indicate the interrelationship that exists between our bodies, souls and spirits. It should not surprise us then to realize that physical, psychological and spiritual components will likely exist in nearly every struggle teens face in life.

For example, if a teenager gets so busy with activities in her life that she neglects her times with God in prayer and His Word and sleeps in on Sunday mornings, could that affect her in other ways?

Certainly. Maybe she will gradually become more and more stressed-out and anxious about her schoolwork. Consequently, she may become irritable with her family and friends, causing them to pull away from her emotionally. Seeing her life begin to get out of control, the girl may experience depression. In her weakened state she could easily fall prey to a current virus, and become quite ill.

So is her problem spiritual, psychological or physical? The answer is *all of the above*. The question really needs to be: *Where is the root problem?* In the case of this teenage girl, it may be she feels such a driven need to succeed that she gets herself in too deep in the rat race of busyness. Or maybe she wants to please people more than God and so finds herself unable to say no to the requests of others. Something has to give in terms of her time and energy and so God gets the pink slip.

At any rate, a biblical solution is called for. She needs to learn to rest in the grace, acceptance and love of God. She needs to realize that in His presence is the fullness of joy (see Ps. 16:11). She may not be ready or willing to hear that until she is flat on her back, sick in bed with the flu! God's ways are higher than ours and His timing is perfect.

The Influence of the Demonic

So what about the influence of the demonic? What role can that play in a teenager's struggles to experience spiritual and mental health?

I (Rich) was speaking at a chapel in a Christian school, sharing some of the statistics about teenagers from the book *The Seduction of Our Children*. The survey asked questions such as:

Have you ever experienced a presence in your room (seen or heard) that scared you?
Do you struggle with bad thoughts about God?
Is it mentally hard for you to pray and read your Bible?
Have you heard "voices" in your head as though a subconscious self were talking to you, or have you struggled with really bad thoughts?
Have you frequently had thoughts of suicide?

Have you ever had impulsive thoughts to kill someone, such as, "Grab that knife and kill that person"?
Have you ever thought you were different from others
(the Christian life works for others but not for you)?
Are you afraid you might be losing your mind?

After finishing my message, I made myself available to talk with
anyone who wanted to. A 16-year-old girl approached me and said,
"I answered yes to every one of those questions you asked."

She told me she had been having trouble sleeping for two years
and that she felt a cold, evil presence staring at her in her room at
night. She was scared to death in her bedroom and usually ended up
sleeping in her mom's bed.

Anger. Hatred. Bitterness (she had been angry with her parents for
eight years because they had moved when she was in third grade).
Guilt about past homosexual experiences. Loneliness. Depression.
Fear of being beyond help or hope. Voices in her head. Awakening
suddenly at 3:00 A.M. The litany of torment went on and on.

Could all these things have been the result of chemical imbal-
ances in her brain? Perhaps, but not likely. Could she have been simply "manic-depressive" as her dad was diagnosed? Maybe.

The Bible says to "seek first His kingdom and His righteousness"
(Matt. 6:33), so I decided to help her resolve the personal and spiritual conflicts that were robbing her of her freedom in Christ and intimacy with God. After about an hour and a half of walking Sharon
through the Steps to Freedom in Christ, her prayer says it all:

Lord, thank You for setting me free from my bondage
and for answering my prayer by sending someone
here to talk to me. Thank You for giving me a second
chance to live for You.

What if things had not improved in Sharon's life after working on
her relationship with God? Assuming she had been honest and thorough in sharing the problems in her life and she had also been complete in her repentance from sin, then other avenues would have had
to be explored, such as a thorough physical examination.

We are whole people who have a whole God who has the whole answer for our whole lives. We do a great disservice to people by sending them to well-meaning "deliverance" ministers who see the problem as purely demonic and neglect developmental issues and human responsibility. We also fail to help others find freedom when we drop them off at the doorstep of counselors who do not know Christ or who deny the reality of the spiritual world.

Sharon's problems were primarily spiritual. She had allowed the devil to gain a foothold in her life by harboring anger against her parents for eight years. She had opened the door to further bondage by experimenting with homosexual behavior. The anger, guilt and

Our problems in life are *always* spiritual because God is always ◗ ◗ ◗ ◗ ◗ present with us, Christ is our life and it is never safe to take off the armor of God.

shame were eating her up on the inside, preventing her from growing close to the God who loves her.

Feeling cut off from God and unable to walk by faith, she was an easy target for Satan's bullying tactics. Sharon had given way to fear and had allowed the devil to intimidate her through the frightening presence in her room at night.

Not knowing completely where all the root problems lay, I walked her through all seven of the Steps to Freedom in Christ. She had to confront issues in all of them—occult dabbling, lies she had believed, bitterness, rebellion, pride, fleshly sin and generational bondage.

It was important that the slate be completely clean, but a few conflicts seemed to be particularly critical for Sharon to resolve. She needed to forgive from her heart those who had offended her—especially her parents. She had to confess and renounce the wrong uses of her body sexually and experience the guilt-releasing power of Christ's forgiveness. She also needed to renounce fear and declare her position and authority in Christ by faith. When she did this, freedom returned and the terrible mental torment left.

The truth of the matter is that our problems in life are *always* spiritual because God is always present with us, Christ *is* our life and it is never safe to take off the armor of God (see Eph. 6:10-18)!

Awareness of Satan's Deceitfulness

Although we can be tempted by our own fleshly lusts and desires (see Jas. 1:14,15), Satan is also called "the tempter" (Matt. 4:3). He is the god of this world (see 2 Cor. 4:4) and he works through the world system and our flesh to tempt us (see 1 John 2:15-17). Jesus was tempted by the devil and we can expect that to happen to us as well.

Satan and his demons would always like us to take matters into our own hands and try to get our needs and wants met apart from God—that is, through the world and the flesh. That attempt to seduce us into evil to bring us into demonic bondage is a constant threat for God's people.

Satan is also called the accuser of the brethren who accuses the saints before God day and night (see Rev. 12:10). He wants us to believe we are helpless, hopeless, worthless, evil, dirty and full of shame and guilt. His tormenting voice can be a constant horror for some people. This living hell was captured by the psalmist when he wrote:

> All day long my dishonor is before me, and my humiliation has overwhelmed me, because of the voice of him who reproaches and reviles, because of the presence of the enemy and the avenger (Ps. 44:15,16).

The devil's most subtle tactic, though, is to deceive. Through human logic and understanding—as opposed to God's revelation—half-truths and outright lies, Satan seeks to lure God's people away from following Jesus. Consider the apostle Paul's wise warning:

> For I am jealous for you with a godly jealousy; for I betrothed you to one husband, that to Christ I might present you as a pure virgin. But I am afraid, lest as the serpent deceived Eve by his craftiness, your minds should be led astray from the simplicity and purity of devotion to Christ (2 Cor. 11:2,3).

How does the devil deceive us from following Christ alone? He tries to get us to follow a Jesus that is different—but often very close—to the real One. He tries to get us to swallow a different gospel that undermines the grace of God. He also tries to get us to listen to a spirit other than the Holy Spirit (see 2 Cor. 11:4).

False teachers, false prophets, false apostles and even false Christs are everywhere, hawking a "new and improved" faith that easily entraps the spiritually gullible. Teenagers are no exception. Easily captivated by a powerful, charismatic figure, young people can be captured by cults, the occult and false religions.

Whether the message comes through personal contact with people or so-called "spirit guides," books, music, magazines, TV or movies, the source is clear in 1 Timothy 4:1:

> But the Spirit explicitly says that in later times some will fall away from the faith, paying attention to deceitful spirits and doctrines of demons.

As parents and youth leaders, we must be on guard against the devil's "antidote" to lonely, confused and hurting teens—demons masquerading as spirit guides, companions or guardian angels. We should take the warning of 2 Corinthians 11:14,15 very seriously:

> And no wonder, for even Satan disguises himself as an angel of light. Therefore it is not surprising if his servants also disguise themselves as servants of righteousness; whose end shall be according to their deeds.

Beware of angels seeking to establish long-term friendships with teens, especially when they identify themselves by name. Only one angel in all Scripture gives his name—Gabriel—and he was pretty special! The angel Michael is referred to by another angel.

Nowhere in the Bible, however, does an angel seek to become a companion of a human. Angels bring messages from God, ministering to God's people by directing them to trust *Him*, and then they leave. The only exception might be when an angel disguised as a human stranger pays a visit (see Heb. 13:2).

Hearing a Strange "Friendly" Voice

Dave Park and I (Rich) had just finished taking the group through the Steps to Freedom in Christ at a "Stomping Out the Darkness" conference when a youth leader and a teenage girl came up to me all excited. Eileen, the youth leader, explained that the girl, Meggan, had just rid herself of Mario.

"Who's Mario?" I asked, wondering if he was a clingy boyfriend Meggan had been trying to dump.

"Mario is a voice that has been speaking to Meggan for a couple of years now," Eileen explained.

"After I went through the Steps, I called out for Mario, but he didn't answer. I said, 'Mario, are you there?' but there was only silence," Meggan said, and had kind of a puzzled look on her face.

"You know, he never said anything bad. In fact, he told me I could come to this conference," Meggan added, almost defending Mario.

"Yeah, but remember the time I tried to take you through the Steps to Freedom in Christ individually? Mario kept you up all night before so that you were too tired to go through it!" Eileen waited for Meggan's nod.

It was clear to me that Meggan was still a bit confused about the identity of Mario, so I asked, "Meggan, what do you think Mario was?"

"I don't know," she responded, her eyes indicating her genuine desire to know.

"Mario was a spirit guide. He was not a friend at all. Even though he never told you anything bad, that doesn't matter. His purpose was to become your companion so that you wouldn't turn to God for help. You learned to lean on Mario instead of leaning on God, and that was wrong."

Meggan seemed to be understanding, so I continued, "If Mario comes back again, don't let him in. Even if *Super* Mario shows up, don't let him come back, all right?"

She laughed, but then at my urging once and for all renounced Mario as a friend and declared she would have no more to do with spirit guides.

After all, who needs advice from a spirit guide (demon)—regardless of how "helpful"—when we can be led by the Holy Spirit (see Rom. 8:14)?

Satan's Effective Strategy

How effective has Satan's strategy of temptation, accusation and deception been? Let me put it this way: What percentage of the Christian teenagers you know are walking in the love and grace of the Father, the life and joy of the Lord Jesus and the freedom and power of the Holy Spirit?

All this talk about demons attacking believers in Christ can be unsettling for some people. Are we saying that Christians can be demon possessed? Do we believe that the bodies of believers can be invaded by demonic powers?

The Bible clearly declares that our bodies are the temples of the Holy Spirit and that we have been bought with a price—the blood of Jesus. We belong to God and are owned by Him (see 1 Cor. 6:19,20). Since to "possess" something implies ownership, a child of God can never be owned or possessed by the devil or a demon.

Can believers be controlled by a lying or deceiving spirit? Certainly, but not against our wills (see Acts 5:3,4). To the extent that we believe the devil's lies, we will be controlled by those lies. If, for example, a teenage boy—whose hormone levels are off the charts anyway—believes the devil's lie that he is not a man until he has "scored" with a girl, will that affect him? You had better believe it! Most of his waking hours (and a lot of his sleeping ones, too!) will be consumed with lustful thoughts, plans and eventually actions.

If he also swallows the devil's lies that he must continue to conquer new girls sexually to feel good about himself, he will soon find himself in deep, sexual bondage.

If truth sets us free (and Jesus said so in John 8:32), then lies keep us in bondage—and bondage is control. That is why our counseling method is better described as a *truth encounter* rather than a *power encounter.* We have all the power we need through the Holy Spirit (see Acts 1:8). Teens, however, will not be able to walk by faith until they reform their belief systems. Once they know the truth, they can walk freely in the power of the Spirit of truth, the Holy Spirit (see Gal. 5:16).

Are you still not convinced that a lie can be so powerful? Consider this: If a precious child of God, chosen by the Father, holy and blameless, forgiven and bound for heaven sees herself as unloved, helpless, dirty, evil or rejected by God, will that affect the way she lives? Will it affect her thought life? How about her emotions? Her behavior? Of course, it will!

Does not the Bible say "as he thinks within himself, so he is" (Prov. 23:7)? In other words, our attitudes will show themselves in our *actions.* What we *believe* will be demonstrated by how we *behave.*

The question whether demons are deceiving from the inside or the outside is difficult to answer. Regardless of how you choose to understand the spiritual battle, the powers of darkness cannot change who we are in Christ, and the solution is the same: "Submit therefore to God. Resist the devil and he will flee from you" (Jas. 4:7).

We are playing right into the devil's hands to quarrel and quibble about the location of the demons that are tempting, accusing, deceiving or otherwise harassing the children of God. Satan would like nothing more than to have us hunker down into our theological bunkers and shoot at one another while the wounded soldiers of God are left unattended on the battlefield!

We need to turn our attention to the *real* battle, which is "not against flesh and blood, but against the rulers, against the powers, against the world forces of this darkness, against the spiritual forces of wickedness in the heavenly places" (Eph. 6:12).

God's Word declares in 2 Corinthians 10:3-5 that a spiritual battle must be fought with spiritual weapons. Paul's words ought to form our strategy for war as they so obviously did his:

> For though we walk in the flesh, we do not war according to the flesh, for the weapons of our warfare are not of the flesh, but divinely powerful for the destruction of fortresses [strongholds, *NIV*]. We are destroying speculations and every lofty thing raised up against the knowledge of God, and we are taking every thought captive to the obedience of Christ.

The devil has been arrogantly raising up thoughts against the knowledge of God ever since the encounter in the Garden of Eden. He hissed to Eve and he whispers to us: *You can't trust God. He's holding back from you. He's got a hidden agenda. He's out for His own skin and doesn't really care about you!*

Far too many teens have swallowed his lies hook, line and sinker and have come to believe that their heavenly Father cannot be counted on. Maybe their distorted view of God comes from abuse or neglect from a family member. Perhaps it developed from a cold, harsh, legalistic church or minister. Whatever its source, a young person must know and believe the truth about our heavenly Father or freedom will never ring in that heart.

If a "wall" has been erected between a teenager's head and heart so that he is unable to experience and enjoy that "Abba! Father!" relationship with God, he must tear down the strongholds of lies and rebuild a fortress of truth. The following exercise is designed to begin to do just that.

Have the teenager read through the following list out loud, slowly, and from the heart. Start with the left column and say, *I renounce the lie that my Father God is distant and disinterested.* Then move to the right column and say, *I joyfully accept the truth that my Father God is intimate and involved.* Then continue down the list in that manner, left to right.

The Truth About Our Heavenly Father

I renounce the lie that my Father God is...

I joyfully accept the truth that my Father God is...

I renounce the lie that my Father God is...	*I joyfully accept the truth that my Father God is...*
1. distant and disinterested	1. intimate and involved (Psalm 139:1-18)
2. insensitive and uncaring	2. kind and compassionate (Psalm 103:8-14)
3. stern and demanding	3. accepting and filled with joy and love (Zephaniah 3:17; Romans 15:7)
4. passive and cold	4. warm and affectionate (Isaiah 40:11; Hosea 11:3,4)
5. absent or too busy for me	5. always with me and eager to spend time with me (Jeremiah 31:20; Ezekiel 34:11-16; Hebrews 13:5)
6. never satisfied with what I do, impatient or angry	6. patient, slow to anger, and pleased with me in Christ (Exodus 34:6; 2 Peter 3:9)
7. mean, cruel or abusive	7. loving, gentle and protective of me (Psalm 18:2; Isaiah 42:3; Jeremiah 31:3)
8. trying to take all the fun out of life	8. trustworthy, and He wants to give me a full life; His will is good, acceptable and perfect (Lamentations 3:22,23; John 10:10; Romans 12:1,2)
9. controlling or manipulative	9. full of grace and mercy, and He gives me the freedom to choose, even when I am wrong (Luke 15:11-16; Hebrews 4:15,16)
10. condemning or unforgiving	10. tenderhearted and forgiving; His heart and arms are always open to me (Psalm 130:1-4; Luke 15:17-24)
11. nit-picking, exacting or perfectionistic	11. committed to my growth and proud of me as His growing child (Romans 8:28,29; 2 Corinthians 7:4; Hebrews 12:5-11)

I am the apple of His eye!

How Can I Point Them to Jesus?

I (Rich) received a phone call recently from a staff member of a major Christian youth organization. He asked me if I could speak at an overnight retreat they were hosting for about 100 or so high-school students.

After checking with the Lord and my wife, I called back and asked him if I could take my family. That was no problem for them, so I agreed to speak at the retreat. Our discussion then turned to the theme of the overnighter.

"We want to help our students obey God and walk in holiness," he began.

"Things have not been going too well in that area then?" I probed.

"Well, I think we need something more than just telling them what they should be doing and not doing." The youth leader's tone of voice clearly communicated to me that he had been seeking the Lord's guidance in this matter. He continued, "Do you have any thoughts on what you could speak about?"

"As a matter of fact I do," I quickly replied. "It sounds to me as if you need some messages with more of a *grace* orientation rather than a *law* orientation. Jesus said, 'If you love me, you will obey what I command' (John 14:15, *NIV*).

"How about one message on who the students are in Christ—

their identity as children of God, and another on who Christ is in them—God's character?" I suggested.

You could tell he was smiling over the phone. "That's exactly what our staff team thought we needed!"

Putting On the New Self

It is easy as parents and youth leaders to fix our attention primarily on the behavior of the teens we love. For example, maybe your teenager or youth-group member has a problem with lying, so you respond by rebuking the teen. "Stop lying! Christians shouldn't lie because the Bible says you should tell the truth!"

Is anything wrong with that method? Well, as a matter of fact, a lot is wrong with it. Let's look at one of the key passages in the New Testament about telling the truth and not lying so you can see what we are talking about:

> Do not lie to each other, since you have taken off your old self with its practices and have put on the new self, which is being renewed in knowledge in the image of its Creator (Col. 3:9,10, *NIV*).

How do we stop lying to one another? We put on the new self. Paul is saying our motivation for telling the truth is that it is a characteristic of who we are now in Christ; lying is part of who we once were in Adam. Colossians 3:11,12 continues this theme of our new identity in Christ and emphasizes the point that *what we do comes from who we are*, not vice versa. Paul writes, "Therefore, as God's chosen people, holy and dearly loved, clothe yourselves with compassion, kindness, humility, gentleness and patience" (v. 12, *NIV*).

Our problem is that we have seen verses such as, "For as he thinks in his heart, so is he" (Prov. 23:7, *NKJV*), and what do we notice in other people? The "so is he." So what do we try to change? The "so is he." If we do not seek to change the "as he thinks in his heart" part first, we will never effect any lasting change on the "so is he."

In other words, what a person *believes* must first be changed; then how he *behaves* will naturally follow.

In recent years, many wonderful campaigns have emerged to help teens "say no" to sexual immorality and to stay pure until marriage. Entire denominations and major parachurch organizations have invested huge amounts of time, energy and finances toward that goal. So how are we doing? Are our Christian young people experiencing great freedom and victory in this area? Some are, to be sure, but many are not.

Rallies, concerts and other youth events are great to a point. Teens will respond to the Spirit of God working through speakers, musicians, positive peer pressure and the excitement of the moment to make real decisions for Christ and commitments to personal holiness. What lasting fruit remains, though, after the event has ended and the emotions fade? Are the young people truly free from the bondage in their lives and able to move on to spiritual maturity? Or are they still trapped in the sins of the past, doomed to give in to the pressures of flesh again and again?

Commitment to spiritual growth without freedom from fleshly and demonic bondage will only yield frustration and defeat.

Freedom from Sexual Bondage

I (Rich) had the opportunity recently to speak to a group of 220 college-age young men. The vast majority were believers in Christ who were sincere in their desire to walk with him. The many genuine questions they asked about how to encourage their sisters in Christ reflected their sincerity and commitment to God.

Knowing the ferocity of the world's temptations in the sexual area, I began to speak about the futility of battling sexual bondage on their own.

"Pornography is so easy to find now. Not only is there the constant temptation from magazines, books and videos, but now we have 900 numbers and smut on the Internet. With a couple clicks of the mouse you can be there.

"Many of you have struggled with secret sin, suffered from secret shame and are now drowning in secret defeat. You have struggled with masturbation, sexual foreplay and intercourse outside of marriage and homosexual desires and actions.

"James 5:16 says, 'Therefore, confess your sins to one another, and pray for one another, so that you may be healed. The effective prayer of a righteous man can accomplish much.'"

At that point I invited the men to come forward with a trusted friend to whom they could confess their sexual sin and with whom they could pray. The response was immediate and overwhelming. When they stopped coming forward, maybe 40 students were left in their chairs.

For 20 minutes or so they bowed their hearts in the presence of God, confessing their sin. They went beyond that, however. They verbally renounced (rejected and disowned) every sexual use of their bodies as instruments of unrighteousness.

After they had all returned to their seats, we prayed a prayer together affirming the completeness of Christ's forgiveness and cleansing (see 1 John 1:9). We announced together that our bodies were not dirty or evil and that God accepted us, and therefore we could accept ourselves. We then committed ourselves to reserve the sexual use of our bodies for marriage only.

I felt impressed to conclude with the story of Jesus and the woman caught in adultery (see John 8:1-11). Remembering our Lord's final words to her, I said on Jesus' behalf, "Neither do I condemn you; go your way; from now on sin no more" (v. 11).

As I sat down they all rose to their feet, bursting out in a spontaneous standing ovation punctuated by a chorus of joyful whoops and hollers that only college guys can do. The freedom and hope in that room were glorious.

What made the difference? In prior messages I had already laid the groundwork of our identity in Christ and the complete acceptance, security and significance we find in Him. The students needed only to find the way of escape from their sexual bondage.

They found "the way" in Jesus who is "the way, and the truth, and the life" (John 14:6).

Neil shares how we can be free from sexual strongholds such as incest, rape, lust and so on in *A Way of Escape*. A youth version of that book, coauthored by Neil and Dave Park, is available as well. This critical work is entitled *Purity Under Pressure*.

Christ Is the Hub

We desperately need to go beyond telling our young people what is right and what is wrong, although that is a critical piece of the puzzle. Telling them what they are doing wrong, however, does not give them the power to do what is right!

If someone understands what it means to be a child of God, is developing an intimate "Abba! ▮ ▮ ▮ ▮ ▮ Father!" relationship with God, and learns how to be filled with the Spirit, the person will almost instinctively do what is right.

What is the solution? Get people connected to Christ! If someone understands what it means to be a child of God, is developing an intimate "Abba! Father!" relationship with God, and learns how to be filled with the Spirit, the person will almost instinctively do what is right.

Paul's Epistles are basically divided into two sections—the *theological* and the *practical*. In our zealousness to provide a quick fix to our teens' problems, it is easy to bypass the former and dive into the latter.

The main problem with that practice is that the first section of those letters provides the foundational truth so that we *can* follow the commands of the second section! For example, Colossians 1 and 2 lay the groundwork theologically so that the reader can obey the commands of chapters 3 and 4.

The following diagram depicts the basic disciplines of a balanced life—spiritual, mental, physical and social. What is missing? The hub. And the hub is Christ.

Without Christ in the center of all we are and do, what results is a subtle form of Christian behaviorism. It sounds like this: "What you are doing is wrong. You should do it this way." Teens respond by saying, "Okay, I'll try harder!" So they try harder and fail harder.

The try-harder method causes young people to become driven by the flesh rather than being led by the Spirit. Even if we progress from a negative legalism (Don't do that!) to a positive legalism (Do this instead!), the results are the same. The farther we move from the hub, the harder we try until something snaps. The result? Guilty burnout, apathy or rebellion.

Jesus said, "By this is My Father glorified, that you bear much fruit, and so prove to be My disciples" (John 15:8). We look at Jesus' words and conclude that we have to bear fruit and get our teens to do likewise. No we don't! What we have to do is abide in Christ and teach teenagers to do likewise. If we abide in Christ, we *will* bear fruit. That is a promise from Jesus.

If we try, however, to bear fruit and do what is right apart from Jesus, we will fall flat on our faces. Jesus also affirmed, "I am the vine, you are the branches; he who abides in Me, and I in him, he bears much fruit; for apart from Me you can do nothing" (John 15:5).

Is anything wrong with the many excellent programs and books available to help teens overcome peer pressure, establish good dating habits, maintain sexual purity, get along with parents and so on?

No, most are good "spokes," and when applied in the right order, they will provide sound advice reflecting biblical insight.

That is what makes the problem we are addressing so subtle, because most of the programs are excellent.

The problem is that we easily put our confidence in programs and strategies instead of in Christ. If God is in it, any program will work. If God is not in it, no program will work. If God is in it, however, a good program will be more fruitful than a bad program.

Colossians 2:6,7 provides a framework for our parenting or discipling young people in Christ:

> As you therefore have received Christ Jesus the Lord, so walk in Him, having been firmly rooted and now being built up in Him and established in your faith, just as you were instructed, and overflowing with gratitude.

The order is critical. It goes like this:

1. First, *receive Christ Jesus as Lord.*
2. Second, *be firmly rooted in Him.*
3. Third, *continue being built up in Him.*
4. Fourth, *walk in Him.*

How does someone receive Christ Jesus as Lord? By grace through faith. How does someone walk in Him? The same way; by grace through faith. Before someone can walk, however, the person must be firmly rooted and continue to be built up.

The following diagram depicts those levels of growth and the conflicts teens typically face in each level. Let it be a guide to show you what to focus on in your teaching to the young people in your home or church. Let it also forewarn you about the conflicts and struggles those teenagers are likely to be facing.

Discipling in Christ[1]
Levels of Conflict and Growth

	Level I:	Level II:	Level III:
	Identity: Complete in Christ (Colossians 2:10)	**Maturity:** Built up in Christ (Colossians 2:7)	**Walk:** Walk in Christ (Colossians 2:6)
Spiritual Life	**Conflict:** Lack of salvation or assurance (Ephesians 2:1-3) **Growth:** Child of God (1 John 3:1-3; 5:11-13)	**Conflict:** Walking according to the flesh (Galatians 5:19-21) **Growth:** Walking according to the Spirit (Galatians 5:22,23)	**Conflict:** Insensitive to the Spirit's leading (Hebrews 5:11-14) **Growth:** Led by the Spirit (Romans 8:14)
Mind	**Conflict:** Darkened understanding (Ephesians 4:18) **Growth:** Renewed mind (Romans 12:2; Ephesians 4:23)	**Conflict:** Wrong beliefs of philosophy of life (Colossians 2:8) **Growth:** Handling accurately the Word of truth (2 Timothy 2:15)	**Conflict:** Pride (1 Corinthians 8:1) **Growth:** Adequate, equipped for every good work (2 Timothy 3:16,17)

Emotions	**Conflict:** Fear (Matthew 10:26-33)	**Conflict:** Anger (Ephesians 4:31), anxiety (1 Peter 5:7), depression (2 Corinthians 4:1-18)	**Conflict:** Discouragement and sorrow (Galatians 6:9)
	Growth: Freedom (Galatians 5:1)	**Growth:** Joy, peace, patience (Galatians 5:22)	**Growth:** Contentment (Philippians 4:11)
Will	**Conflict:** Rebellion (1 Timothy 1:9)	**Conflict:** Lack of self-control, compulsive (1 Corinthians 3:1-3)	**Conflict:** Undisciplined (2 Thessalonians 3:7,11)
	Growth: Submissive (Romans 13:1,2)	**Growth:** Self-control (Galatians 5:23)	**Growth:** Disciplined (1 Timothy 4:7,8)
Relationships	**Conflict:** Rejection (Ephesians 2:1-3)	**Conflict:** Unforgiveness (Colossians 3:1-3)	**Conflict:** Selfishness (Philippians 2:1-5; 1 Corinthians 10:24)
	Growth: Acceptance (Romans 5:8; 15:7)	**Growth:** Forgiveness (Ephesians 4:32)	**Growth:** Brotherly love (Romans 12:10; Philippians 2:1-5)

Far more is required in pointing people to Jesus than having good, biblical teaching content. Far more is required in discipleship and counseling than just knowledge. "Knowledge puffs up, but love builds up" (1 Cor. 8:1, *NIV*) and the person who has knowledge without love is nothing (see 13:2). The old adage is true: Teens really don't care how much you know until they know how much you care.

The apostle Paul spoke of the priority of character in ministry when he wrote to his spiritual son, Pastor Timothy (2 Tim. 2:1,2):

You therefore, my son, be strong in the grace that is in Christ Jesus. And the things which you have heard from me in the presence of many witnesses, these entrust to faithful men, who will be able to teach others also.

So what kind of person does God use to help young people find freedom in Christ? What character qualities does it take to become one of God's ministers of mercy to bring healing and restoration to spiritually afflicted teenagers?

Building Character Qualities

About halfway through each semester of the seminary class I (Neil) taught on pastoral counseling, I asked the students to take out blank sheets of paper. On their papers they were to write the most horrible and shameful thing they had ever done—the one thing they hoped nobody would ever find out about them!

Can you imagine what thoughts were going through minds as they tried to decide what to write? *Why does he want us to do this? What is he going to do with this information? There is no way I'm going to write that down on a piece of paper!* Most were probably thinking of writing about number 10 on their "Grossest Hit List," but certainly not numero uno!

I waited a minute until the level of anxiety was unbearable. Then I told them to stop because I did not really want them to expose the gunk in their souls on paper. I just wanted them to feel for a moment the intensity of anxiety a person going in for counseling might be experiencing.

Put yourself in the shoes of a hurting person. Suppose some deep, dark, horrible secret were eating away at you, and you just could not live with it any longer. You knew you needed some help to resolve the issue. If another person were going to help you, would that person need to know that secret? Of course the person would, or he or she would be unable to help you resolve it.

By this time the students in my seminary class were ready to learn an important point. So after everyone's blood pressure had simmered down and their pulse rates returned to normal, I asked the students to answer the question:

If you *had* to share with another person your worst secret in order to be free, what character quality would you want that person to possess?

In other words, what kind of person would the helper have to be

When teens have the courage to share something intimate, ▮ ▮ ▮ ▮ ▮ they are looking for acceptance and affirmation. Not advice and certainly not criticism!

or not be, and what kind of behavior would he or she demonstrate or not demonstrate?

As the students shared their conclusions, I wrote them on the board. Typically their responses would be: *confidentiality, loving, godly, kind, nonjudgmental, compassionate, accepting, patient, understanding* and *able to help.*

Then I had the students look at the list and ask whom those qualities described. They always came up with the same answer. It is Jesus Christ! That is the core issue of Christ-centered counseling and parenting—being like Jesus! I challenged the class by asking, "If you have not done so before, would you now commit yourself to becoming that kind of person?"

Acceptance and Affirmation

When teens have the courage to share something intimate (and that is a rare and precious moment!), what are they looking for at first? Acceptance and affirmation. Not advice and certainly not criticism!

When you confess to God, what do you get? Acceptance and

affirmation. Hebrews 4:15,16 paints a gracious picture of our high priest, the Lord Jesus:

> For we do not have a high priest who cannot sympa-
> thize with our weaknesses, but One who has been
> tempted in all things as we are, yet without sin. Let us
> therefore draw near with confidence to the throne of
> grace, that we may receive mercy and may find grace
> to help in time of need.

Jesus knows the pain of being tempted in suffering, therefore, "He is able to come to the aid of those who are tempted" (2:18). He did not float His way through life, oblivious to the difficulty of walking with God. He is fully human, so He knows the reality of pain. He is also fully God, so He knows the path to victory and freedom.

Praying for Compassion and Mercy

The first time I (Rich) ever sat in on a "freedom appointment," I had the privilege of serving as a prayer partner in a session led by Ron Wormser. Ron and his wife, Carole, have taken hundreds of people through the Steps to Freedom in Christ, and God has used them in a powerful way.

The counselee was a woman who had been horribly abused as a child by her father. Her mother had been so terrified of her husband that she had passively stood by while the abuse took place. The abuse victim had to forgive her mother as well as her dad. I can remember her gut-wrenching, sobbing prayer of forgiveness as if it happened yesterday.

"Father, I forgive my mom for standing by and letting my dad sexually abuse me. She should have tried to stop him, because mothers are supposed to protect their little girls." Her voice had become like a small child as she prayed and wept with the agony of that painful memory.

Ron's eyes began to fill up and then overflow. The path those tears took down his cheeks followed the same course of countless others that had gone before. In contrast, my eyes were dry.

Deeply shaken at my own insensitivity to the pain of others, I left that meeting crying out to God, "O Lord, Your Word says to 'weep with those who weep.' Why couldn't I cry with that woman? Please tear away the crust around my heart that chokes off the flow of your compassion and mercy!"

I praise God for the work He has done and continues to do in that area of my life. Jesus, who wept at the tomb of Lazarus, truly longs to fill our hearts with that same kind of tenderness. I have come to learn that compassion is not a sign of weakness in a man, but of strength.

We are to be like the high priest of Hebrews 5:2 who "can deal gently with the ignorant and misguided, since he himself also is beset with weakness." None of us has "arrived." Working through our own struggles is what qualifies us to tenderly help others.

Harsh, cruel and judgmental Christians have forgotten or never experienced the depths of God's grace freely given to them. Proud, conceited people are unaware of their own need for mercy. Therefore they are incapable of giving mercy to others.

Many people do not see the Church as a house of mercy, and in some cases, they are right. They receive more mercy and less judgment at the local bar or the secular 12-step program than in some churches!

The Church has the grace in Christ to help in time of need, but it won't be given the chance to give it if we cannot withhold judgment and be merciful. Jesus said, "Be merciful, just as your Father is merciful. And do not judge and you will not be judged; and do not condemn, and you will not be condemned; pardon and you will be pardoned" (Luke 6:36,37).

People in pain can't handle one more ounce of condemnation. They are battling self-recrimination and tormenting accusations from the enemy. Our message is, "There is therefore now no condemnation for those who are in Christ Jesus" (Rom. 8:1)!

To simply tell people they need to "get right with God" or "confess their sins and get on with life" ignores the reality of bondage and the battle for the mind. Chances are they *want* to get right with God but don't know how. Odds are they have confessed their sins many times already but feel trapped in an endless cycle of "sin, confess, sin, confess, sin, confess" ad infinitum.

The Biblical Profile of an Effective Counselor

Does any biblical passage describe the person God can work through to help others in bondage? Yes. It is 2 Timothy 2:24-26:

> The Lord's bond-servant must not be quarrelsome, but be kind to all, able to teach, patient when wronged, with gentleness correcting those who are in opposition, if perhaps God may grant repentance leading to the knowledge of the truth, and they may come to their senses and escape from the snare of the devil, having been held captive by him to do his will.

We will spend the rest of this chapter analyzing this passage of Scripture.

The Lord's Bond-Servant

First of all, we must be the Lord's bond-servant. The ministry of helping young people find freedom in Christ requires total dependence on the Lord. Just as a servant of a human master does not act on his own initiative, but rather waits for his master's direction, so we must rely upon the guidance of the Holy Spirit. The temptation (especially after gaining some experience) is to lean on our own understanding rather than trusting in the Lord with all our hearts (see Prov. 3:5,6). It is easy for pride to creep in, especially after we have seen some success.

I (Rich) had been "on a roll." Over the course of several weeks I had seen many people wonderfully set free as I took them through the Steps to Freedom in Christ. During one of those counseling appointments I said to myself (and of course God overheard!), "If anyone comes into my office and truly wants to be free, I can lead them to freedom."

It doesn't take a prophet to know that I had subtly slipped into the sin of pride and arrogance. I needed to be humbled and God did not waste any time. The next person who came in for counseling left in just about the same condition as when he came in. His case remains to this day a mystery to me, and a constant reminder that the Lord said, "But to this one I will look, to him who is humble and contrite of spirit, and who trembles at My word" (Isa. 66:2).

In 2 Samuel 5, God's Word records a short but fascinating account of two military victories—very similar yet very different. Shortly after David had been anointed king, the Philistines launched an all-out offensive against Israel. They came and spread out in the Valley of Rephaim, poised for attack.

Wisely, "David inquired of the Lord, 'Shall I go and attack the Philistines? Will you hand them over to me?'" (2 Sam. 5:19, *NIV*). God's answer was "Go for it!" and so David and the army routed the enemy. The Philistines fled so rapidly that they left their idols behind. David immediately gave orders for those false gods to be burned (see 1 Chron. 14:12), thus protecting his people from spiritual enemies as well.

Apparently the Philistines decided they had not had enough and so they regrouped in the same valley. Obviously, they were not very imaginative in their military strategies! It would have been easy for David to figure, *Hey, same attack plan, same counterattack plan, same result, right?* Wrong!

Fortunately, David did not rely on his experience or his own understanding. Once again he inquired of the Lord, and it was good he did. This time, God's strategy was totally different! The Lord commanded:

> "Do not go straight up, but circle around behind them and attack them in front of the balsam trees. As soon as you hear the sound of marching in the tops of the balsam trees, move quickly, because that will mean the Lord has gone out in front of you to strike the Philistine army" (2 Sam. 5:23,24, *NIV*).

David obeyed God's unusual battle plan and won another major triumph! Who in the world would have thought of such a path to victory?

That is precisely the point—no one *in the world* would or could have devised such a plan! Only God has that kind of wisdom.

We need to humble ourselves before God and realize that every counseling situation is different, because every human heart is different. Our problems can be extremely complex, and the enemy's strategies of deception are myriad.

It is tempting to rely on methods, techniques or the personal skills of the counselor. We must learn to rely completely on the finished work of Christ and the leading of the Holy Spirit. Only He can open someone's eyes to the truth. Only He can empower a believer to choose the truth and walk according to it. Only He can bring a person to the point of turning away from sin and turning back to God.

Nothing is wrong with ministry tools, methods and techniques. The Steps to Freedom in Christ is a tool, and like any tool it is only as effective as the one using it. A Spirit-filled believer in Christ who is yielded and sensitive to the leading of the Lord, however, will be far more fruitful in this ministry than one who is not—even if the latter has had much more counseling experience!

Not Quarrelsome

Second, the Lord's bond-servant must not be quarrelsome. As encouragers (counselors), we must never make it our goal to change a teenager's mind or heart. Only God can do that. We must speak the truth in love (see Eph. 4:15), but if the counselee denies the truth or rejects the love, that is not our responsibility. We would do well to apply the definition of "successful counseling," originally developed by Campus Crusade for Christ in the area of personal evangelism:

> Successful counseling is simply taking the initiative in the power of the Holy Spirit to lovingly present the truth and leaving the results to God.

As the poet said, "A man convinced against his will is of the same opinion still." This applies double for teenagers. You may be able to elicit from a teen a positive response to your forceful arguments, and you may walk away totally convinced (and deceived!) that the young person you are counseling has genuinely been persuaded. Unless the Spirit of God has moved him or her to repentance, though, no change has actually occurred.

Beware, too, of the danger of getting drawn into an argument by the teenager you are counseling. Avoid generalities such as "all rock music is bad" or "I know all teenagers are rebellious."

The devil would like nothing more than for you to lose your credibility with the teen you are counseling. Do not add fuel to his fire by offering your own moralistic opinions or by reacting to harsh or critical comments from the counselee. Listen to the wisdom of Solomon, "A fool does not delight in understanding, but only in revealing his own mind" (Prov. 18:2).

It would be far better to bring God into the discussion rather than drawing up battle lines between your opinion and your teen's. Encourage the young person to pray something like this: *Lord, would you show me if this music (or rock group or movie, etc.) is good for me or not?* Then wait for him to respond. If he still seems confused, take him to Philippians 4:8 and have him evaluate the item in question through that grid.

Kind to All

Third, the Lord's bond-servant must be kind to all. For the most part, teenagers live in a cruel, unforgiving world. They are constantly feeling the pressure to measure up, and if they do not, they can experience harsh rejection and degrading humiliation. It is bad enough when young people experience this in school; it is devastating when they encounter it at home.

One young lady who had been sexually abused by her family described herself as she walked through the Steps to Freedom in Christ as worthless, stupid, can't do anything right, unprotected, vulnerable, helpless, afraid, unloved, terrible, wrong, childish, not part of the family, trapped, second rate, inferior, weak, a victim, rejected, taken advantage of, used, violated, invaded, unwanted and betrayed. She felt as though people would not like her unless she had sex with them. She said she felt as if the very insides of her had been taken away.

Is it any wonder Scripture makes "kindness" such a critical attribute of the counselor? Kindness is communicated by the words said, the tone of voice in which they are said and the facial expressions used when speaking. Beyond that, though, kindness is demonstrated by *listening* to the teenager's story.

Too many teens never have the chance to be heard. They are more accustomed to being interrupted by advice, cut off by harsh criticisms or humiliated by belittling remarks.

James wrote, "This you know, my beloved brethren. But let every one be quick to hear, slow to speak and slow to anger; for the anger of man does not achieve the righteousness of God" (Jas. 1:19,20). By using genuine kindness you give a teenager your ear and you will likely win his heart.

Able to Teach

Fourth, the Lord's bond-servant must be able to teach. Although godly character is the most critical factor in successfully counseling teens, there is no substitute for knowing the Word of God. We are up against the father of lies, and we can only stand against him with the truth. God's Word is truth (see John 17:17). When undergoing direct spiritual attack, that truth must be spoken out loud to resist the devil, just as Jesus did when tempted in the wilderness (see Matt. 4:1-11; Luke 4:1-13).

Why speak out loud? Because only God perfectly knows the thoughts and intentions of the heart (see 1 Kings 8:39). The devil is able to figure out at times what you are thinking (based on body language and so on), and he is able to plant thoughts in your brain, but he cannot perfectly read your mind. Therefore we must always remember to submit to God inwardly and resist the devil outwardly. It is the spoken Word of God, the sword of the Spirit (see Eph. 6:17) from which the prince of darkness flees.

The first piece of protective armor against the enemy is the "belt of truth" (Eph. 6:14, *NIV*), and we are to gird our "minds for action" (1 Pet. 1:13). Therefore, Paul admonishes us, "Be diligent to present yourself approved to God as a workman who does not need to be ashamed, handling accurately the word of truth" (2 Tim. 2:15). Satan is a master at playing "Twister" with the truth (see Matt. 4:6), so be sure what you are believing and teaching is in accordance with the entire Bible and is not just taken out of context.

We have to know the truth because the truth sets captives free (see John 8:31,32). Look again at 2 Timothy 2:24-26. When God grants repentance it leads to a knowledge of what? The truth. The

Holy Spirit is "the Spirit of truth" (John 14:17) who guides us "into all the truth" (16:13).

Remember, at the root of all wrong behavior are wrong beliefs. Teenagers are living in bondage to the lies they believe. We must be able to teach the truth in love, trusting the Holy Spirit to open their eyes so they can respond in faith and be set free.

Some common lies that pop up as you go through the Steps to Freedom in Christ are the following: *God doesn't love me; I'm differ-*

There is simply no substitute for ▪ ▪ ▪ ▪ ▪ knowing and accurately using the Word of God.

ent from others; I could never do that; This isn't going to work; I'm hopeless, I'll never get out of this; and *God won't help me, I've sinned too much.*

We must be able to refute those lies from below with the truth from above. "For the word of God is living and active and sharper than any two-edged sword, and piercing as far as the division of soul and spirit, of both joints and marrow, and able to judge the thoughts and intentions of the heart" (Heb. 4:12). There is simply no substitute for knowing and accurately using the Word of God.

Patient When Wronged

Fifth, the Lord's bond-servant must be patient when wronged. Some teens do not want to hear the truth, even if it is shared in love. They may not want to get well. They have made the conscious choice to live in their sin. Many resent being required to go to counseling because they feel they were tricked or trapped into being there by a well-meaning parent or youth leader.

Maybe they are looking for a "quick fix" to get out of their pain, and they want you to do all the work and "fix" them. They may not like it when you honestly tell them the truth—that you can't fix them, only God can. They may react when they are told God will heal them only after they assume their responsibilities to confess sin, forgive others, renounce lies and choose the truth.

Whatever the reason, teens who are hurting often say hurtful things. Much of their angry outbursts are not really directed against you, the encourager (counselor). They may be ticked off at God, their parents, a boyfriend or girlfriend or themselves. You just happen to be around, so you are the one "taking the hit." Of course, if you say something that foolishly and unnecessarily provokes them to anger, you should not be shocked at their outbursts!

So what should you do if teens express anger? Let them vent their anger and then move on with the session. Do not take the outburst personally. Love covers a multitude of sins, and if you truly love the teens you are counseling, you can handle their anger. Proverbs 12:16 (*NIV*) also gives a wise piece of advice:

> A fool shows his annoyance at once, but a prudent man overlooks an insult.

Gentle

Sixth, the Lord's bond-servant must be gentle. The only time Jesus ever described His character was in Matthew 11:29: "I am gentle and humble in heart." If a person was mighty in the Spirit of Christ, how would that power be demonstrated? We believe it would be in gentleness—power under control.

We simply cannot run roughshod over people and push too hard and fast for resolution. If we move ahead of God's timing, we will turn off a teen. If whatever we do cannot be done in love, it is better to leave it undone. If whatever we say cannot be said in love, it is better to leave it unsaid.

This spirit of gentle patience is critical in taking teens through the Steps to Freedom in Christ. It takes time to go through the "Steps" thoroughly. We need to be willing to sit down for as long as it takes a young person to resolve the personal and spiritual conflicts in his or her life.

How the counseling profession ever decided on 50-minute weekly sessions we have no idea. That process is not based on a theology or philosophy of resolution. You can't resolve anything in 50-minute time slots! If you open a wound in counseling (as often you must), make sure you close it up in that same session—no matter how long it takes.

We strongly recommend that you take teens through the entire Steps to Freedom in Christ process in one session. Set aside a four-hour period for that purpose. Although typically a session with a teen can be completed in two to three hours, allow enough time so that neither you nor the counselee feels rushed.

"Love is patient" (1 Cor. 13:4). We have had many counselees look at us in amazement after the session and exclaim, "I can't believe you spent that much time with me!" They respond to our love shown by our willingness to take all the time needed to help them.

We will say to a young person as we prepare to go through the Steps to Freedom in Christ, "We will stay here with you for as long as it takes for you to find your freedom." Sometimes the person will shake her head in unbelief, saying, "You don't have enough time to do that!" In all sincerity, though, we will respond, "We'll stay here all night and work through these issues, if that's what it takes."

We mean it, too. So you had better mean it as well, or the teens you are counseling will feel they are being a burden to you. That will only serve to reinforce their feelings of rejection and worthlessness.

Proverbs 19:22 says, "What is desirable in a man is his kindness." Let us say it again: Compassion, kindness, patience and gentleness are essential character traits for good parents and for those who want to help others find freedom in Christ. They are all results of the work of the Holy Spirit in our lives (see Gal. 5:22,23).

Committed to the Truth

Finally, the Lord's bond-servant must be committed to the truth and know without question that God and only God can grant repentance, leading people to the knowledge of that truth. Teens in bondage are being held captive by Satan to do his will. God wants to set them free to do His will.

Only God can bring teens to their senses so that they escape from the snare of the devil. That is the exact terminology Jesus used of the prodigal in Luke 15:17—"He came to his senses." Suddenly the curtains were drawn back and the light came pouring in. The fog lifted and everything became clear. That is what it took for the younger son to come home. That is what it takes for each counselee as well. It takes the work of God in a human heart.

What is the role of the Church? What is the role of the parent? To make sure that when the prodigal teen comes home he or she finds the forgiving Father before running into the judgmental older brother.

The Role of the Church

We conclude this chapter with a story of a pastor's daughter who had been horribly abused as a child. I (Neil) had the privilege of helping her resolve the conflicts in her life that she was aware of. At the end of the counseling appointment, I told her to go look in a mirror.

"Do I look that bad?" she asked. She had been through a gut-wrenching time of forgiving those who had abused her.

"No, you look that good!" I replied with a smile.

She wrote the following and gave it to my wife, Joanne, and me for Christmas:

While on vacation as a child one year I happened to find a gold watch that I had noticed was lying on the ground. It was covered with dirt and gravel and was facedown in the parking lot of our motel. At first glance it did not seem worth the effort to bend down and pick it up. But for some reason I found myself reaching for it anyway. The crystal was broken, the watchband was gone, there was moisture on the dial.

From all appearances there was no logical reason to believe this watch would still work. Every indication was that its next stop would be the trash can. Those in my family who were with me at the time laughed at me for picking it up. My mother even scolded me for holding such a dirty object that was so obviously destroyed. As I reached for the winding stem, my brother made comments as to my lack of intelligence.

"It's been run over by a car," he chided. "Nothing can endure that kind of treatment."

As I turned the stem, the second hand on the watch began to move. My family was wrong. Truly odds were against the watch working, but there was one thing no one thought of. No matter how broken the outside was, if the inside was not damaged it would still run.

And indeed it did keep perfect time. This watch was made to keep time. Its outward appearance had nothing to do with the purpose for which it was designed. Although the appearance was damaged, the inside was untouched and in perfect condition.

Twenty-five years later I still have that watch. I take it out every once in a while, and wind it up. It still works. I think that as long as the inside remains untouched, it always will. However, unless I had bothered to pick it up and try to wind it years ago, I never would have known a part of the watch that really mattered was still in perfect union with God.

Although it looks like a piece of junk it will always be a treasure to me, because I looked beyond the outside appearance and believed in what really mattered—its ability to function in the manner for which it was created.

Thank you, Neil and Joanne, for making the effort to pick up the watch and turn the stem. You're helping me to see that my emotions may be damaged, but my soul is still in perfect condition. And that is what was created to be with Christ, the only permanent part—the part that really matters.

I know that deep within my heart, no matter what my feelings are telling me, this is true. I also believe with the help of God's servant, even the casing can be repaired and maybe even that will become functional again.

Isn't that the role of the Church—to pick up the watch and turn the stem? We have a ministry of reconciliation, bringing people to Christ and bringing Christ to people.

It is the only answer we have. It is the only answer that brings freedom. It is the only answer that brings hope.

chapter five

This Means War!

I (Rich) was talking on the phone recently to a woman whose 13-year-old daughter is suffering from a severe case of anorexia. This poor girl has been in and out of hospitals for several years now, but has seen no real progress. Recently she was in such despair that she tried to take her life, and would have died had not her father unexpectedly come home early from work.

Believing that Jeremiah 32:27 is absolutely true—"Behold, I am the Lord, the God of all flesh; is anything too difficult for Me?"—I started talking about my convictions of the power of prayer.

"Do you realize what incredible authority you have as husband and wife to agree together in prayer for your daughter? Sure, I can pray for her and so can your church, but those prayers are meant as a *supplement*, not a *substitute* for your prayers."

To my surprise my statement proved to be a revelation to the mother.

"You know, I had never thought about it like that. That's really good to know. Up until now I had always had some hope for our daughter's healing because you or others from my church were praying."

How many parents, we wonder, operate that way? Because their children are not doing well spiritually, they feel inadequate, guilty and worthless. Therefore, they cry out for others to pray for them, neglecting the tremendous spiritual authority they wield as parents!

Now do not get us wrong. We are not saying it is wrong to ask others to pray for you or your teens! The apostle Paul urged us to pray for one another and entreated others to pray for him in Ephesians 6:18-20.

In fact, we encourage you to form an intercessory team for your teenage children or the teens in your youth group. Find the true intercessors in your church—the people who love nothing more than spending extended time in the presence of God, lifting up praises and petitions to Him. You can also ask individual intercessors to prayerfully consider "adopting" a particular young person in prayer, until your whole family or youth group is covered!

Concerning parental authority in prayer, consider the following Scripture references:

> "I will give you the keys of the kingdom of heaven;
> and whatever you shall bind on earth shall be bound
> in heaven, and whatever you shall loose on earth shall
> be loosed in heaven" (Matt. 16:19).

After making a similar statement in Matthew 18:18, the Lord Jesus added the following truths:

> "Again I say to you, that if two of you agree on earth
> about anything that they may ask, it shall be done for
> them by My Father who is in heaven. For where two or
> three have gathered together in My name, there I am in
> their midst" (18:19,20).

Now, it would be wonderful if we could all just gather as believers and agree together that Satan and all demons would be banished to the planet Mars until the Second Coming of Christ. Scripture, however, does not provide any instruction to do that. Authoritative praying in the Spirit must originate in heaven, not on earth. What the two or three are agreeing upon is the direction the Holy Spirit is leading them in prayer.

So what authority do we have to "bind" and "loose"? The Pharisees had accused Jesus of casting out demons by Beelzebul (a name referring to Satan). Jesus countered by saying, "How can anyone enter the strong man's house and carry off his property, unless he first binds the strong man?" (Matt. 12:29). Jesus is the One who ties up the strong man (Satan) and carries off his property.

Satan gains the right to operate in people's lives because of ground they have given him—through occult/cult involvement, unresolved anger, pride, rebellion, sexual sin and so on. To recapture that ground we have to first bind the strong man by the authority we have in Christ.

James 4:7 says, "Submit therefore to God. Resist the devil and he will flee from you." The order is critical, both for the one praying and the one being prayed for.

As parents, to wield spiritual authority in prayer, you must first be submitting to God—both individually and as a couple. If both you and your spouse are believers, are you walking in humble surrender to the lordship of Christ? If not, we encourage you to make that your number one priority—to get right with God individually and then be reconciled to one another. Can you see how perhaps the devil has crippled the Lord's rescue efforts of your child by spiritually immobilizing you as parents?

Unfortunately, too many people have James 4:7 all backward. Instead of submitting to God and resisting the devil, they are resisting God and submitting to the devil! The result is that they will find God Himself opposing them (see Jas. 4:6), not to mention Satan as well.

If you happen to be a single parent or have an unbelieving spouse who is unwilling to pray, do not despair. Find a person of the same gender as yours who has spiritual authority in your church (e.g., pastor or pastor's wife) to agree with you in prayer. Do not believe the lie that you are hopelessly handicapped in the realm of spiritual authority. First Corinthians 7:14 provides encouragement in that situation:

> For the unbelieving husband is sanctified through his wife, and the unbelieving wife is sanctified through

her believing husband; for otherwise your children are unclean, but now they are holy.

Because as parents (or youth leaders) we are called to be stewards of those entrusted to us, we should then commit to the Lord our marriages, families, ministries, homes and everything in them.

Job made it a regular practice to consecrate his children, rising up early in the morning to offer burnt offerings for them all. He did this as a spiritual safeguard in case his children had turned against God in their hearts (see Job 1:5).

The following list, adapted from a list by Dr. John Maxwell, provides some helpful tracks on which to pray. Feel free to add to it other prayer items and Scripture references that pertain to your teenagers.

How to Pray for Your Teens

1. That they will know Christ as Savior and follow Him as Lord, daily seeking and longing for Him (see Ps. 63:1; Rom. 10:9,10; 12:1,2).
2. That they will know their identity, position and authority in Christ (see Rom. 6:1-14; Eph. 1:3,14; 2:6; Jas. 4:7).
3. That they will hate sin and walk in freedom from bondage to it (see Prov. 8:13; Gal. 5:1,13; Heb. 12:1-3).
4. That they will be caught when guilty, suffering constructive consequences for sin, and experiencing a repentant heart (see Ps. 119:67,71; Rom. 2:4).
5. That they will have tender, forgiving hearts and not harbor grudges (see Matt. 6:12-15; 18:21-35; Eph. 4:31,32).
6. That they will be protected from the evil one in every area of life, and have the ability to take every thought captive in obedience to Christ (see 2 Cor. 10:5; 2 Thess. 3:2,3).
7. That they will respect those in authority (especially parents) over them and reject a spirit of pride and rebellion (see Rom. 13:1-5; Eph. 6:1-3; 1 Pet. 5:5).
8. That they will desire and find godly friends and be

protected from the moral corruption that comes from bad company (see Prov. 13:20; 18:24; 27:5,6,9,17; 1 Cor. 15:33).

9. That they and their future mate will remain sexually pure until marriage (see 1 Cor. 6:18-20; 1 Thess. 4:3-8).
10. That they will be kept from the wrong mate and saved for the right one (see Prov. 18:22; 2 Cor. 6:14-18).
11. That they will have God's wisdom for life choices (college, business, ministry and so on) (see Prov. 3:5,6; Jas. 1:5-8).
12. That they will develop a compassionate heart for all people and especially for the lost (see Matt. 9:35-38; 2 Tim. 4:1-5).
13. That they will experience a lifetime of godly character development in the power of the Holy Spirit (see Rom. 8:29; Gal. 5:16-18,22,23; Eph. 5:18).

Praying for God's Protection

Every night I (Rich) pray for God's protection over my children. I pray for their bodies that they would be guarded from illness and injury. If they are sick, I pray for speedy healing and protection from complications.

I also pray for protection over their souls—that they would believe the truth and reject the devil's lies. I pray for protection from nightmares and other nighttime attacks of the enemy. I pray that their minds would be filled with happy thoughts and good dreams. I also pray that they would fall deeply in love with Jesus and grow to trust Him in all areas of their lives.

Then, as steward of the house in which we live, I commit our land, cars, house, appliances, furniture and utilities to the Lord and stand against any intrusion of evil—either human or demonic. Finally, I ask the Lord to especially set apart our children's rooms and Shirley and my bedroom as places of grace, peace and rest for the night.

Does that mean we have a perfect marriage and perfect kids? I am afraid not. My *wife* still has some areas of her life to work on (and I do, too!). Does that mean we are always in perfect health and always get the perfect night's sleep? Well, Michelle only threw up nine times the other night. Does that mean our house is in perfect shape and nothing ever needs repairing? Not quite—especially in a 120-year-old farmhouse!

We all live in a fallen world in which we will have tribulation (see John 16:33); but when we foolishly refuse to submit to God and resist the devil, we open ourselves wide to his attacks in addition to everything else.

Prayer is the greatest weapon, ııııı because when we pray we bring God into the situation.

Whether your children are young (like Rich's) or teens, you can pray for them. They may not listen to you, but you can pray for them. They may run away and leave your home, but you can still pray. Jesus told a parable in Luke 18 "to show that at all times they ought to pray and not to lose heart" (v. 1).

Prayer is the greatest weapon, because when we pray we bring God into the situation. Only God can soften a hard heart. Only God can bind up a broken heart. Only God can humble a proud heart. Only God can light a fire in an apathetic heart. Only God can bring home a runaway heart. Only God.

Preparation for the Freedom Appointment

The prayers at the end of this chapter are designed to be models to jump-start you in your intercession for the teens you love. Let the Lord lead you beyond these generic prayers into specific petitions. Do not give up.

Prayer is critical for the success or failure of the "freedom appointment" as well. Prayer ahead of time helps the counselees come to their senses so they will seek help by going through the Steps to Freedom in Christ.

That is why we make it our policy not to hunt for teens to take through the Steps. We make it known that we are available to help those who desire freedom, but we wait for the hurting young person to come to us. Why? It is a humbling thing to admit you need help and God "gives grace to the humble" (Jas. 4:6). Until teenagers are desperate enough to seek help to overcome their spiritual bondage, they are probably not ready to go through the Steps to Freedom in Christ anyway.

We also recommend that young people either attend one of our youth conferences or read *Stomping Out the Darkness* and *The Bondage Breaker Youth Edition* prior to going through the Steps. The content they will find there will put the "freedom appointment" in its proper biblical context, providing much smoother going.

The exception to that rule might be if the young person experiences so much mental disruption from the enemy that he or she is simply unable to concentrate on the material. Some well-meaning teens will be mercilessly bombarded by distracting or tormenting thoughts while trying to read or listen. It is possible in severe cases for young people to be deafened while trying to listen to a conference speaker live or on tape. They may also find their vision clouded or blinded while trying to read the books. In these cases, a "freedom appointment" should be conducted, assuming the teen is agreeable.

Once again, prayer is key *during* the "freedom appointment" as well. If at all possible we have an adult of the same gender as the teen-counselee sit in on the session to bathe the whole time in prayer. This practice also serves to train the "prayer partner" for future ministry of leading others through the Steps to Freedom in Christ. It is best if the prayer partner is already trusted by the young person being counseled and will have an ongoing accountability relationship with that teen.

What about really "tough issues" such as eating disorders? Can the Steps to Freedom in Christ help young people trapped in that kind of serious bondage? Absolutely. Some important cautions need to be kept in mind, though.

Seek Medical Care When Needed

First, in no way are we implying that the Steps are a substitute for proper medical care. Teens who are suffering from anorexia or bulimia need to be supervised by a doctor's watchful eye and hospitalization may be required to stabilize electrolytes and rebuild body weight to safe levels. To neglect to do so could result in death.

Make no mistake about it; young people die from eating disorders. Piously deciding to shun a physician's care to simply "trust God" for a teenager at risk from anorexia or bulimia could be a fatal mistake. Consulting a doctor is not an act of unbelief. The apostle Paul himself had his own personal, traveling physician—Luke.

The Steps Are Not a Cure-all

Second, taking someone through the Steps to Freedom in Christ does not necessarily mean the war has been won. For many teens, going through the Steps will provide sufficient help to set them on the road to full recovery. For others, however, months of compassionate counseling/care (often outside the home) could well be necessary. This is especially true in the cases of those whose self-esteem has been severely damaged through traumatic rejection or abuse. Victims of eating disorders are especially prone to relapses.

A Christian care facility that can provide consistent and loving medical, psychological and spiritual treatment is certainly best, especially if the staff understands the power of our identity in Christ and how to resist the evil one's influence in a believer's life. When insurance plans do not provide the needed finances for this normally costly care, the church has the responsibility to assist parents in need in every way possible.

Both anorexia and bulimia can be extremely complex conditions that defy conventional means of treatment. That is why a broad-based spiritual inventory such as the Steps to Freedom in Christ can be a critical piece of the healing process.

For example, an anorexic teen is almost certainly "paying attention to deceitful spirits and doctrines of demons" (1 Tim. 4:1). She will need to renounce that practice in Step One.

One particular demonic teaching specified in 1 Timothy 4:3 is "abstaining from foods, which God has created to be gratefully shared in by those who believe and know the truth." The teenager will need to confess that she has not been grateful for food, but has instead viewed it as an enemy.

First Timothy 4:4 goes on to say, "For everything created by God is good, and nothing is to be rejected, if it is received with gratitude; for it is sanctified by means of the word of God and prayer." A helpful exercise for an anorexic teenager is to make the following renunciation and affirmation:

> Lord, I renounce the lie that food is evil and to be rejected. I choose instead to believe God's truth that says food is good and to be received with gratitude. I now affirm that this food placed before me is made holy through the Word of God and this prayer. Give me strength through the Holy Spirit to eat this food and even enjoy it. In Jesus' name, amen.

The Battle of Anorexics and Bulimics

The battle for the mind of anorexics and bulimics was vividly portrayed on ABC's 20/20 program December 2, 1994. Peggy Claude Pierre, director of "The Mansion" in Victoria, Canada, described the battle as "a civil war going on in their heads."

One anorexic patient confided, "I have a lot of voices in my head, telling me not to eat, telling me to exercise, telling me how bad I am, telling me I can't trust these people."

Mrs. Claude-Pierre described the mental torment of her patients as their "brain yelling at them for having the audacity to eat." Some sufferers, she confided, even go into absolute trances. "They go into their head to listen to the voices telling them not to eat," she added.

Mrs. Claude-Pierre, who has seen phenomenal success through her program of intensive, round-the-clock care, loving affection and affirmation, tenderly counseled a woman in her facility. As the cameras rolled, the battle for this young lady's mind was intense.

"We love to love you," Mrs. Claude-Pierre gently told her.

"I'm not to be loved," she responded quietly.

"Why don't you think you're to be loved?" Mrs. Claude-Pierre was holding her, face-to-face, compassionately communicating love.

"I'm a terrible, bad person."

"You're not a bad person. We wouldn't have you here if you were a bad person."

The litany of self-condemning words flowed on, though. The young lady told Mrs. Claude-Pierre that "it's a mistake that I'm here." She said, "I'm worthless, I'm not to be saved."

Why is there such an awful spiral of self-destructive behavior of, as Mrs. Claude-Pierre puts it, "eating less and less so that they become smaller and smaller so they will simply disappear." Why such a heart-rending sense of worthlessness, with a level of pain and suffering only other anorexics and bulimics can imagine?

Anorexics and bulimics, according to Mrs. Claude-Pierre, tend to be perfectionists, obsessed with an unattainable goal to make everything right around them. When they fail, they start to feel worthless. When they realize they can't fix things, they begin an unconscious attempt at suicide. Eating disorder victims, she says, do not believe they deserve to live.

It usually starts with an attempt to control the one thing they feel they *can* control. They may even get some encouragement from others who say they "look good." They feel better as they watch their weight drop.

Then the voices in their head take over, however, refusing to let them eat, making them feel, as one young lady said, like a "fat pig, hideous, disgusting, vile, obese, overweight, tarnished"—even when they are near starvation.

Although not understood by Mrs. Claude-Pierre to be the tormenting voices of demonic powers that they are, she does not deny they are there. Speaking of those voices she concluded, "They're happening. They're real to them [the patients], and that makes them very real."

Very real indeed. A child of God, however, has the authority in Christ to "Submit therefore to God. Resist the devil and he will flee" from him or her (Jas. 4:7).

That is just the first of seven major areas, though, that could be possibly contributing toward the anorexia.

Renouncing the Lies

In Step Two she will have to confess that she has believed the lie that she is fat and that eating normal amounts of food will make her fat. She likely will have to renounce more lies such as: "I'm ugly," "I'm evil," "Nobody loves me," "I'm worthless" and others.

It may take a period of loving, tender counseling and speaking the truth in love before an anorexic or bulimic will be convinced those things are actually lies. Mrs. Claude-Pierre's treatments typically take 9 to 12 months before full healing takes place.

God is also able to do a marvelous work of healing in a much shorter time. One young lady came to our conference and made real progress in overcoming her eating disorder. She had believed that 120 pounds was the "fat line." If she weighed more than that, she was certain she would become overweight. The Lord opened her eyes to that deception and she renounced it. Her joyful, public testimony showed that she was well on the way to freedom.

In Step Two, the whole practice of lying about eating (when she really hasn't eaten), cleverly hiding food, wanting to eat by herself and other deceptive practices must be renounced as well. Anorexics and bulimics will sometimes wear hidden ankle weights to appear heavier when being weighed. Some will poison their food so they have to throw it up. Others will compulsively exercise, even in bed, frantically trying to burn calories.

Satan loves the darkness and wants anorexic and bulimic teens to keep things hidden. Walking in the light is the only path to freedom and cleansing (see 1 John 1:7).

Another root lie that anorexic and bulimic teens usually believe is that their value and worth comes from their physical appearance. Therefore they are obsessed with staying thin, fearful that becoming fat will bring a sense of worthlessness. This lie, too, must be rejected.

Teenage anorexics can also be controlled by a fear of growing up. They dread the responsibilities and pressures of adulthood and so sabotage their physical development by starving themselves. They are controlled by the fear of failure, having believed the lie that they are incapable of handling teenage or adult life. Learning to trust God to protect and provide for them will be a key factor in seeing healing take place.

Addressing Bitterness and Unforgiveness

In Step Three, any areas of bitterness and unforgiveness will be addressed. In some cases, teenage girls can use their eating disorder as a weapon of revenge against parents who they feel have controlled them too much. If this is the case, it can be cleared up here.

A big issue in many eating disorder cases is sexual abuse. If the teen has been so treated she will need to forgive the abuser. That can be one of the roughest portions of this journey and can seem like an impossible mountain to climb.

Although there are no tunnels through it or convenient detours around it, the Lord Jesus graciously promises to walk with her all the way to the top—the top of that "mountain" of forgiving others to the freedom that awaits on the other side.

Covering Issues of Rebellion and Pride

Step Four focuses on rebellion, and certainly teens who refuse to eat, or who vomit or expel through laxatives what their parents or doctors try to feed them are guilty of that sin.

Step Five covers issues of pride, and this is a big one with eating disorders. Anorexics can cling desperately to this one area of control—food—refusing to give it over to the Lord.

Sometimes they feel so smothered in their lives that they believe controlling their eating is the only choice left to them. They need to humble themselves before the Lord and let Him dictate how to treat their bodies.

An important Scripture to teach teens who have eating disorders is 1 Corinthians 6:19,20:

> Or do you not know that your body is a temple of the Holy Spirit who is in you, whom you have from God, and that you are not your own? For you have been bought with a price: therefore glorify God in your body.

Once again, the control of one's own body can be a tool for controlling others. Sometimes, in a twisted sense, an anorexic young person can feel she is being good to the family by suffering from this condition. The person sees that everyone else in the family pulls together to battle this crisis, thus creating a sense of "harmony" that may not have been there before. Therefore, subconsciously the teen may be reluctant to be healed for fear of having the family split up again.

For many who have suffered from eating disorders for an extended period of time, it is a frightening thing to give up this one area of control, although it may be killing them. A measure of security is felt in that which is familiar, no matter how destructive it might be. Indeed, "all change is met with resistance and accompanied by grief." Those trapped in any addiction or bondage know this pain all too well.

Renouncing Wrongful Uses of the Body

Step Six is critical in having the teenager renounce the use of her body as an instrument of unrighteousness. It would be beneficial to have her specifically renounce the wrongful use of her eyes, nose, mouth, stomach, hands and feet in practicing anorexia.

A special prayer renouncing perfectionism and drivenness (see the Steps to Freedom in Christ in the second section of this book) will be a critical factor in gaining complete freedom.

If sexual abuse has occurred, she can find complete freedom during Step Six from any sinful bonding that took place with the abuser. By renouncing every way in which her body was wrongfully used sexually, she can take a definitive step toward putting the past behind her.

Confronting Generational Bondage

Finally, in Step Seven, any generational bondage will be dealt a death blow. Certainly this is a causative factor in many cases of anorexia. In coordination with the declaration and prayer in this Step, it would be very healing for any parent or other relative contributing to the anorexic condition to ask forgiveness of the teen.

A Story of Freedom and Victory

Many stories of freedom and victory could be shared from those struggling with eating disorders. The following story comes from a 17-year-old girl who is well on the way to freedom from bulimia that started after being sexually molested. She is not all the way there yet, but she has come a long way!

I for one know the power of the Freedom in Christ material and all the freedom that it brings if you allow that healing to take place! Looking back now, I would not have changed a thing in the way that I had to deal with everything that came out in both the freedom appointments I was involved with. Although for sometime I had wished I could keep everything secret for years to come.

I no longer feel scared of any of Neil Anderson's books and most importantly I can read my Bible! (Something that I could never do, or never thought that I could do again!)

The incredible thing is that before I went through the seven steps the second time I was extremely bulimic. I was throwing up at least 3 to 6 times a day, after barely eating anything. But I would never have admitted that to anyone before.

Since the last time I saw you guys [about a month] I can't say that I have not been sick or my eating habits are completely normal, but I can confirm that I have only been sick about 5 times since. You have NO clue how good that feels, to have conquered some of the major battles that I have to face every day concerning my eating! It feels so good to be able to go to any restaurant and order whatever I want, without worrying about it after I'm done!

Thank you so much for taking the time to talk to me. I really needed to go through the steps again. It has once again changed my life, and I am more than willing to say that it was for the better. I don't ever want to lose my freedom again, and if for some reason I do, I now have the tools to get it back.

It is often helpful for a person—as it was for this girl—to go through the Steps to Freedom in Christ more than once. This is especially true when several major areas of trauma have occurred in the person's life.

For some, freedom comes like peeling the skin off a banana. One shot is all that is needed. For others, bondage comes off in stages, like the thin layers of skin of an onion. The Lord is gentle and knows how much we can handle. Our role as "encouragers" is to be sensi-

A.D.D. and A.D.H.D could almost be called the "in" maladies of the ▮▮▮▮▮ '90s. For some, they are nothing more than scapegoats to dodge responsibility.

tive to the gentle Jesus and not push people beyond what they are able to handle during a session.

The "In" Maladies of the 1990s

Another common problem with teenagers is what is called attention deficit disorder (A.D.D.) or attention deficit hyperactive disorder (A.D.H.D). These could almost be called the "in" maladies of the '90s. For some, these are no doubt helpful and accurate diagnoses. For others, they are nothing more than scapegoats to dodge responsibility.

A local juvenile court judge was reviewing the case of a local teenager who had been rebellious to authority. The young person stated confidently, "I'm A.D.D." He was, no doubt, expecting clemency or at least some sympathy.

The judge looked at him sternly and said, "Everybody who comes in here says they are A.D.D. Son, you better not use that as an excuse for your poor behavior." He was put on a tight probation.

To be honest with you, we would have to add our hearty amen to the judge's warning.

Be assured, we are not advocating a carte blanche negation of all the medical world is saying about this disorder being a chemical problem.

Many parents have found Ritalin and other stimulants to be life-savers when they were at the end of their ropes in handling their hyperactive teens.

What we are saying, however, is that the mere fact that a drug helps alleviate symptoms does not mean it is curing the root problem. An aspirin will reduce the pain of a headache and allow a person to function, but what caused the headache in the first place? A tranquilizer can calm someone's nerves so that he can sleep, but has the real source of his stress been truly overcome?

Remembering Jesus' admonition to seek first the kingdom of God and His righteousness (see Matt. 6:33), why not see if there are any spiritual roots to the problem? Perhaps he is hearing voices that are driving him to bounce off the walls. Maybe the enemy is feeding distracting thoughts into his mind so he can't concentrate.

If, after going through the Steps to Freedom in Christ the condition persists, you have lost nothing. At the very least, he will be really ready for communion next Sunday!

A close friend of one of our staff was diagnosed with A.D.D. and had just sort of accepted it as a fact of life. Many passively accept the medical diagnosis and assume "that's just the way I am, I guess." The staff member was skeptical in this case, so he asked, "When do you struggle the most with being able to concentrate?"

"Oh, whenever I'm in church or when I'm trying to read my Bible," she said matter-of-factly.

"Think about that for a minute. If this were simply a chemical problem in your brain, why would you struggle more with concentrating while trying to draw close to God?"

The lights began to turn on in her brain and she recognized that she may very well have been deceived. Going through the Steps to Freedom in Christ confirmed that her A.D.D. was in reality a battle for her mind. She is now learning to stand in her authority in the Lord and take every thought captive to the obedience of Christ. The difference is profound.

Complete the Entire Steps Process

In any counseling situation with a teenager, we recommend going through the entire seven Steps to Freedom in Christ. That goes for the teen who just can't seem to get motivated to walk with God all the way to those involved with the occult, satanism and witchcraft.

Our tendency is to take a piecemeal approach to counseling and to work on the most obvious symptom, thinking that will cure the problem. What we see may be just the surface symptom of a deeper problem. A teenage boy who sleeps too much may be more than lazy; he may be very depressed. A teenage girl who breaks curfews and hangs around a new crowd may be more than "going through a phase"; she may be dabbling in the occult.

When we walk a teenager through the entire process of the Steps to Freedom in Christ, we give the Spirit of God ample opportunity to surface the root issues. Rather than trying to figure out what they are on our own, we let God do the detective work. Paul gave a great principle for counseling when he wrote:

> Therefore do not go on passing judgment before the time, but wait until the Lord comes who will both bring to light the things hidden in darkness and disclose the motives of men's hearts; and then each man's praise will come to him from God (1 Cor. 4:5).

In other words, let God run the show. Have the counselee invite the Holy Spirit to bring to mind the things that need to be renounced. He will bring to the surface what is necessary at the right time. By gently and patiently working through the entire seven Steps, you give Him the opportunity to shine His light into the dark areas of a young person's life. Then once the light has penetrated the shadows and hidden corners of that teen's life, he or she will find the joy again of experiencing the affirmation and praise of God Himself!

So what can we expect to take place in a teen's life as he or she goes through the Steps to Freedom in Christ? To answer that question we must first differentiate between "freedom" and "maturity." Consider the following chart:

Freedom	Maturity
Freedom is being released from the hold the enemy had over us because of our sin.	*Maturity is being transformed through a renewed mind so that the flesh and habits of the self-life are in submission to the Holy Spirit.*
Freedom is being able to choose by faith to believe the truth regardless of feelings.	*Maturity is a lifestyle of focusing on things that are true, honorable, right, pure, lovely, etc. (see Phil. 4:8).*
Freedom is being able to experience the broad range of human emotions while not being controlled by them.	*Maturity is the character of Christ evidenced by the ripening (not perfection) of the fruit of the Spirit and the expression of godly emotions.*
Freedom is being released from bitterness, hatred and anger by choosing to forgive others from the heart.	*Maturity is developing a heart of compassion, kindness, mercy, gentleness and patience.*
Freedom is having a renewed hunger for God's Word and prayer and having the ability to concentrate on them.	*Maturity is a deep love and trust in God through a lifestyle of prayer, time in the Word, obedience and endurance through hard times.*

Freedom is meant for every child of God, teenager or not, no matter how young or old that person is in Christ. Maturity, on the other hand, is the lifelong process of becoming like Christ. We never reach perfection this side of heaven, but we are always to be reaching ahead toward greater and greater maturity (see Phil. 3:13).

Run Strong in the Race

The Christian life could be compared to a horse race. Many Christians are like horses trapped in a starting gate that is stuck, never able to join the others already flying around the track toward the finish line. Others "pull up lame" somewhere along the way and are not able to finish.

Freedom allows a believer to get into the race and begin to run strong. Maturity enables the Christian to finish the race and win.

Freedom allows a believer to get into the race and begin to ▮ ▮ ▮ ▮ ▮ run strong. Maturity enables the Christian to finish the race and win.

Without first experiencing freedom, there can be no hope for maturity and victory.

The writer of Hebrews put it this way:

> Therefore, since we have so great a cloud of witnesses surrounding us, let us also lay aside every encumbrance, and the sin which so easily entangles us, and let us run with endurance the race that is set before us, fixing our eyes on Jesus, the author and perfector of faith (Heb. 12:1,2).

Freedom is laying aside the things that weigh us down and getting untangled from the sins that slow us down so that we can run. Maturity is fixing our eyes on the finish line, Jesus, running the race of life with endurance.

It is a long race and at times a difficult one, but unlike the horse races and track events of today, we are not competing against the other runners. We have the joy and opportunity to run together with our brothers and sisters in Christ, locking arms and locking armor together as we all strive toward the "finish line" of falling into the arms of Jesus.

We hope it is clear by now that we do not believe the Steps to Freedom in Christ are a cure-all for a person's struggles. Struggles, pain, difficulties and hardships are a natural part of the race of life, and the Christian life is no exception. Most teenagers will not be particularly excited about this reality, but they need to know it. Otherwise the enemy will have no problem ambushing them as the trials of life occur.

We indeed have been called to a battle with the world, the flesh and the devil, but these are winnable battles because Christ already won the war.

Jesus warned us of the "war of the world," and gave us words of comfort in John 16:33:

> "These things I have spoken to you, that in Me you may have peace. In the world you have tribulation, but take courage; I have overcome the world."

Paul described the Spirit versus flesh war in Galatians 5:16,17:

> But I say, walk by the Spirit, and you will not carry out the desire of the flesh. For the flesh sets its desire against the Spirit and the Spirit against the flesh; for these are in opposition to one another, so that you may not do the things that you please.

The war continues when we encounter the powers of darkness. We are commanded to put on the armor of God so that we can "be strong in the Lord and in the power of His might" (Eph. 6:10, *NKJV*). The language of warfare showed up again when Paul wrote:

> For we do not wrestle against flesh and blood, but against principalities, against powers, against the rulers of the darkness of this age, against the spiritual hosts of wickedness in the heavenly places (v. 12, *NKJV*).

We do a great disservice to teens if we give them the impression that going through the Steps to Freedom in Christ means the end of the battles they have been facing. What they will find, however, is an increased ability to hang in there, fight and win the battles for their minds, rather than giving up and giving in.

The Steps to Freedom in Christ are a training tool. Every time a teenager (who sincerely wants to do business with God) walks through that process, at least two critical things happen.

First, that young person sees the awesome liberating power of God unleashed in his life. Second, the teen is trained in how to handle the sin in his life so that if he becomes aware of something later on that day, or the next day, or the next...he will not have to call the encourager for help. He will have the Steps to refer back to and will know what to do.

Get Rid of Life's Garbage

Imagine for a moment that an elderly lady lives next door to you. She is a bit eccentric, but basically harmless. One day, however, you walk out your door and see swarms of flies enveloping her house. Then you catch a whiff of an odor that drives you back inside real fast. You are sure it is coming from her house.

Not wanting to cause any problems for the old woman, you call the police, mention your concern and ask them to investigate. Pretty soon you see a patrol car pull up in her driveway and two uniformed police officers casually stroll up to her door and knock.

As the door swings open, a stench greets the nostrils of the officers like nothing they have ever smelled before. Practically gagging, they notice that the hallway behind the woman is filled with garbage bags—stacked all the way to the ceiling! They have to duck as they are dive bombed by what seems like a plague of flies. The problem is obvious: The elderly lady has not taken out the garbage in her house for years!

"Oh, it's such a nuisance at times, officers, but for the most part I've learned to cope." The old woman smiles kind of weakly at the men in blue.

"But ma'am, don't you realize that if you just take it to the curb, someone will come and take it away for you? I bet that will go a long way toward clearing up your fly problem, too. Here, let us help you carry it down."

The old woman is overjoyed as she begins to see pieces of her furniture, areas of carpet and beautiful paintings on the wall reappear after years of being hidden. She had long ago lost hope of ever seeing beauty again, but slowly, painstakingly it happens right before her very eyes.

After hours of arduous labor, the mountain of garbage is moved to the curb. The officers open the windows, toss the drapes in the washing machine and begin washing the floors and carpet. Meanwhile, the elderly woman cleans the upholstery and polishes the wood furniture. By the end of the day, the dirt is all gone and so are the flies. The place smells fresh and clean again.

"I just can't thank you boys enough for all your help," she tearfully cries as she dances a little jig on her freshly cleaned carpet.

"Well, you've made a lot of progress today, ma'am, but you've got to remember to take your trash down to the curb. Otherwise, eventually the same thing will happen to you again, do you understand?" The officers gaze intently at the woman, making sure she nods before they tip their hats and say good-bye.

That's what the Steps to Freedom in Christ are all about. We take out the garbage in our lives—by confessing sin, renouncing lies and forgiving those who have hurt us—so that Jesus can carry it away. We open the windows to our hearts—through humility and submission—so the fresh breezes of the Spirit of God can blow again. We spiritually "scrub" those tough-stained places in our souls by tearing down strongholds so the "lord of the flies" (Satan) takes off for smellier places.

- Confession
- Repentance
- Renunciation of lies
- Forgiveness of offenses against us
- Tearing down strongholds of wrong thinking and fleshly living

That's the way to freedom.

We suppose you could spend all your time swatting flies and you would make some progress. Wouldn't it be simpler and more effective, though, to remove the garbage? Get rid of the waste matter and the flies will go.

The powers of darkness are attracted to sin the way flies are attracted to garbage. James 4:7 provides the solution: "Submit therefore to God. Resist the devil and he will flee from you." That, in essence, is what the Steps to Freedom in Christ are—a practical guide for applying James 4:7 to our lives.

Once the hard work is finished, what a joy that newfound freedom is to us; not to mention how wonderful it is for all those within "sniffing" distance.

A Teenager's Parable of Life

The following testimony was graciously submitted for our use by a Christian teenage girl. She had started writing it while going through counseling at age 17. She was unable to finish the story until she went through the Steps to Freedom in Christ at age 19.

I am a gardener. That is what I do. It seems I have always done it. Even as a child I knelt beside my mother as she worked in the soil. I used to find such joy and excitement in my garden. It was thrilling to be a part of such a glorious gift from God. I loved to feel the unplanted soil in my hands. I looked forward to the moment I would plant my seeds. I cherished watering and feeding them, knowing I was nourishing a living thing. It was often necessary for their survival for me to care for my plants. I felt important and needed. I even looked forward to weeding. I would get on my knees and pull out those pesky invaders, who hoarded the soil, food and water.

Yet through the years I began to lose interest. It became boring and mundane. I was too busy with more important matters than to care for my garden. I rushed from task to task, neglecting an activity that once meant so much to me. I often scurried out the front door, leaving the growing weeds to overpower the plants I had once tenderly cared for.

Years went by and my once radiant and blooming garden turned into a wasteland of weeds. I honestly couldn't stand the sight of it. It nearly made me sick to my stomach. I began to leave my drapes closed so I wouldn't have to look at the mess.

I considered hiring a gardener but decided against it, believing I would one day get back to my garden. I believed I could do it myself.

I never did anything about the weeds until a dear, old friend gently persuaded me to allow him to take a look at my garden. He shared with me that while he had the power and strength to take care of the weeds on his own, it would be more beneficial if I were to join him. He reminded me that the garden was my responsibility. After much thought I decided he was right!

One gloomy, cold day we began the vigorous and difficult work. My friend and I worked so hard on the weeds—I often grew tired and wanted to quit but drew strength from my friend's seemingly never-ending energy. At the end of some days, I would find blisters on my hands. It was exhausting work, and seemed unending. I never realized how large my yard truly was. But, eventually the agonizing work paid off.

There came a day when all that could be seen in my yard was dirt. It was a rewarding day. I felt exhilarated! It was freeing to see that the weeds were gone. With the weeds finally gone we began the replanting process. We carefully chose plants that would refill the barren expanse made by the freshly removed weeds. We planted and planted until we had filled every available morsel of land. It took time before we actually saw the fruits of our labor, but eventually we began to see little green sprouts popping up out of the ground.

It wasn't long until weeds began appearing again among my growing plants. I felt discouraged. My dear, patient friend reminded me that the removal of the weeds wasn't a "once and for all" process. It would still be necessary for me to deal with those weeds. Only this time I could take care of them before they got out of control.

I once again have found joy in my garden. At the first sign of weeds, I am able to deal with them without them overcrowding my beautiful plants. And while my plants are still growing and developing I know that the once overcrowded wasteland of weeds will never return.

The Parable Explained

This story is about my life. I had a garden just like the gardener in this story. Only my garden was inside of me. It began as a beautiful, peaceful garden. I was a child relatively free of trauma. The garden of my heart and emotions were, to an extent, clear of debris. After facing the excruciating pain of sexual abuse, weeds of anger, bitterness, unforgiveness and rage began to creep into my inner garden. Through the years, the weeds inside of me grew just as the weeds in my character's garden grew. I could not even acknowledge what had happened to me. It was too painful. I ignored the signs of trouble for a long time.

The dear old friend in my story was actually Jesus in my life. I had chosen to be a follower of Christ at a very young age, but because of the bondage in my life Jesus had been all but crowded out. There came a time in my life when the Lord gently convinced me to take a look at my "garden." I went to counseling and dealt with some issues, but only made a dent in the "weeds" and "debris."

Not until I read the books *Victory Over the Darkness* and *The Bondage Breaker* did I began to understand I was not only in bondage to my past, but I also did not know my identity in Christ.

A trained lay encourager led me through the Steps to Freedom in Christ. In going through the Steps, I confessed and renounced sin and forgave those who had hurt me. Just as the layers of an onion must be peeled off one layer at a time, so too did the layers of my heart.

It was still necessary for me to go through the Steps on my own as the Lord revealed new areas of bondage in my life. Eventually came a day when, just like in the story, I could see no more "weeds." By the grace and power of the Lord Jesus Christ I was freed from my painful past.

That is when the process of replanting or renewing my mind began. It is also when harmful habits began to be replaced by healthy ones. Weeds do pop up again, though, just as my gardener discovered; but now I know that I am a child of the One True Living God, and that I share an inheritance with Christ. So when the "weeds" begin to rear their ugly heads, I know how to quickly dispose of them. What a thrill it is to know who I am in Christ, and that the truth has set me free (see John 8:32).

Parents' Prayer for Protection
of a Christian Teen

Dear heavenly Father,

I bring (name of teen) before Your holy throne. Nothing is hidden from Your sight, and I thank You that You look upon my child, Your son (daughter) with deep compassion and complete understanding. Lord, please strengthen and protect (name of teen) from the evil one. Open his eyes to every scheme, temptation, accusation or lying deception that the enemy would seek to unleash against him today. I pray that he would put on the Lord Jesus Christ this day and make no provision for the flesh in regard to its lust. I pray that (name of teen) would seek You with all his heart and fall deeper in love with You each day. May his love for You grow so strong that he would not love the world or the things in the world. Teach him, Lord, to fear You and stand in awe of Your great holiness, so that he would hate all sin and turn from it. Please provide godly companions for him that would be an encouragement to his faith. Give my child a holy boldness to witness for Christ and to stand firm today against the godlessness around him. In the name of the Lord Jesus Christ, I pray that You, Lord, would place Your hedge of protection around (name of teen). Teach him, Lord, how to win the battle for his mind today. Especially, Lord, shield him from sexual sin and may a pure heart be his greatest longing. May the words of his mouth and the meditation of his heart be acceptable in Your sight, O Lord, my Rock and my Redeemer. In Jesus' name I pray. Amen.

Parents' Prayer for a
Rebellious Teen

Dear heavenly Father,

I bring my daughter (son), (name of teen), before Your throne of grace. She is in need of Your great mercy and grace. Lord, please have mercy on her and bring her to her senses. Grant her repentance so that she may come to the knowledge of the truth and escape from the snare of the devil who has held her captive. Please tear down the strongholds of anger, pride, rebellion, bitterness and fleshly sin that have deceived her. Lord, it is Your kindness that leads to repentance. Open (name of teen)'s eyes to see Your manifold grace and mercy at work in her life. As I pray, Lord, search *me* O God and know my heart. Try me and know my anxious thoughts, and see if there be any hurtful way in me, and lead me in the everlasting way. (Spend a quiet time allowing the Lord to speak to you and confessing any sin He reveals.) Lord, I confess any part I played in (name of teen)'s rebellion, and I here and now cancel out any and all access that the enemy gained in her life through my sin. I ask for and look forward to seeing the complete victory of Jesus' crucifixion, resurrection, ascension and glorification at work in my daughter's (son's) life. Show me, Lord, how to show Your tough and tender love to her today. Give me wisdom, Lord, to set proper limits for (name of teen) while always demonstrating the grace and acceptance of Jesus. In His name I pray. Amen.

Prayer for a Hurting Teen

Dear heavenly Father,

You are the Father of mercies and God of all comfort. I bring before You today Your child, (name of teen). Lord, You are the God who daily bears our burdens, so I know that You are deeply aware of the pain that he is going through. Father, would You minister Your grace and mercy to (name of teen) so that he can choose to walk hand-in-hand with You through this time of pain. Enable him to forgive those who have hurt him so that Your healing power could be poured into his broken heart. Enable him to forgive himself as well. Strengthen him today to fix his eyes on Jesus Christ and His finished work at the cross. May he not give in to sin or give up on life. Remind him that Jesus came to give him life and life more abundantly. Lord, (name of teen) needs to experience that precious "Abba, Father" intimacy and affection with You through Your Spirit. As he submits his life fully into Your faithful hands, give him courage to resist the devil by putting on the full armor of God. Please bring other godly people into his life to wrap their arms and their armor around him as well. May the pain that You have allowed him to go through serve as a purifying process so that his faith like gold would shine even brighter with Your glory. Give me wisdom, Lord, so that I would know how to pray for (name of teen) and how I could be Your servant to encourage his faint heart. I pray in the name of the gentle, humble Jesus who is our Healer. Amen.

Part Two

Walking Through the Steps

chapter six

Setting the Stage

O nce a person experiences the freedom for which Christ has set us free (see Gal. 5:1), it is the most natural thing in the world to want to help others find their freedom in Christ as well. That is the way it should be!

So who is "qualified" to take others through the Steps to Freedom in Christ? First, you do not have to be a trained, professional counselor to use this ministry tool. Already thousands of parents and other laymen (as well as clergy) have been trained to use the Steps effectively.

Nor should you feel constrained to master all the material in this book before leading others through the Steps. I (Neil) knew little of this material when I first began, and I learned most of it through trial and error. A lot of trial and quite a few errors!

Walking others through the Steps does not require a special spiritual gift, although God will use the gifts you have as you minister.

What it does require is dependence upon God, a Christlike heart of love and the ability to apply the truth of God's Word to another's need. You need to be personally walking in your freedom in Christ—consistently living in submission to God and resisting the devil in your own life (see Jas. 4:7).

If you have read *Victory over the Darkness* (or *Stomping Out the*

Darkness) and *The Bondage Breaker* (adult or youth edition), have a clear understanding of the concepts in those books, and have a genuine, caring and nonjudgmental attitude toward young people, you can start taking teens through the Steps to Freedom in Christ today!

So with whom do you start? *Anyone* who desires a one-on-one appointment to walk through the Steps is a candidate. The word "desires" is critical here. Often I (Rich) will receive a phone call from a parent who is very concerned about a rebellious or apathetic teenager. The parent is hoping I can "fix" him.

My first question is always, "Does he *want* help?" More often than not the answer is no.

The Steps to Freedom in Christ is not going to be an effective tool if the young person going through them does not want to be there. The person will feel trapped, anxious and probably resentful of the "encourager" (counselor) as well as the person who made him or her come in the first place.

The next thing I ask of the parent who calls is whether she and her spouse would be willing to come in for individual freedom appointments first. In working with teenagers, it is crucial—if at all possible—to work through the lines of authority in the home. Once Dad and Mom come to grips with the personal and spiritual conflicts in their lives, they are in a far better position to help their children. Many times—though certainly not always—their children will then *want* help as well.

Parents' Newfound Freedom
Encouraged Their Teens

At a youth conference I (Rich) conducted in North Carolina, two incidents occurred to drive home this truth to me. A husband and wife were at the end of their rope, clueless how to help their rebellious son. Both of them humbled themselves and went through the Steps to Freedom in Christ, and Christ indeed set them free. Without a further word of encouragement from his parents, the boy showed up the next morning at the conference, wanting to go through the Steps himself. God set that whole family free that weekend!

Another mother recognized her bondage to fear and perfectionism and went through a personal freedom appointment Saturday afternoon during the conference. She found her freedom in Christ. At the same time, her daughter went through the Steps with 400 other teens in a group setting, and was one of the young people who went up front to share what God had done in her life.

Guess from what the Lord had set her free? That's right: fear and perfectionism.

Preliminary Preparation

The best preparation for teens wanting to go through the Steps to Freedom in Christ is to have attended a *Stomping Out the Darkness* youth conference or to have read the books *Stomping Out the Darkness* and *The Bondage Breaker Youth Edition*. Generally speaking, the more truth a young person can digest before going through the Steps, the better.

The teens will have some understanding of what the personal and spiritual conflicts in their lives are all about and how to resolve them in Christ. They will have received some critical teaching about their identity in Christ and their position and authority as believers.

If a young person is unwilling to take the time and personal responsibility to attend a conference or read the books, we would question how serious he or she is about getting well. Some teens want attention from people, but are not sincere in wanting to get right with God. Having them take a step of action and responsibility like this helps you discern their sincerity.

The exception to this principle might be in the case of young people who are being so bombarded by accusing, distracting, harassing or blasphemous thoughts that they are finding it impossible to concentrate on the material. In that case, it is all right to take them through the Steps first.

The Freedom Appointment

Generally speaking, a freedom appointment with a teenager will take between two and four hours. We encourage you to set aside a chunk of time when both you and the counselee will be unhurried and able to go through the entire process.

Greater resolution results when you hear young people tell their stories, and confront all their sin and pain while the memories and emotions are at the surface and fresh on their minds. Going through one step at a time (for example, at a weekly youth group) will leave those young people vulnerable to the enemy's attacks.

A surgeon who opens a wound is careful to cleanse it and close it up during the same operation. If not, infection is sure to set in, and the healing process will be thwarted. Unfortunately, most counseling sessions focus on the opening-up process, but fail to bring the counselee to resolution. The devil acts like a bacterial infection and will gladly take advantage of and attack the open wounds in a teenager's soul.

The Ministry Team
In most cases, the best setup for the freedom appointment is for an adult male encourager and an adult male prayer partner to work with a teenage boy, and an adult female encourager and an adult

■ ■ ■ ■ ■ Teenagers must feel the complete freedom to air any and all dirty laundry in their lives, or they will not truly find freedom.

female prayer partner to work with a teenage girl. Where this is not possible, at least one of the ministry team should be of the same gender as the counselee.

If one or both of the ministry team members has an ongoing relationship with the teen, so much the better. He or she can provide continuous encouragement and accountability, which are critical in helping the young person maintain freedom after the appointment is finished.

As we have stated before, it is the exception rather than the rule for parents to be able to take their own teens through the Steps to Freedom in Christ.

If, however, a strong relationship of love and trust flourishes within the family, and no adversarial relationship exists between parents and teen, it is possible for parents to minister in this way to their kids. Teenagers must, however, feel the complete freedom to air any and all dirty laundry in their lives, or they will not truly find freedom.

Parents should be extremely sensitive here and not force this issue with their teenagers. Let the young people themselves call the shots on whether mom and/or dad should be in on the counseling process.

Sometimes teens will ask to bring one of their teenage friends along for the appointment. Explain that their freedom depends upon their being totally open and honest about everything in their past and present lives. If having that friend there would inhibit that honesty, it would be better for the friend not to be there. In addition, if that friend has serious personal and spiritual conflicts in his or her life, the person should go through a freedom appointment first before sitting in as a prayer partner.

On the other hand, we must respect the need teens have for safety and security. This process can seem intimidating to a young person. The person may be afraid of some violent demonic encounter. The counselee needs to know that he or she will be respected, believed and helped in a calm, controlled way. Having a trusted friend sitting in may give that teenager the needed sense of security.

The prayer partner is there to bathe the entire session in prayer, lifting up specific requests as the process progresses. When issues of conflict arise that are difficult for the counselee to handle, the prayer partner immediately does spiritual battle on his or her behalf. This frees up the encourager to focus on the young person, providing encouragement and biblical truth to defeat the enemy's lies.

The prayer partner also is present for training purposes. After going through classroom or textbook training on how to take others through the Steps to Freedom in Christ, the next logical step is to observe a session led by a trained encourager. Often after sitting in as a prayer partner once or twice, the "trainee" is ready to take the next step and work as an encourager.

Realize, however, that some gifted intercessors play a more strategic role by remaining in the role as prayer partners. These precious prayer warriors should be encouraged to remain in that role and not feel as though they are second-class ministers!

If a teenager is under the care of a trained, professional counselor but still wants to go through the Steps, the option should be given to bring that caregiver to the appointment. Knowing which issues were covered during the freedom appointment will enable that counselor to more effectively follow up and continue the process of recovery and discipleship.

The Location

Where you conduct the freedom appointment is important. Look for a quiet place that provides comfortable chairs, proper room temperature and freedom from interruptions such as phone calls, pets and people walking through the room. Be aware that the enemy would love to disrupt the session in any way possible. A private room in your church would likely be a better environment for the appointment than the home of the counselee.

Make sure there is easy access to a rest room. Provide water to drink, tissues and a wastebasket for the tissues to be discarded.

What to Expect

It is important as well that the counselee have a general idea of what to expect beforehand. Assuming he or she has read through the books or attended the youth conference, give the following explanation:

1. During the freedom appointment, a leader will hear her story and then take her through the Steps to Freedom in Christ.
2. The appointment will most likely last from two to four hours.
3. There is nothing to be afraid of, although condemning, doubting and fearful thoughts may try to prevent her

from keeping the appointment. The appointment will be a quiet, controlled process of helping her resolve personal and spiritual conflicts.

4. Nothing will be done to violate her will. She is free to come and free to leave at any time.
5. At least one prayer partner will be present.
6. What she shares will be held in strict confidence unless the leader feels the counselee is personally in danger or endangering the safety of another. *(Note: This will be discussed later in this chapter.)*
7. There is no financial charge for this appointment.

Some encouragers prefer to have the teen fill out a "Confidential Personal Inventory" (CPI) prior to going through the Steps. The inventory is most helpful when the young person can fill it out and return it in advance of the appointment so the leader can be aware ahead of time of probable areas of conflict. If this is not possible, we recommend that the encourager use the questions on the CPI as a guide for obtaining a brief history of the counselee prior to beginning Step One.

Bathe the Room in Prayer

If possible, it is helpful for the ministry team to arrive at least 15 minutes prior to the counselee to pray in the room they will be using. We have the privilege of being good stewards of that which the Lord has entrusted to us.

Start by asking the Lord to search your hearts in case there is any "anxious thought" or "wicked way" in you (see Ps. 139:23,24). Give each team member time to hear from the Lord and then out loud commit yourselves and the room to Him in prayer.

Some find it helpful to ask the Lord to surround the room with His protecting angels and to place a hedge of protection from the influences of the enemy.

Take your stand in Christ's authority and verbally declare that you are servants of Jesus, the One who has all authority in heaven and on earth (see Matt. 28:18) and therefore Satan has no authority in this time, place or in your lives.

Prepare for the Counselee

Make sure the room is ready and contains a copy of the Steps to Freedom in Christ for each person. A pen and pad of paper should be available for use by the encourager and counselee during the session.

Arrange the chairs so that the young person will be seated across from the encourager at a close but comfortable distance. Seat the prayer partner(s) to the side, out of the direct line of vision, between the encourager and the counselee.

When the counselee arrives, make sure everyone warmly introduces themselves to the young person. Then have the teen fill out the "Statement of Understanding" (see appendix), explaining that you are not a professional counselor or therapist (unless you are), but an encourager of the Christian faith. Remind the counselee that there is no charge for the counseling and that he or she is free to leave at any time.

The leader should express, on behalf of the ministry team, his or her commitment to maintain confidentiality after the session is finished. There are, however, two primary exceptions to that rule. These must be explained briefly to the counselee:

1. If the young person is under age 18 and still living under parental authority, the encourager must honor that parent-child relationship by graciously answering any questions a parent asks about the session. However, the encourager should try to keep his answers as general as possible while encouraging the parents to talk personally with their child about the session.
2. In the event the teen discloses he is presently in danger himself (e.g., suicidal, an abuse victim, etc.) or is a danger to others (e.g., an abuser), the encourager is under both legal and moral obligation to get help for the teen and/or to protect others from the teen.

Honor Legal Requirements

Most states require abuse to be reported to a state agency or law enforcement official. To protect the teen, society and yourself (from legal consequences), find out what procedures the laws in your state require in the case of reported abuse.

The following excerpts from the laws of the state of Tennessee are fairly typical of state statutes in this regard:

> Any person, including, but not limited to, any:....(3) Practitioner who relies solely on spiritual means for healing....(8) Neighbor, relative, friend or any other person; having knowledge of or called upon to render aid to any child who is suffering from or has sustained any wound, injury, disability, or physical or mental condition which is of such a nature as to reasonably indicate that it has been caused by brutality, abuse or neglect...shall report such harm immediately, by telephone or otherwise, to the judge having juvenile jurisdiction or to the county office of the department or to the office of the sheriff or the chief law enforcement official of the municipality where the child resides.

Beyond what you are legally required to do, taking a young person through the Steps to Freedom in Christ will help her deal with the pain and bitterness from the abuse and be set free from any spiritual bondage resulting from it. As she comes to experience a fresh intimacy with her faithful, caring heavenly Father, she will be able to begin to move on with her life in Christ's love. Ultimately, that is the greatest help you can provide for an abuse victim.

For other issues that surface, consult an attorney, if necessary, to protect yourself legally and obey the laws of your state. For example, what are you legally required to do in the event the counselee confesses to a crime he has already committed? What should you do if he discloses his intention to commit a crime?

In times of uncertainty it is always wise to pray "The Jehoshaphat Prayer": "We do not know what to do, but our eyes are upon you" (2 Chron. 20:12, NIV). Your pastor may be aware of your legal requirements in these cases.

In any event, it is always wise to encourage the teen to make restitution for any crime committed (see Matt. 5:23,24) and repent of any intention to commit a future crime.

Persistent suicidal thoughts or urges the teen discloses (beyond just a fleeting thought) must be taken very seriously, even if the young person seems to gain significant resolution during the Steps. Once you have concluded the Steps to Freedom in Christ, discuss again with the teen your legal and moral obligation to inform parents, stepparents or guardians of this struggle.

Go with the teenager to make sure he follows through on this step. Certainly a trusted pastor, youth pastor or counselor should also be brought into the loop for protection and accountability.

Do not assume that complete healing and resolution has taken place through the Steps. That is often the case, but it is not worth the risk of losing a teenager's life to make that presumption. Commit yourself to being a continuing source of prayer and encouragement for that young person as well.

Create a Relaxed Atmosphere

The ministry team should seek to create a warm, relaxed atmosphere during the freedom appointment. The counselee may already be struggling with thoughts such as: *This isn't going to work. This is a waste of time. I can't trust these people. This is going to be too painful or embarrassing. If I tell them what's really bothering me they'll reject me or laugh at me.*

The ministry team can help alleviate those fears by graciously communicating an unconditional acceptance of the teen, no matter how he dresses, acts, talks or the attitude he conveys.

After your introductions, the following assurances will help comfort the counselee:

Nothing you could share would shock or embarrass me. Nothing you could share would cause me to think less of you. We know who the enemy is and he is the devil, not you. You might be surprised to hear this, but after hearing a young person's story, we find ourselves caring more deeply for him or her because now

we can understand some of the terrible trauma the
person has experienced.

Introduce the Steps

After sharing those encouraging words, go ahead and read the
Preface to the Steps to Freedom in Christ to the counselee. As you
become more and more familiar with this introductory material, feel
free to paraphrase it, but not neglecting any of the key principles
contained therein. After years of using the Steps, I (Rich) still basically stick to the script and that works fine for me.

The Lord Jesus is the "Wonderful Counselor" and so He should be ▮ ▮ ▮ ▮ ▮ in control of the session. He exercises His authority through the Church.

Have the counselee follow along silently in her copy of the Steps
while you read out loud from yours. The key points to cover are the
following:

1. An overview of the biblical basis for the Steps to
   Freedom in Christ;
2. A brief description of what spiritual freedom is;
3. A reminder that it is our responsibility as Christians to
   do what is necessary to gain and maintain our freedom;
4. A word of encouragement regarding Christ's victory
   and Satan's defeat—opening the way for our restoration and healing;
5. A caution about how to deal with opposing thoughts or
   physical discomforts that can arise during the session.

The Lord Jesus is the "Wonderful Counselor" (Isa. 9:6) and
so He should be in control of the session. He exercises His author-

ity through the Church and so He will use the ministry team to maintain control of the session. The prayer partner's role is to be continually binding the activity of the devil in prayer. The encourager's responsibility is to be alert to interference the counselee is experiencing and to seek to expose it before it becomes overwhelming.

That is why the leader needs to encourage the young person to share that interference as soon as it is experienced. That interference is always designed to somehow short-circuit God's process of setting the counselee free. Some possible forms of interference include:

1. *Deception*—the teen verbalizes a belief that is clearly untrue (e.g., "I don't think I need to say all these prayers out loud. It seems stupid to me"). The best response is to gently take the young person to the truth of God's Word because it is the truth that sets us free.

   In this case you might say, "I know it might feel a little uncomfortable at first to pray out loud, but James 5:16 says, 'Therefore, confess your sins to one another, and pray for one another, so that you may be healed.' We're here to help you and pray for you so that you may be healed. That's why you're here, right? (Wait for positive response.) All right then, let's move on."

2. *Fear and flight*—the teen gets up and leaves the room. In this case, never attempt to restrain him or hold him back. Simply pray together as a ministry team and wait patiently. Usually he will return a short time later. This kind of behavior happens very rarely. Sometimes a young person will blurt out, "I feel like I should get out of here!"

   If that happens, gently thank him for sharing that thought. Tell him he can leave anytime he chooses, but the enemy is trying to provoke him to flee because he doesn't want him to be free. Usually the person will stay.

3. *Mental interference*—confusion, noise, racing thoughts or nagging, accusing or threatening voices in the head. Watch the counselee's eyes. Are they clouding over?

Does she seem to be losing focus or drifting away mentally? If so, bring her back to attention by asking her what is going on in her head. It is critical that she share the thoughts she is having or you may lose control.

Once she verbalizes it, thank her for doing so and move on. No matter how vile or threatening the thought may be, don't belabor the point. You can ask the teen, "Is that thought true?" Normally the teen will shake her head. Then simply continue with the process.

4. *Physical interference*—pounding headaches, nausea or other physical symptoms. Usually just having the counselee acknowledge them will cause them to stop or subside. If they persist and are a distraction to the young person, address the problem directly in prayer, affirming that the enemy is a defeated foe and has no authority to inflict bodily pain. Then move on.

The important principle to remember at this stage of the freedom appointment is not to allow the devil to set the agenda by causing you to try to put out lots of little fires. Address any issue that surfaces briefly (as just described) and move on. Most (if not all) interference will diminish and disappear as you faithfully move through the Steps.

The prayer and declaration at the beginning of the Youth Steps acknowledge our dependence upon Christ and our authority in Him. As you read the declaration, insert in the blanks the first name of the counselee:

Prayer
Dear heavenly Father,

We know that You are always here and present in our lives. You are the only all-knowing, all-powerful, ever-present God. We desperately need You, because without Jesus we can do nothing. We believe the Bible because it tells us what is really true. We refuse to believe the lies of Satan. We stand in the truth that all authority in heaven and on earth has been given to the resurrected Christ. Because we are in Christ, we share His authority in order to make followers of Jesus and set captives free. We ask You to protect our thoughts and minds and lead us into all truth. We choose to submit to the Holy Spirit. Please reveal to our minds everything You want to deal with today. We ask for and trust in Your wisdom. We pray for Your complete protection over us. In Jesus' name. Amen.

Declaration
In the name and the authority of the Lord Jesus Christ, we command Satan and all evil spirits to let go of (name) in order that (name) can be free to know and choose to do the will of God. As children of God, seated with Christ in the heavenlies, we agree that every enemy of the Lord Jesus Christ be bound to silence. We say to Satan and all of his evil workers that you cannot inflict any pain or in any way stop or hinder God's will from being done today in (name)'s life.

Review the CPI
If the young person has already filled out the CPI, ask any clarifying questions that came to your mind as you reviewed it beforehand. The idea is for you to gain a basic understanding of the key events in the teen's life that have contributed to her current struggles. If the CPI was not filled out ahead of time, take some time and ask the questions and encourage the young person to briefly answer. After you walk through a brief history of her life, ask if other incidents come to mind that need to be shared.

Listen patiently and attentively. The mere fact that an adult is taking the time to listen without harsh reactions or unpleasant interruptions can be a tremendous encouragement to a young person.

Remember, however, that not all details need to be shared at this point. What is necessary for the counselee's freedom generally surfaces in sufficient detail as you process each Step.

Delving into the teen's history, however, can provide important clues about the source of that young person's struggles. It is helpful to find out about the teenager's parents and grandparents. Are they Christians? Did they ever participate in any cult or occult practices? We want to know if any generational issues might be contributing to the person's problems.

Beyond that you would like them to briefly discuss the following:

- Home life from childhood to the present;
- Any family problems (e.g., separation, divorce, alcoholism, abuse);
- Is the counselee adopted? In foster care?

Continue to affirm your love for the young person no matter what he or she shares. Mention that you will be jotting down notes to remind yourself of important issues; but maintain as much eye contact as is possible with the teen.

What are some of the primary issues you are seeking?

- A dysfunctional family background: mental illness, chronic depression or illness, addictions, involvement in the occult or false religions, extreme legalism, control, permissiveness or neglect, an adoption, living overseas under pagan influences;
- Personal problems such as depression, fear, anxiety, anger, bitterness, lust, pride, rebellion, addictions, the occult, mental or physical illness, rape, abuse, abortion, compulsive behavior, an evil or frightening presence, sexually deviant behavior;
- Spiritual problems such as a lack of assurance of salvation, false beliefs about God, themselves, the Church or Satan.

Again, don't become overwhelmed here. The more you take young people through the Steps, the more you will learn for what to look. God will be faithful to surface the critical issues as you lean on Him. Just be careful not to get bogged down in hearing the story. Rarely will you need more than a half hour to do this. Once you have a good idea of the key events in the teen's life, it is time to move into the first Step.

The Counselee's Status
The Steps to Freedom in Christ are designed for a teen who already has a personal relationship with Christ. Nevertheless, many young people who don't have the assurance of their salvation want help.

That is not surprising because many are being harassed by the enemy and have swallowed his lies—hook, line and sinker. The very fact that they are concerned about their walk with Christ and are turning to you for spiritual help suggests they are already Christians.

Be aware that the accuser of the brethren, Satan, wants us to question and doubt our salvation because he seeks to steal, kill and destroy our hope. He will often put thoughts in a young person's head such as, *How can you be a Christian and sin like that?* or *I don't see how God could love me, I'm so evil.* Sincere Christians who are caught in the web of sin express these concerns frequently, so do not assume the counselee does not know Christ.

If their answers to your questions about when and how they knew they were saved are vague or clearly indicate a "works" view of salvation, however, you may simply ask, "Would you like to follow me in a prayer of faith right now to make sure of that relationship with Christ?" If they are interested, lead them in a prayer such as the following:

> Lord Jesus, I thank You for dying on the cross to pay the full penalty for my sins. I now confess with my mouth that You, Jesus, are my Lord, and that You rose from the dead. I now open my heart to You and receive You as Savior and Lord. Thank You for coming into my life, forgiving my sins, and making me a child of God my Father.

A Successful Example

I (Rich) met Jay at a teen Bible study at the home of his youth pastor. Jay was an earnest young man who was very excited about learning spiritual truth, but he had a problem that was tormenting him. He was addicted to pornography.

Jay's youth pastor and I met with him to take him through the Youth Steps after school one day. As we chatted, it became clear that Jay was spiritually hungry, but had never trusted Christ to save him. Joyfully we shared the gospel with him and Jay eagerly received Jesus as Savior and Lord.

We proceeded to take him through the Steps anyway (it did not take long), and the change was profound. Before he left to go home, God had stripped him of his addiction to pornography and he knew it had no more hold on him. He went home and trashed the moun-

We are not simply asking people to recite prayers by rote; we are trying to help people connect to God.

tains of pornographic magazines he had stashed in his room and never looked back.

In many cases, however, the only person unsure of the counselee's salvation will be the counselee himself! As he goes through the Steps, he will rekindle his relationship with the Lord and find the assurance of salvation as well.

Ask for the Lord's Leading

As you walk a young person through the Steps to Freedom in Christ, maintain your sensitivity to the Lord's leading. We are not simply asking people to recite prayers by rote; we are trying to help people connect to God.

You will learn to recognize evidence of a stronghold or lie the counselee has believed as you take more and more people through the Steps.

For example, when Sue went through the Steps, she first spoke of a supportive family and love for her mom and dad. Later on, she revealed that someone had robbed her of her innocence by sexually abusing her as a young child.

Unfortunately, when she told her dad about it, he did nothing and even questioned her sincerity. Suddenly in the session, she blurted out, "I hate my father!" She had been unwilling to face and acknowledge that hatred before.

The way her father had related to her, as well as the abuses suffered from other men, had developed a stronghold in her life that kept her from trusting men and God as her Father.

When Sue recognized and renounced the lies that she was worthless and could not trust anyone, she won the battle. Later on, she gave me (Neil) a hug, which was significant because of her previous mistrust. She said, "I believe I can trust now."

Teens Need to Fight Their Own Battles

A major battle is often going on for the minds of the young people you help. Though you can pray for them and encourage them, you can't fight the battle for them. The battle will only be won as they personally choose truth. Their freedom will be the result of what *they* choose to believe, confess, forgive, renounce and forsake.

While the battle is raging and painful memories are surfacing, the natural tendency is to lovingly reach out and hold their hands or pat their shoulders. Most of the time it is best to avoid touching the counselee until the session is completed.

In severe cases, until the young person is free, the conflict within her may cause resistance to the Holy Spirit within you, and touching could actually hinder progress. In addition, sexual abuse victims can easily misinterpret the purpose of the touch.

Instead, it is safer to communicate your compassion through facial expressions, words and tears (if genuine) during the session. Afterward, an appropriate hug might be in order.

Finally, recognize that some strongholds, particularly addictions, will need more work after the end of the session. Even when those areas of bondage are exposed, confessed and renounced, further discipleship and support will likely be needed.

Gain, but Also Maintain Freedom

Tim was caught in a web of homosexual behavior. After going through the Steps in a personal appointment, he was elated about the sense of freedom and joy he felt. A letter received a few weeks later announced his belief that he was now free from the weight of his past. A second letter, though, sent a few months after the first, gave a different picture.

Tim had taken a backward step, but he had not forgotten what he had learned by going through the Steps. He realized he had not won a "once-for-all" victory and that it is one thing to gain freedom and another thing to maintain it.

After confession, he began practicing resisting the enemy and choosing truth daily. When we saw him nearly a year after first taking him through the Steps, Tim was *maintaining* his freedom daily.

Many times additional issues will surface after the freedom appointment has ended. Immediately the devil launches his attack and sneers, *You see, it didn't work! Nothing's changed!* In reality, what is happening is simply that another layer of the onion skin is being revealed. Encourage the young people you work with to be faithful to handle each issue the Lord brings to the surface and freedom will be maintained.

What if teens struggle with remembering the past? What if they pray and nothing surfaces? Then point them to their identity in Christ because that is where their hope lies anyway. As Paul said, "Forgetting what lies behind and reaching forward to what lies ahead, I press on toward the goal for the prize of the upward call of God in Christ Jesus" (Phil. 3:13,14).

chapter seven

Unmasking the Enemy

Step One:
Counterfeit Versus Real

The first Step to freedom in Christ is for the young person to renounce all past or present involvement with any activity or group that denies Jesus Christ, offers guidance contrary to the Bible, or requires dark, secret ceremonies or covenants. This includes all occult, cult and false religious beliefs, practices and objects associated with them.

Webster's New World Dictionary defines the word "renounce" as: "To give up, usually by a formal public statement; to cast off; disown; deny all responsibility or allegiance to."[1]

In the New Testament, the word translated into English as "renounce" is the Greek word *apeipon. Vine's Expository Dictionary of Old and New Testament Words* defines *apeipon* as literally "to tell from," signifying an act of disowning. In its use in the Septuagint in 1 Kings 11:2, it carries the meaning of "to forbid." Therefore, the concept of renouncing also may hold the sense of "forbidding the approach of the things disowned."[2]

Paul uses a form of the root word *apeipon* in 2 Corinthians 4:1,2:

> Therefore, since we have this ministry, as we received mercy, we do not lose heart, but we have **renounced** [our emphasis] the things hidden because of shame, not

walking in craftiness or adulterating the word of God, but by the manifestation of truth commending ourselves to every man's conscience in the sight of God.

The public declaration "I renounce you, Satan, and all your works and all your ways" has historically been a part of the Church's profession of faith since its earliest days. Even today, Catholics and members of other liturgical churches make that same pronouncement at confirmation. For the renunciation to be complete, however, it must be more than generic. It must be specific (e.g., "I renounce any and all involvement with fortune telling").

To renounce a group, activity, belief or practice means to express verbally your decision to turn your back on it. When done genuinely, it is a verbal declaration of a heartfelt repentance.

Biblical Examples of Repentance

Biblically, repentance always means a change of heart or mind demonstrated by a change of lifestyle. John the Baptist captured this flavor of repentance when he scolded the Pharisees and Sadducees who were coming for baptism:

> "You brood of vipers, who warned you to flee from the wrath to come? Therefore bring forth fruit in keeping with your repentance" (Matt. 3:7,8).

John questioned the religious leaders' motives of being baptized, challenging them to give evidence of a change of heart and life by bringing forth fruit. Genuine repentance will always begin inwardly and manifest itself outwardly.

The biblical precedent for open renunciation is found in Acts 19:18-20. Many of the brand-new Christians in Ephesus had been deeply involved in false religions and the occult through worship in the Temple of Artemis. Luke writes in verse 18: "Many also of those who had believed kept coming, confessing and disclosing their practices."

The open disclosure of occult practices was followed by the positive action of ridding themselves of anything associated with that darkness. "And many of those who practiced magic brought their books together and began burning them in the sight of all" (v. 19). The value of the books (50,000 pieces of silver) was high, but did not deter the believers from destroying them. Their repentance was clearly genuine.

Some believers balk at verbally renouncing evil practices, fearing that they might be guilty of pronouncing a "railing judgment" against Satan, a practice forbidden in 2 Peter 2:10,11 and Jude 8,9. In reality, to renounce one's involvement in the occult is obedience to James 4:7, which commands us: "Submit therefore to God. Resist the devil and he will flee from you."

We need to resist Satan verbally because he cannot read our minds, therefore he is under no obligation to obey our thoughts (God alone knows our innermost thoughts: 1 Kings 8:39; 1 Chron. 28:9; Jer. 17:9,10). Jesus Himself resisted the devil verbally during His temptation in the wilderness, thrice speaking the Word of God out loud to Satan (see Matt. 4:1-11). If any human being should have been able to resist the devil with just a thought, it would have been Jesus, but He intentionally spoke the Word (*rhema*) of God (see Deut. 8:3; 6:13,16). We also are told to take up that sword of the Spirit, which is the spoken Word (*rhema*) of God (see Eph. 6:17).

Nothing even remotely close to pronouncing a "railing judgment" against Satan is contained in the practice of renouncing our own sinful practices. Only God can pronounce judgment against the devil anyway. We are simply declaring our decision to have nothing more to do with the evil one or any of his ways. That is the God-ordained responsibility of every child of God.

Exposing *All* the Strongholds

When we walk young people through the Steps to Freedom in Christ, we are not always aware of what still needs to be exposed. Even the counselee may not have realized that certain religious or occult experiences have given a foothold to the enemy.

In this first Step, the teens will pray and ask God to bring to their minds all previous involvement with cult or occult practices, false religions and false teachers, whether done knowingly or unknowingly. Often God will bring to their memories things long forgotten, things that have deeply affected them.

One 16-year-old girl, after praying for the Lord to reveal to her mind the things she needed to renounce, started listing a whole array of things such as automatic writing, visionary dreams, fortune-telling, Bloody Mary (the occult game, not the drink!) and others. Then she recalled that as a child she had been visited day and night by a "little girl" in a white dress. They would talk and play together. The real little girl had drowned years before. The counselee's "friend", of course, was a demon masquerading as the deceased girl's "spirit."

Up until the freedom appointment, this teenager had forgotten about her childhood "friend," considering it an innocent relationship. She needed to thoroughly renounce that friendship, which she gladly did.

Two important objectives will be accomplished during Step One. First, strongholds from false belief systems will be exposed and broken by agreeing with God through verbal renunciation. Second, young people will be equipped to handle lies and strongholds that may surface later.

As you begin this Step, you are helping teens take back any ground gained by the enemy in their lives, issue by issue, step by step.

Explain that everything said in the session is said out loud, because no evidence in the Bible reveals that the devil can read our minds. God alone knows our innermost thoughts, but Satan is not God and it is always dangerous to ascribe divine attributes to him.

After reading to the counselee the introductory paragraph, have the teenager begin by praying the first prayer in Step One aloud:

Dear heavenly Father,
I ask You to guard my heart and my mind and to reveal to me anything I have done or anyone has done to me that is spiritually wrong. Reveal to my mind any and all involvement I have knowingly or unknowingly had with cult or occult practices, and/or false teachers. I ask this in Jesus' name. Amen.

It is critical for the young people to understand that even if they participated in something as a game or a joke, they need to renounce it. Even if they stood by and watched others do it, they need to renounce their passive agreement and involvement.

Satan is a wily opportunist who can take advantage of any violation of God's holy law, even when those transgressions are done in ignorance (see Eph. 4:27). Express to the teen that we do not know the specific ways the devil may have gained a foothold in his life, so we will take the safe route and be thorough by dealing with everything that comes to mind.

The "Non-Christian Spiritual Experiences Checklist"

Have the counselees read the "Non-Christian Spiritual Checklist" and put a check mark in the box next to any and all activities in which they have been personally involved. They have already asked the Lord to show them those areas, so trust that the Lord will answer their prayers.

■ ■ ■ ■ ■ **God grants repentance, leading to the knowledge of the truth, so that we may escape from the snare of the devil.**

God grants repentance, leading to the knowledge of the truth, so that we may escape from the snare of the devil (see 2 Tim. 2:25,26). It is essential not to overlook anything God wants to bring to the surface, therefore they should take seriously any impression they receive and check the appropriate box. If they are unsure of their participation, they can feel free to verbalize their renunciation as: "Lord, I confess that I may have participated in..."

The Non-Christian Spiritual Checklist itself is far from exhaustive, so after scanning it and checking the ones that apply, ask them to jot down any others God is bringing to mind.

If a young person has a genuine question about what one of the items on the checklist is (because the person suspects he did it), go ahead and explain what that particular practice or belief is. It is not necessary, however, for the counselee to know the definition of each and every item on the list to complete this exercise.

"Sexual spirits" is an item that sometimes needs explanation. It refers to attacks by spirits seeking to arouse a person sexually, usually (but not always) in the teen's bedroom. If the young person allowed the sexual spirits to operate, she will need to renounce it; if she resisted at the time, nothing needs to be renounced.

Sexual spirits can be introduced into a young person's life through sexual molestation and abuse, sexual experimentation in childhood and exposure to pornography. If a child or teen demonstrates an unhealthy and unusually strong knowledge, curiosity or compulsion in the sexual area, sexual spirits may be involved.

Beware of being drawn into lengthy explanations of each item on the list. This can be a laborious effort and can cause an unnecessary delay in the counselee's resolution of his or her own issues.

If a young person confesses that he was a serious practitioner of a cult or false religion prior to coming to Christ (for example, Mormonism), encourage him to renounce very specifically the practices and beliefs of that group. Studying the *Book of Mormon*, attending services, participating in baptisms for the dead and so on are examples of specific things to be renounced.

A fascination or obsession about things of the occult, demonstrated by a hunger to know details about things dark, hidden and mysterious, needs to be renounced. If you sense that is the case with the counselee, have the person renounce that curiosity along with the other items checked.

The "Anti-Christian" List

In today's youth culture, much of what is dark, evil, sinister, grotesque and horrifying is considered "cool." The section below the checklist provides spaces for the teen to fill in "Anti-Christian" movies, music, TV shows, video games, books, magazines and comics he or she has seen, heard, read or played.

Although certain rock groups, movies and so on are obviously focused on the devil, we do not list them here for obvious reasons. First, the list would be outdated almost before it was published because the culture changes so rapidly. Second, we are trusting the Spirit of God to reveal to the young person's mind the things *He* wants him or her to expose. God has His list for each teenager who comes for a freedom appointment.

Usually, if a teen is ready to do business with God, there will be little resistance at this point. If the teen can't seem to think of anything, encourage her to ask God again and to write down everything that comes to mind, no matter how "okay" *she* may think it is.

Do not allow yourself to get into an argument at this point. Simply encourage the teen to be obedient to what the Lord has shown her to do.

Encourage the counselee to be sensitive to the Lord, revealing things he participated in that glorified Satan, were gruesomely violent or caused fear or nightmares in the counselee. Things he watched years ago should be renounced as the Lord brings them to mind.

Seven Questions Regarding Evil Spirits

After finishing the Anti-Christian lists, have the counselee move on to the following seven questions:

1. Have you ever heard or seen or felt an evil spiritual being in your room?
2. Do you now or have you had an imaginary friend, spirit guide or angel offering you guidance and companionship?
3. Have you ever heard voices in your head or had repeating negative, nagging thoughts such as *I'm dumb, I'm ugly, Nobody loves me, I can't do anything right,* etc. as if a conversation were going on in your head? Explain.

4. Have you ever consulted a medium, spiritist or channeler?
5. What other spiritual experiences have you had that would be considered out of the ordinary (contact with aliens, etc.)?
6. Have you ever been involved in satanic worship of any kind or attended a concert at which Satan was the focus?
7. Have you ever made a vow or pact?

The counselee can either write down his answers or discuss them with you verbally. Either way, encourage him to briefly describe his experiences.

Question one is designed to surface any direct intimidation tactics of the devil—attacks upon that young person's sense of safety and security. Sometimes a stronghold of fear can develop in childhood from these kinds of incidents and remain a driving mechanism for a person's teenage life. Have the teen renounce any and all such frightening incidents as well as any fear that may have taken hold in his life as a result.

Question two explores ways demons may have been invited into young people's lives under the guise of "spirit guides" or "imaginary friends."

If they answer that question in the affirmative, ask for any name(s) associated with those beings and have them write them down in the blank space. Those guides should be renounced by name, if the name is known. A continuing relationship to an imaginary friend keeps the doorway open to the operation of that masquerading demonic spirit.

Every child, of course, has a wonderfully vivid imagination, creating games, fantasies and characters. If the imaginary friends talk back, give counsel or become primary companions of that child or young person, though, they are not imaginary!

Those involved with the occult or New Age often seek a guide or guides who come to them from the spirit world. They frequently identify themselves as "guardian angels" and give their names. They can even use the name "Jesus." It is not unusual for people to express reluctance or even sorrow at the thought of breaking off their relationships with spirit guides, thinking their lives will be somehow diminished by renouncing them.

Question three focuses directly on the battle for the mind. Those who hear audible voices, noises or have recurring, nagging thoughts recognize they are being harassed. Many others, however, have believed they themselves were the *source* of their negative thoughts.

The devil is the accuser of the brethren. Almost everyone at one time or another has faced condemning thoughts that come directly from the enemy or indirectly from harmful programming of their minds. In either case, these damaging thoughts must be taken captive and not allowed the power to control our lives (see 2 Cor. 10:5).

The issue is: Who will set the agenda? Who will decide what we think about? You may want to share the following with the teen counselee:

> Suppose you were watching TV and a seductive beer commercial came on. You have the remote control in your hand so you have complete control over what you watch and don't watch. You could quickly change the channel and watch something healthy or you could sit passively by and watch the commercial. In the same way, the enemy tries to barge into your mind with temptations, lies and accusations. When he does, you have a choice to make. You can choose to allow those thoughts to come into your mind or you can "change the channel" and think about something that's good for you. If you do nothing, you let him set the agenda. To take your thoughts captive, you must actively choose to think and believe on what is true and right and pure.

Some young people may not realize they can choose which "program" they are going to allow into their minds. Encourage them to make the tough, responsible choice at this point to take control of their thought lives and focus on true and good things.

If they have made it a practice of passively allowing anything and everything into their minds or have believed the enemy's lies about God or themselves, it would be helpful for them to pray the following:

> Lord, I confess that I have paid attention to the enemy and believed the nagging, condemning voices and thoughts in my head. They are against what is true and what I truly believe. I renounce any and all influence and involvement with those lying voices and thoughts, and I thank you that in Christ I am forgiven.

Question four addresses the practice of seeking guidance from sources other than God. This is clearly forbidden in Leviticus 19:31, Isaiah 8:19,20 and other passages of Scripture. As believers, we have the privilege of being led and guided by the Holy Spirit. To look for direction through occult means is an offense against a holy God, which must be renounced. It also opens the young person to fraudulent or counterfeit guidance that, if believed, can function as a curse or self-fulfilling prophecy, keeping that teen under its cruel power.

Question five relates to religious or supernatural experiences that were not from God. This includes venturing into "haunted" houses and seeing a ghost, being contacted by "aliens" or even participating in unbiblical practices in a church.

Though there are certainly legitimate and authentic spiritual gifts, there are also counterfeits—both of the flesh and the demonic. New Age healers and cultists practice speaking in tongues and perform occult healings, for example. If a teen verbalizes concern about an incident in which a "gift" was exercised over him or imparted to him, he can simply pray, "Lord, if this gift of _____ is not from You, I renounce it in Jesus' name." Let the *Lord* bring it to his mind; then after encouraging him to pray, simply move on.

Testing of the spirits (see 1 John 4:1) is best done by the counselee. If the young person is unclear about the source of the gift, experience or "prophecy," encourage him to pray, asking the Lord to show him the true nature of it.

A young man said that the voice in his head was pleading, "Don't send me away. I want to go to heaven with you." Being prompted, he prayed, "Lord, please show me the true nature of this voice." Before he could finish the prayer, he cried out in disgust. He knew at once that it was not from God.

Question six mentions satanic worship. This includes any kind of rituals practiced in a group or individually, whether done actively or just passively standing by. This also includes any participation in rock concerts in which songs were performed to worship or in any way glorify or promote the devil or diabolical violence, sex, drugs or rebellion.

If any history of satanic or secretive rituals exists in the family or personal life of the counselee (or any suspicious blocked memories), have her read through the "Kingdom of Darkness, Kingdom of Light" list in Step One following the prayer of confession and renunciation.

Question seven relates to any unholy agreements made between the counselee and another person, or between the counselee and a supernatural being. We are to live only under the promises and conditions of our new covenant with Jesus Christ through His shed blood. Any other blood pacts must be renounced. Any angry vow or promise made against God should also be renounced.

Once the checklist and questions have been reviewed, help the counselee confess his or her involvement with every item that has surfaced, by repeating the following prayer aloud. The prayer should be repeated separately for each individual item that needs to be renounced.

> Lord, I confess that I have participated in _____. I renounce any and all influence and involvement with _____, and I thank you that in Christ I am forgiven.

Stay Alert to Special Needs

For you to maintain control while leading young people through the Steps means that you are aware of what is happening with the teens you are helping. So stay alert. Watch their eyes and facial expressions and listen for any omissions from the checklist or questions previously filled out. If the counselees seem to be struggling, ask them to describe any interference they may be having, either mentally or physically.

Usually the simple act of telling you what is going on in their minds or bodies is enough to break its hold. If not, encourage the counselees to exercise their authority in Christ by praying against the enemy's activity. If the attack is severe, the encourager and prayer partner can pray out loud as well.

An important principle to remember is that the encourager should only exercise his or her spiritual authority on behalf of the counselee to the degree necessary to allow that counselee to exercise

> **Counselees must learn to lean on God, not the encourager, ▮ ▮ ▮ ▮ ▮ during the freedom appointment, so that future struggles are taken to the Lord.**

her own authority in Christ. The process of going through the Steps to Freedom in Christ is training designed to equip young people to obey James 4:7, learning to submit to God and resist the devil themselves. Counselees must learn to lean on God, not the encourager, during the freedom appointment, so that future struggles are taken to the Lord, not to you.

Most of the young people you lead through the Steps will not require the "Kingdom of Darkness, Kingdom of Light" renunciations. You will need to use them, though, if any of the following are true:

- Actual memories of satanic ritual abuse or other satanic activities;

- Family history of occult or cult involvement;
- Large number of cult or occult items checked on the list;
- Severe nightmares;
- History of being molested as a child;
- Family history of Native American spirit worship or religion.

These renunciations/annunciations should be read across the page, left to right, proceeding down the list of statements in that manner.

Young people who have been involved in satanic rituals and other practices need to renounce each one as the Lord reveals them. Some will already be aware of the issues, but others may have memories surface as they work through the "Kingdom of Darkness, Kingdom of Light" statements.

Although cases of teenage multiple personality disorder (MPD) no doubt exist, they are rare and it is highly unlikely you will encounter one. In addition, MPD is a complex issue and is beyond the scope of this book. We encourage you to read pages 150-151 in *Helping Others Find Freedom in Christ* for more information about this subject.

We need to be aware that not everything counselees claim happened to them indeed occurred. The enemy can create false memories in an effort to bring a slanderous accusation against a parent or Christian leader. "Memories" that surface through dreams or so-called "words from the Lord" that have no corroboration with external evidence are highly suspect and should never be trusted.

If you discern that what they are "recalling" is nothing but deceptive lies, have them pray, asking the Lord to reveal the source of their memories. If they persist in believing their dreams or "words from the Lord," have them forgive those who they believe hurt them (see Step Three) and move on.

The bottom line is that as you trust the Holy Spirit to guide you, He will. It is impossible to prepare you for every possible "glitch" in the smooth flow of the process of going through the Steps to Freedom in Christ. The human mind and heart is far too complex for that anyway.

Watching, Learning, Doing

The first two times I (Rich) sat in as a prayer partner, I watched Ron Wormser and then his wife, Carole, take people through the Steps. I left those sessions shaking my head, wondering how in the world I could ever have the kind of discernment, love and kindness they demonstrated.

Before long, the Lord "kicked me out of the nest" and said, "Okay, Rich, your turn." So feeling great fear and trepidation, I started taking others through the Steps. Others sat in as prayer partners, as is our normal practice.

I figured, "Well, Lord, the same Holy Spirit who works through Ron and Carole is alive and active in me as well, so please give me wisdom and discernment beyond my years." To my astonishment, He did!

The amusing thing was that those who were involved as my prayer partners came out of the sessions shaking their heads, saying, "I could never have that kind of discernment and insight that you showed."

I laughed and told them that was the exact thing I had said a few weeks before. God is gracious and filled with mercy. He wants to set the captives free and He is the One who does it. He is simply looking for and eager to use any yielded vessel.

If issues surface that are not specifically covered in this (or any) of the Steps, just allow the Spirit to direct you.

One woman had been led into a life of prostitution by her mother. She remembered that at a very young age a fortune-teller said to her, "Honey, you have a beautiful face and body. That will help you make it through life." She was encouraged to renounce that curse and the lie that she should use her appearance and body to meet her needs, and she was encouraged to announce out loud the truth that her body is a temple of the Holy Spirit and that God would supply all her needs (see 1 Cor. 6:19 and Phil. 4:19).

An important rule of thumb is that every time counselees renounce a lie or counterfeit experience, they should affirm the corresponding truth and Christian practice. That model is given to us in scriptural passages such as Ephesians 4:20-24, which admonish us to "put off the old self" and "put on the new."

Freedom Costs, but So Does Bondage

Finally, as you conclude going through this Step with a teenage counselee, you may need to encourage that young person to discard or destroy any books, photos, materials, fetishes, artifacts, music or any other items or gifts he owns that may be tied to any past practices. The repentant sorcerers in Acts 19:19 did so, destroying a fortune in occult paraphernalia.

To some, that may have seemed like an unnecessary "waste" of money. "Those books or scrolls could have been sold and the money used for feeding the hungry or something!" the pragmatist and materialist of the day surely cried out. Those kinds of people, though, can never understand the purity of worship that comes from sacrifice, such as breaking the alabaster jar of perfume poured over our Lord prior to His burial. All they could see were the dollar (or *drachma*) signs slipping from their greasy fingers. The heart of the repentant one, though, never counts dollars and cents when it comes to the price of freedom.

Neither, incidentally, does God. Jesus Himself believed our salvation and freedom were so valuable that He bankrupted the vaults of heaven to make it possible. He shed His own precious blood to make it a reality. He did not even consider equality with God something to be held onto in view of the value of redeeming us from our sins.

True freedom always costs us something, but so does bondage. The choice is always ours: Lose your life and find it or find your life and lose it.

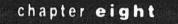

chapter **eight**

Facing the Truth

Step Two:
Deception Versus Truth

I (Rich) can't recall praying harder for anyone in the ministry than I did for Paul. He was not only a friend, but also a faithful servant of the Lord in full-time youth ministry. His mind, however, was a complex tangle of wrong thinking and distorted beliefs. I knew the truth could set him free, but could he sink his teeth hard enough into the truth to hold on and not let go?

"To the Black Hole and Back"

His story, which I have titled "To the Black Hole and Back," is being played out in myriad forms in the lives of parents, Christian workers and Christian teens across this country. Paul's story is one of intense pain, centered around a battle between truth and deception that raged in his mind. It is also a wonderful testimony of victory in the truth—Jesus Christ. It is a "before" and "after" story containing an 18-month period of healing in between. You will notice the remarkable change immediately. First, the "before."

The "Before"
Rich, as I was praying this morning I asked the Lord to show me the junk that has been plugging up my thought life regarding my identity in Christ.

Most of what I've described are nagging thoughts that pop into my mind from time to time. Some things are deep rooted.

So much of what I've written is based in feelings of fear and personal unworthiness. While I've recognized this for a long time, where I'm having trouble is in screening the lies out. Why do I struggle with this so much? I need some help in "locking in" on the truth and internalizing it.

I just don't know if I can do this job. You [talking to himself] started out with a ton of hopes and dreams and three years later very little has changed here. Who are you trying to kid? God is not going to use you to do the things you want to see happen—a spiritual movement with dozens of kids coming to meetings, excitement about Christ, kids coming to Him, etc.

Other people have been used like that but not you. It looks like God's plan for you is one of gutting it out, trying to remain faithful but seeing less fruit than you want. You're going to have to accept being less than you want.

Those in authority over you have lost confidence in your leadership, Paul. You have not received any new personnel in more than four years. They are watching you to determine if you are really able to do your job. Remember what they said about Will [another youth minister]?—"He's been around for eight years and nothing's happened yet; it's time to move on." Well, Paul, your turn is coming.

The reason you are struggling here so much is that you don't know what you're doing. You can't seem to figure out what God is trying to do in this place. You started out full of dreams, and one by one they have crashed and left you with nothing but confusion over what God wants to do.

You must be full of pride. How can you say, let alone even think, that God's will for your life is less than best for you? Why don't you just settle in and be content in your daily walk with God? You are screwed up.

You've got a big problem with your son, Samuel. He's got so much anger and rebellion built up in him. He is going to struggle like this his entire life and cause himself and you and Margie [Paul's wife] a great deal of heartache.

You're one of those guys who likes to talk the talk, but when it gets down to action, you can't deliver the goods. You never have, you never will.

Paul's battle with depression was born out of a sense of helplessness, feeling trapped in a situation that looked as though it would never change. We spent time on the phone, working through each one of the lies he had believed. Paul renounced the lies and chose the truth. The rest of the story speaks for itself:

The Rest of the Story: The "After"

Thank you for giving me the opportunity to write down and recount the good thing God is doing in my life. It grieves my heart, and is almost scary to me, to look back at my letter to you. My heart breaks with compassion for that poor soul who wrote those words...yet they came from my own hand and heart. Life is so different for me now. I cry with gratitude to God for setting me free from those awful chains of fear and self doubt.

I used to be plagued with accusations regarding my own worthiness and readiness for ministry. I had a phantom in my mind as to what a "real youth minister" should look like and perform like—how many students should be involved, what kind of students they should be, what youth meetings should look like, how many teens should be coming to Christ, etc. Whenever reality did not meet my expectations—which was often—I would be plagued by guilt, condemnation and doubt. Jesus Christ has set me free from that awful cycle.

In addition, I can honestly say that I now no longer struggle with negative thoughts regarding my leadership's view of me. I have learned how to ward off the accusations from the pit regarding my worthiness as a leader and I see regular victory in this area.

I was also haunted with fear regarding one of my children. Attacks would come like: he's going to end up in prison, we're in for a lifetime of pain and misery, etc. They would come regularly, and fear and despair would confuse me as to what steps were appropriate to help him. Those attacks are gone! Fear and doubt have been replaced by hope and trust that God is in control, even when it is hard to know what to do.

Victory and growth have been a gradual process for me, yet the change is real. I do not feel like "that person," the one who wrote that painful letter. As to why the change has occurred, I give all the credit to Jesus Christ. I am free because He has set me free. I believe that in His kindness and love for me He brought you and Neil's teachings on this topic into my life. Having read Victory over the Darkness *and* The Bondage Breaker *on my own, our ministry team went through the video series for both of these books. I also went through training in how to lead others through the Steps to Freedom in Christ.*

My point? My mind was renewed by the truth. The old lies were replaced by the truth of my identity. Even so, I would still stumble my way back into bondage at times. I think our phone conversations were what helped me crystallize in my mind what was happening. I knew the principles were true, yet they didn't seem to last—because I was not guarding my mind diligently from the return of the lies.

Over a period of weeks, perhaps months, I read the identity verses almost daily. I would regularly pray warfare prayers for myself as well. Then I started praying in my authority in Christ for my children every night when I put them to bed. God was replacing the garbage with His precious truth.

Gone are the days when I condemn myself over my failures and faults. God is doing so many things in my life right now that I can hardly keep up! When I find myself awakened during the night with "gloom & doom" thoughts, I resist Satan and command him to leave. By the authority of Jesus Christ, Satan's days of bullying me and my family around are over.

God's goodness is so constant, His presence is so real, His faithfulness is so abundant. His plan is just right. I am more excited about my ministry than I have ever been. It is stronger than ever, and I am enjoying it more!

Truly, Jesus said it best in John 8:32: "Then you will know the truth, and the truth will set you free" (NIV). He has done just that in my life.

Acknowledging Truth

Paul's testimony illustrates a crucial point, and the subject of Step Two. Believing the truth about who Christ is, why He came and who we are in Him is the essence of the liberating gospel. Girding our loins with truth (see Eph. 6:14) is our first line of defense against Satan, "the father of lies" (John 8:44). We need to acknowledge truth in the inner man (see Ps. 51:6), deep down in our hearts, though, because genuine faith goes beyond mere intellectual assent or accumulating knowledge.

God's truth is meant to penetrate the heart, the very core of our beings (see Heb. 4:12). Only then will His truth bring about the freedom and lasting change we desire our young people to experience.

A commitment to the truth, however, implies more than believing the truth in your head. It is a lifestyle of committing to "walk in the light" (1 John 1:7), "speaking the truth in love" (Eph. 4:15) and "laying aside falsehood" (v. 25).

One major characteristic of teens in bondage is this: they lie. Jesus put it this way: "For everyone who does evil hates the light, and does not come to the light, lest his deeds be exposed" (John 3:20).

Bulimics lie about their bingeing and purging. Alcoholics hide their addictions and secretly stash bottles around the house. Those involved with the occult carry on secret rituals and practices. In fact, the word "occult" means hidden or secret. Sex addicts can keep their sin hidden for years. The first step to recovery in any of these areas is to get out of denial or deception, get the bondage out into the light and face the truth in the presence of God and caring people.

Satan operates like a roach, scurrying around in the dark, and fleeing for cover when the lights are turned on. He tries to convince young people that the truth is the enemy, so they are often afraid to walk in the light and own up to what they have done. They fear rejection or condemnation by God or people. They are convinced that it will be too hard to repent and change. They are convinced that they could never cope with life apart from their secret sins.

Truth, however, is never the enemy. Jesus, the full embodiment of truth (see John 14:6) is the best friend any of us could have.

The power of Satan is in the lie and the battle for a young person's life is won or lost in the mind. If the devil is able to deceive Christian teens into believing things that are not true about God or about who they are in Christ, they will live in spiritual defeat. When the lies are exposed and replaced with the truth, however, Satan's power over the believer is broken.

A Bulimic's Story

Sharon came up to me (Rich) during one of the breaks in a conference at which I was speaking. Her mind was a confused jumble of anger, fear and sadness. She had suffered from sexual abuse in the past and was presently bulimic. She had an awful compulsion to cut on herself and struggled with staying in the room while God's Word was being preached.

The most devastating distortion in her belief system, however, came from her view of God. She had come to believe that God was evil, mean, uncaring and untrustworthy, while concluding that the things the devil had to offer her were good. It was almost a complete reversal of the truth.

By the end of the conference, she tearfully went forward to share that "maybe God isn't the awful person that I thought He was." She had come light-years in less than a 24-hour period! Her twisted view of herself is being changed by the truth, as she wrote in a letter to me after the conference:

We are not called to dispel the ♦♦♦♦♦ darkness; we are called to turn on the light.

This seminar has been a turning point for me and it's scary and exciting at the same time! What a difference it makes to see your identity—that your worth comes from Christ and not your body shape. I know that it's the truth that is and will set me free. It's amazing how my insurance has paid over half a million dollars on me in the last five years for hospitals and counseling, compared to all that has happened to me and all I have learned at a $30 seminar! I have been completely off the diet pills for over a week and as of today I haven't purged for three days!

Choosing the Truth

The battle indeed is for the minds of young people and Satan will twist Scripture or tell half-truths to subtly deceive. We must remember that the weapons we fight with are not of the world. On the contrary; they have divine power to demolish strongholds. In Step Two, we use truth to "demolish arguments and every pretension that sets itself up against the knowledge of God, and we take captive every thought to make it obedient to Christ" (2 Cor. 10:5, *NIV*).

During Step Two, be alert to possible interference in the counselee because most of the enemy's attacks occur in the first two Steps.

The primary approach is to maintain control by exposing the lies and revealing the battle for the mind, and then ignoring it. Help the young people you work with understand the concept of not paying attention to deceiving spirits. Remember, freedom doesn't come from swatting flies (constantly exercising authority over the enemy's harassing tactics); it comes from taking out the garbage (confessing and renouncing sin).

The way we overcome the father of lies is by choosing the truth. We are not called to dispel the darkness; we are called to turn on the light. The teen counselee will experience increased freedom from the enemy's torments as she progressively walks through the Steps to Freedom and resolves her personal and spiritual conflicts. Any noise in her head is just an attempt by the enemy to derail her from the track that leads to freedom.

As you begin working through Step Two in the Youth Steps, read the introductory material. Then have the young person humbly acknowledge her need for and commitment to walk in the truth by praying the introductory prayer out loud:

Dear heavenly Father,

I know You want me to face the truth, being honest with You. I know that choosing to believe the truth will set me free. I have been deceived by Satan and I have deceived myself. I thought I could hide from You, but You see everything and still love me. I pray in the name of the Lord Jesus Christ, asking You to rebuke all of Satan's demons that are deceiving me. By faith I have received You into my life and I am now seated with Christ in the heavenlies (Eph. 2:6). I acknowledge that I have the responsibility to submit to you and the authority to resist the devil, and when I do, he will flee from me (Jas. 4:7).

I have trusted Jesus alone to save me, so I am your forgiven child. Because You accept me just as I am in Christ, I can be free to face my sin. I ask for the Holy Spirit to guide me into all truth. I ask You to "Search me, O God, and know my heart; try me and know my anxious thoughts; and see if there be any hurtful way in me, and lead me in the everlasting way" (Ps. 139:23,24). In the name of Jesus, I pray. Amen.

Confessing Three Lists of Items

Following that prayer, the counselee may need to confess sins found in three lists: (1) "Ways you can be deceived by the world," (2) "Ways you can deceive yourself" and (3) "Wrong ways of defending yourself."

Identifying areas of deception by the world and by themselves, and fleshly self-defenses, is another way for young people to discover wrong beliefs so they can choose to walk in the truth. You can have the counselees read through the lists silently or you can read the lists out loud to them.

A prayer of confession follows the first list. The counselee need only pray through the prayer once, filling in the blank with any and all items from the list that need to be confronted. The prayer goes like this:

> Lord, I confess that I have been deceived by _____.
> I thank You for your forgiveness and I commit myself to only believing Your truth. Amen.

Another prayer of confession follows the second list. Once again, the counselee need only pray through this prayer once:

> Lord, I confess that I have deceived myself by _____. I thank You for Your forgiveness and commit myself to believing Your truth.

Most young people will work through the second list with little difficulty. Some explanation may be necessary for items in the first list, but refrain from arguing with the counselee. If necessary, look up the Bible references, read them in context and let the Word of God speak for itself. Then invite the teen to pray the prayer of confession as applicable.

Another prayer of confession follows the list of "Wrong ways of defending yourself." The process is similar to the previous list and prayer, though this one is worded somewhat differently:

> Lord, I confess that I have defended myself wrongly by
> _____. I thank You for Your forgiveness and commit myself to trusting in You to defend and protect me.

For teenage abuse victims, that may be a difficult prayer to pray. Many have used anger and withdrawal as shields to protect themselves from further abuse and are afraid to trust God. You can encourage them by explaining that as they realize their true identity in Christ and their child-Father relationship with almighty God, they will come to realize more and more that He is the only defense they need. In time, abused young people will learn to cope with pain in life in new and healthy ways.

The Truth About Our Heavenly Father

The next exercise is designed to help teens develop that intimate "Abba, Father" relationship with God. By beginning to destroy "speculations and every lofty thing raised up against the knowledge of God (2 Cor. 10:5), young people can be set free to worship God in spirit and truth and seek Him earnestly, perhaps for the first time in their lives.

It is a process of renouncing lies and choosing truth about who God is. This is basically the same chart entitled "The Truth About Our Heavenly Father," which is found at the end of chapter 3 of this book.

Have the counselees read down through the chart, left to right, left to right, and so on down the lists. Every phrase describing who God is *not* (on the left side of the chart) should be prefaced with the words, *I renounce the lie that my heavenly Father is....* Every phrase describing who God *is* (on the right side of the chart) should be prefaced with the words, *I accept the truth that my heavenly Father is...*

This exercise can be an incredibly liberating moment for those who have struggled with experiencing an intimate relationship with

God. One young lady who had felt that the Lord was just like her angry, controlling and absent dad finished this exercise and then moved on to the next prayer. She began praying *Dear heavenly Father...*, and then she stopped. She looked up at me with a smile and said, "I have prayed prayers to my heavenly Father all my life, because that's how you're taught to pray. But just then, when I prayed those words, was the first time I ever *felt* something."

What was happening to her? The wall between her head and heart was crumbling down! She had all the right doctrine and could

Jesus Christ is to be our only Master, because God is the only legitimate object of fear. He alone is omnipresent and omnipotent.

■ ■ ■ ■ ■

quote John 3:16 backward and forward; but she had never been free to experience God's Father heart of love—until then.

Satan is a bully, wanting to drive us away from the God who loves us. Sometimes he does it by slandering God's good character, and sometimes he does it by initiating intimidating attacks of fear. Our "adversary, the devil, prowls about like a roaring lion, seeking someone to devour" (1 Pet. 5:8). He wants to create fear in us so we will not walk by faith in God.

Fear is the antithesis of faith. Fear weakens us, causes us to be self-centered and clouds our minds so that all we can think about is the thing that frightens us. Fear, though, can only control us if we let it.

God, however, does not want us to be "mastered by anything," including fear (1 Cor. 6:12). Jesus Christ is to be our only Master, because God is the only legitimate object of fear. He alone is omnipresent and omnipotent.

Begin the next critical exercise in Step Two by having the teens pray:

Dear heavenly Father,

I confess to You that I have listened to the devil's roar and have allowed fear to master me. I have not always walked by faith in You, but instead have focused on my feelings and circumstances (2 Cor. 4:16-18; 5:7). I thank You for forgiving me for my unbelief.

Right now I renounce the spirit of fear and affirm the truth that You have not given me a spirit of fear but of power, love and a sound mind (2 Tim. 1:7).

Lord, please reveal to my mind now all the fears that have been controlling me so that I can renounce them and be free to walk by faith in You.

I thank You for the freedom You give me to walk by faith and not by fear. In Jesus' powerful name, I pray. Amen.

A variety of fears can plague a young person—fear of death, Satan, crowds, failure, rejection, disapproval, embarrassment, crime, pain or insanity. They can be afraid of never being loved or never having a boyfriend or girlfriend. They can be afraid of what will happen to them in the event their parents get divorced. They can be afraid of becoming homosexual, of being a hopeless case, of losing their salvation and being rejected by God. They can also be afraid of the future, fearful that they will never make it.

For each fear that surfaces as a controlling force in that young person's life, have him or her say out loud the following renunciation. As was the case with the exercises earlier in Step Two, it is only necessary to say the renunciation once, filling in the blank with all fears the Lord brings to mind.

I renounce the fear of (name of the fear) because God has not given me a spirit of fear. I choose to live by faith in God, who has promised to protect me and meet all my needs as I walk by faith in Him (Ps. 27:1, Matt. 6:33,34).

After the teens have finished renouncing all specific areas of controlling fear, have them pray the next prayer out loud from the heart:

> Dear heavenly Father,
> I thank You that You are trustworthy. I choose to believe You, even when my feelings and circumstances tell me to fear. You have told me not to fear, for You are with me; not to anxiously look about me, for You are my God. You will strengthen me, help me and surely uphold me with Your righteous right hand (Isa. 41:10). I pray this with faith in the name of Jesus, my Master. Amen.

Understanding Faith

After completing these exercises, read the material in the Steps prior to the "Statement of Truth" out loud to the counselee. Discuss any questions the young person might have regarding the content of this section, which is a proper understanding of faith.

Many people struggle with walking by faith. Their emotions and experiences may shout so loudly into their belief system that they doubt the trustworthiness of God and His Word.

One of the values of being led through the Steps by another believer is having an outside, objective source helping you take an honest look at your life. The most difficult teens to work with are those who are highly subjective and passive mentally. They believe every little thought that comes into their minds, having never taken responsibility for their own thought life.

Their thoughts and feelings tell them they are hopeless, and that they need someone to do something *for* them. They are prime candidates for cults or sick, legalistic pastors who exercise cruel control over their people by telling them what to believe and do and making them feel guilty if they fail to tow the line.

These teens believe God does not hear their prayers, that they do not have enough faith, or that it works for others but not for them. Seeing themselves as "different," they believe they are hopeless and helpless cases.

Before you can make any progress with these kinds of young people, you may need to have them make a renunciation similar to this:

> I renounce the lie that I am a helpless victim, with no hope of ever changing. I renounce the lie that Christianity works for others but not for me and that I am the exception to the rule. I choose to believe that God's Word is true for me and I reject all lies in my thoughts and feelings that oppose the truth.

Ed Silvoso, an evangelist and church planter, offers a definition of a stronghold: it is a "mind-set impregnated with a sense of hopelessness that causes us to accept as unchangeable that which is known to be contrary to the will of God." Before the stronghold itself (e.g., alcoholism) can be attacked and torn down, the young person must be convinced that real change is possible, though its walls most certainly will not come tumbling down without a fight. The following illustration may help:

> Suppose a dirt road leads to your house in the country. Week after week you drive your pickup truck over that road through rain and mud. Ruts form in the road, and are dried by the sun, hard as concrete.
>
> You are used to driving down the road in those ruts, but a smoother road runs outside the ruts. If you make a half-hearted attempt to steer the truck out of the ruts and onto the smoother surface, your vehicle will resist your efforts. If you really want to get out of the rut, you have to make a deliberate choice to do so and it will take some work to get the truck out of the rut.
>
> In the same way, if you no longer want to be controlled by the strongholds or "rut thinking" that the world, the flesh and the devil have cemented in your mind over the years, you need to commit yourself wholeheartedly to breaking those strongholds and choosing to believe the truth. Take every thought captive to the obedience of Christ and don't let your mind

passively follow your feelings. As you "let the Word of Christ richly dwell within you," you will experience the peace of Christ ruling in your heart (Col. 3:15,16).

Statement of Truth

Have the counselee then read through the "Statement of Truth" out loud. No matter how difficult it may be for him to finish it, have him persevere. This is an opportunity for him to affirm what he truly believes and directly counteract the devil's lies that may have distorted his concept of God, himself and the Christian life.

Some young people may have learning disabilities or may read at a below average level. Be patient with them, helping them pronounce difficult words and defining new words as necessary.

For those who are unable to read because of a physical or educational problem, you can have them repeat it after you, phrase by phrase.

Do not assume, though, that the difficulty in reading necessarily has a natural explanation. It is not uncommon for counselees to experience blurred vision or distracting thoughts that hinder their ability to read or comprehend. Some experience a tightness in their throats or a sense that their tongues are thick, making it difficult to enunciate.

Some may say, "I feel like I am just reading words." Help that young person by asking, "Is it your desire to be sincere in what you are saying? Then renounce the lie that you are just reading words, and declare the truth that this Scripture is what you choose to believe."

It will be clear to you when someone has difficulty reading the Statement of Truth because of a spiritual conflict. Critical points of truth will be contested by the enemy and the young person will struggle with speaking the words. As the counselee perseveres in spite of the opposition, an important battle of truth over deception will have been won.

I (Neil) have often used the Statement of Truth as a litmus test to show a counselee his or her newfound freedom after completing all seven of the Steps to Freedom in Christ.

I have said to many, "Remember how difficult it was to read through that Statement of Truth earlier? Why don't you read through it again and see if you can tell any change." Some can hardly believe the difference. Suddenly it is understandable, as is the Bible. Most have a hunger and thirst for the Word of God in a way they have never experienced before.

Letting Go, and Letting God Be in Control

Sarah was a teenager emotionally tied up in knots. Coming from a broken home (her dad had left when she was five), she had tried her best to keep her life from falling apart, though she was deeply hurt by the divorce.

She had been a Christian for years, but only three months prior to our meeting Sarah had dedicated her life to full-time Christian service. That was when things really began to get rough for her. She was overwhelmed with feelings of inferiority, worthlessness, guilt and overwhelming shame. She had doubts about God's love for her, her salvation and even her sanity.

"I'm having so much trouble with my mind going crazy with questions and worries," she confessed.

Struggling with intense anger, hatred, bitterness, loneliness and depression, she had even come to fear that she was beyond help or hope.

The one problem that screamed out louder than any other to me was Sarah's desperate attempt to control the people and circumstances around her. Consequently, she worried about everything. In particular, she was constantly anxious about losing a close group of friends who had recently seemed a bit aloof. Frantically wanting not to lose their closeness, she was inadvertently driving them farther and farther away.

Of particular concern to her was the driving goal she had to marry one of the boys in that close group. Sarah was convinced that she could not be happy unless Jason married her. A voice in her head tormented her, saying, *I'm not worthy enough. I'm not pretty enough for him.* Not surprisingly she was plagued by envious and jealous thoughts of other girls in church whom she perceived as being prettier than her.

After renouncing the lie that she was "on her own" and that she had to be in control or her world would fall apart, she joyfully affirmed that God loved her enough to take care of her. She was able to let Jason go, knowing that God could be trusted to provide the right guy at the right time.

We read through Matthew 6 and she was reminded of the Father's care for the birds of the air and flowers of the field. She also came to understand on an experiential level that she was of much more value to her heavenly Father than even the sparrows and lilies.

And then the peace came. And the joy flooded her heart. And the voices were gone. And the smile returned to Sarah's face. And that is the truth.

The Freedom of Forgiveness

Step Three:
Bitterness Versus Forgiveness

I (Rich) was speaking on the subject of "Forgiving from the Heart" to a group of high school students, when to my left I noticed a young man in a wheelchair crying. Some friends of his were gathered around him, obviously trying to comfort him in his pain.

The Miracle of Forgiveness

After I had finished speaking, Jeffrey slowly wheeled over to me and asked if we could get together and talk.

"Tonight has been the most important night of my life," he said. So we agreed to meet early the next morning along with his good friend and youth pastor, Larry.

Jeffrey's story was a sad tale of pain, anger and disillusionment. He had been born prematurely, and while being transferred from one neonatal facility to another, he was not given the precious oxygen his body needed. As a result, he suffered serious damage to his body. His legs became useless. His hip was constantly going out of joint, throwing his upper body to the side or into a slumped-over position. His barely usable hands were locked in a clawlike position.

Jeffrey's condition was clearly a matter of human error and negligence, as the courts had later ruled. The large monetary remuneration Jeffrey received, however, did nothing to remove the intense anger and bitterness boiling inside him against those negligent medical technicians. Then he heard the message about forgiveness and chose to let go of his anger. He was finally able to forgive those medical men from his heart.

So a miracle took place that day. No, Jeffrey did not get up out of his wheelchair and walk. He remained a "prisoner" of that wheelchair, but he was a free man on the inside! He knew it was impossible to turn back the clock and change his past, but that courageous young man was given new hope and joy and freedom to walk with God; and ultimately that is what matters most.

How many Christian young people are walking around with strong, able bodies, but they are prisoners spiritually and emotionally, in crippling bondage to bitterness?

Of the hundreds of people we have had the privilege of helping find their freedom in Christ, forgiveness has been the primary issue, and in some cases, the *only* issue that needed to be resolved. Without a doubt, forgiving others from the heart is the number-one ticket to freedom for God's people—both young and old.

For some who have been abused, forgiveness seems unthinkable or at best a cruel joke. They see it as just another way to be victimized, a continuation of the weak, sickening saga of codependency.

Although forgiving others may feel as though it is a violation of a young person's sense of justice, that is a misconception. On the contrary, forgiveness is a courageous act, requiring the grace of God. Forgiveness is not excusing or tolerating sin; it is letting go of the anger and hatred against the offender while setting scriptural boundaries against future offenses.

Turning Away from Anger and Revenge

Oftentimes teenagers do not want to forgive because they desperately want the one who hurt them to pay. They feel it is only fair that the offender suffer in return for the suffering he has inflicted. So they punish their abusers again and again in their minds with their bitter anger, replaying the painful incident(s) time and time again in the "VCR" in their brains.

They may also try to ruin the offender's reputation, slandering him behind his back. Or they take direct revenge, seeking to damage that person with their words and actions.

Seeking revenge, however, is forbidden by God. Paul writes, "Never take your own revenge, beloved, but leave room for the

> ▪ ▪ ▪ ▪ ▪ **While trying to play God by meting out revenge, we instead sink to the same level as the abuser.**

wrath of God, for it is written, 'Vengeance is Mine, I will repay,' says the Lord" (Rom. 12:19). While trying to play God by meting out revenge, we instead sink to the same level as the abuser.

Trying to cover up our unforgiveness does not fool anyone either, least of all ourselves, because "the heart knows its own bitterness" (Prov. 14:10). Bitterness acts as a cancer that eats us up on the inside and spreads to others, defiling them as well (see Heb. 12:15).

Frederick Buechner put it this way: "Of the seven deadly sins, anger is possibly the most fun. To lick your wounds, to smack your lips over grievances long past, to savor to the last toothsome morsel both the pain you are given and the pain you are giving back—in many ways it is a feast fit for a king. The chief drawback is that what you are wolfing down is yourself. The skeleton at the feast is you!"

You might want to use the following illustration to drive home to the young people you meet how critical this matter of forgiveness is:

> Imagine for a moment that you have been suffering from a cold and bronchitis for a long time. You can't seem to shake it. You are growing increasingly alarmed because you are starting to cough up blood with your mucus. So you see a doctor who runs a bat-

tory of tests on you, including X rays and an MRI (Magnetic Resonance Imaging).

A few days later you receive a call from your physician. He has discovered a large mass in your lung that he highly suspects is cancer. The good news is that it is operable and he thinks he can get it all. He waits for your decision about what you want to do.

Would you say to him, "Okay, Doc, let's operate. You get in there and try to remove most of that lump. Don't worry about getting it all, though, 75 to 85 percent will be fine"? Of course not! You would want him to get every last cancer cell out of there! Why? Because you know that if any of the cancer is left in your lung it could easily spread again and eventually kill you.

Scripture says, "Get rid of *all* bitterness, rage and anger, brawling and slander, along with *every form* of malice. Be kind and compassionate to one another, forgiving each other, just as in Christ God forgave you" (Eph. 4:31,32, *NIV*, emphasis added).

In many of the freedom appointments with young people, we have had our hearts wrenched listening to the painful memories of unspeakable atrocities perpetrated on innocent children. It is almost unbelievable what people are capable of doing to one another.

I (Neil) have said to hundreds of people in counseling sessions, "I'm so sorry that happened to you." Instead of having fathers who would protect and provide for them, they had fathers who took advantage of them sexually. Instead of having mothers who would comfort and encourage them, they had mothers who verbally or physically abused them. Instead of having pastors who would shepherd them in love, they had legalistic men who tried to control them under a cloud of condemnation and guilt. What some thought would be safe dates turned into date rapes. The litany of horror goes on.

Forgiving the Perpetrators

In the entire process of helping young people find freedom in Christ, no other Step requires greater patience, sensitivity or skill than this one. By way of introduction, gently read the content before the opening prayer in Step Three. Then invite the teen to pray the prayer out loud, telling him that it is a request for God to reveal to his mind all the people he needs to forgive.

The prayer is as follows:

> Dear heavenly Father,
> I thank You for Your great kindness and patience, which has led me to turn from my sins (Rom. 2:4). I know I have not always been completely kind, patient and loving toward those who have hurt me. I have had bad thoughts and feelings toward them. I ask You to bring to my mind all the people I need to forgive (Matt. 18:35). I ask You to bring to the surface all my painful memories so I can choose to forgive these people from my heart. I pray this in the precious name of Jesus who has forgiven me and who will heal me from my hurts. Amen.

When he has finished praying, ask him to write down the names that are coming to his mind. Some encouragers prefer to write the names down themselves as the counselee names them out loud. Either way, encourage the young person not to fill in any details of the offenses done to them at this point. That will come later.

First names or titles (such as Mom, Dad, first-grade teacher) are sufficient. If he never knew or can't remember the person's name, usually a face will come to mind and a way to identify them, such as "the mean man with the beard." Usually the names at the top of the list are the ones that have hurt the teen most deeply—often parents.

The ministry team should sit quietly and prayerfully while the list is being made. Listen carefully in case the name of a person mentioned earlier as a source of hurt is overlooked by the counselee. In that case, go ahead and remind him or her to jot down that person's name. The list may be long or short depending on the young person's history. Perfectionists tend to have shorter lists because they more often than not blame themselves rather than others. Be patient and allow the counselee adequate time to complete the list.

We have had some people pray the prayer and then conclude, "Well, I don't think there is anybody I need to forgive." Or they may say, "Oh, I've already done that. I've already forgiven everybody."

You can respond, "That may be the case, but would you share the names that are coming to mind right now?" Don't be surprised if a list of 10 to 15 names suddenly appears and you will spend the next half hour or so helping that teen work through it!

Some young people will express confusion about why a certain name is coming to mind. Assure them that when they get to that person, the Lord will reveal the reason. Many times the "forgiveness" a teen has already exercised toward an offender has been superficial. Fearing the pain and not wanting to come to grips with the intense hatred and anger they felt, they have suppressed their emotions, stuffing them down inside. Thus their forgiveness has failed to touch the emotional core, and they have yet to truly forgive *from the heart* (see Matt. 18:35). Those emotions often surface during the freedom appointment, once the counselee lets down her guard and allows the gentle, healing Jesus to work.

If the counselee continues struggling to think of more names, you can gently suggest people that were mentioned during the earlier parts of the freedom appointment. You can also suggest categories of people such as relatives, classmates, teammates, teachers, coaches, employers, people at church and so on.

Do not badger the young person, though. People cannot be forced beyond their understanding of the issues or their willingness to forgive. We must think of the possibility, too, that in some cases he or she has truly done a thorough job of forgiving others from the heart. In these rare instances, the reason many names are not coming to mind is because few are left to forgive—praise God!

Letting Yourself Off the Hook

Some young people are their own worst enemies. They have harbored anger and bitterness against themselves, beating themselves up for past or present mistakes, sins and faults. They need to write "myself" on their list. The concept of "letting go" of self-loathing, guilt, shame and self-condemnation may not have ever occurred to some of the teens you counsel. They may have always thought they deserved to feel bad for what they have done or not done.

That is the beauty of the Cross. "He made Him who knew no sin to be sin on our behalf, that we might become the righteousness of God in Him" (2 Cor. 5:21). Because God has already forgiven us all our sins (see Eph. 1:7), removing them "as far as the east is from the west" (Ps. 103:12), hurling them "into the depths of the sea" (Mic. 7:19), we can forgive ourselves. To choose *not* to accept God's for-giveness by forgiving ourselves is to declare in essence that Christ's death was not sufficient payment for our sins. Jesus, however, cried out on the cross, "It is finished!" or literally "Paid in full"!

It is a fleshly deception that motivates young people to atone for their own sins. We are warned not to let anyone "keep defrauding you of your prize by delighting in self-abasement" (Col. 2:18). Instead, we are commanded to hold "fast to the head" (v. 19), which is Christ. What is the prize spoken of here? The freedom from being judged or condemned by anyone, and that includes yourself!

Forgiving ourselves is saying in effect: "Lord, I do believe that You have forgiven me and cleansed me of those sins I have confessed to You. Because of Your great love and grace—not because I deserve it—I choose to no longer hold those things against myself. I receive Your forgiveness and I renounce all guilt, self-loathing and shame either coming from my conscience or from the accuser of the brethren."

Resolving Anger Against God

Bitterness toward God is far more common than you might expect. Young people often harbor anger against God because He failed to answer a prayer in the way they expected (e.g., a loved one died or parents divorced). Sometimes they are mad at Him because He did not give them what they feel they need to be successful in life (e.g., good looks, athletic ability, money). In the case of abuse victims, they can hold on to anger against God because He allowed those atroci-ties to happen to them. If not resolved, a young person's anger toward God can become a wall that blocks him from experiencing that deep, intimate "Abba, Father" relationship.

It is a dead-end street to try to explain why God allows the things He does. It is a mystery of His sovereignty that He allows evil men to inflict pain and suffering upon innocent people. Do not try to defend God to hurting young people. The key issue is not where *was* God, but where *is* God. You might want to say something like this:

> I can't even begin to explain why God allowed you to suffer the way you have. But you are here in this place and so is God so that you can be set free from the pain of your past. We can't turn the clock back and undo what was done to you, but you don't have to allow your past to control you. You can be free to move on with your life and experience the healing touch of Jesus, but it only comes through truly forgiving those who have hurt you.
>
> One thing that helps me is to realize that one day God will make all the injustice done in the world right at the judgment seat of Christ. You want justice now, and that is a natural reaction. God, however, has His timetable and we can't change that. For now, God wants you to focus on finding your freedom from the past through forgiving others from your heart.

Obviously, God does not need to be forgiven because He is incapable of ever doing anything wrong. "Angry thoughts against God," however, will need to be added to the counselee's list and those thoughts "let go" for freedom to be found. Scripture says we are to destroy "speculations and every lofty thing raised up against the knowledge of God" and we are to take "every thought captive to the obedience of Christ" (2 Cor. 10:5).

It is often helpful to explain to teens that there is a definite line in life between things God says He will do versus the things in life that are our responsibility to do. God alone can save us from sin, empower us to live the Christian life, convict another person of sin, and so on. If we try to save ourselves, live the Christian life in our own power, or try to be another person's conscience, we will mess it up every time.

On the other hand, God commands and expects us to do certain things. No amount of pleading on our part will cause God to budge one bit.

For example, we must confess our sins, renounce lies, forgive those who hurt us, put on the armor of God, submit to His lordship and resist the devil. God will not and cannot do those things for us. If we fail to do them, we will experience struggles and pain in life.

Sometimes young people harbor resentment toward God because He refuses to respond to their angry demands. In reality, that should bring security, not insecurity, to the teens you counsel. After all, who would ultimately trust a God that could be badgered or bargained with to do our will?

Renewing Relationship with the Heavenly Father

Jeffrey (the young man in the wheelchair) had harbored a lot of anger against God for allowing his crippled condition. That anger was intensified when his sister was involved in an industrial accident. A piece of heavy machinery had fallen on her foot, crushing it. After three months of that disability, his sister went to a healing service and was supernaturally healed by God.

Although Jeffrey was glad for her healing, a part of him cried out to God in anger, "I've been crippled for 19 years and she was only disabled for three months! God, why did You heal her and not me? Why?"

As he shared that incident, I prayed that nothing I told Jeffrey would sound like a hollow cliché to him. He had experienced far more pain and suffering in 19 years than I have in my whole life. So I spoke gently and carefully.

"Jeffrey, your happiness in life simply can't be dependent upon your physical condition. Otherwise God is a cruel and unjust God."

He nodded his head and replied, "I know that."

After further encouragement, Jeffrey was able to let go of his anger toward God. He confessed that he had felt justified in harboring resentment against the Lord because He had not healed him. It opened the way for a beautiful renewal of that young man's love relationship with his tenderhearted heavenly Father.

Then Jeffrey took a further step toward spiritual healing by thanking God for each of the parts of his body that did not work well. That was not all. Then he prayed and asked God to glorify Himself through that crippled body bound to a wheelchair. Such a sweetness about his praying could be felt that as the tears flowed from his eyes, I could not help but be touched as well.

It would have been futile to try to tell Jeffrey, "Well, you shouldn't feel that way about God!" That would have come across as a subtle form of rejection of him and probably would have shut the door on any further deep sharing on his part.

God knows exactly how we feel toward Him (even hatred) and He does not condemn us (see Rom. 8:1). We need to give people the full freedom to vent their emotions during the appointment, and once they have been real with us, then we can gently point them to the truth that will set them free.

The Meaning of Forgiveness

Once the counselee's list is complete, it is time to address the meaning of forgiveness. We can't assume that people know how to forgive from the heart, so take time to read and discuss with the teen you are counseling the explanation in Step Three of the Steps to Freedom in Christ.

The key points to emphasize are found in the bold print in the Youth Steps and are as follows:

1. Forgiveness is not forgetting.
2. Forgiveness is a choice, a decision of the will. Since God requires us to forgive, it is something we can do.
3. By forgiving, you let them off your hook, but they are not off God's hook.
4. You forgive for your sake, so that you can be free. Forgiveness is mainly an issue of obedience between you and God. God wants you to be free; this is the only way.
5. Forgiveness is agreeing to live with the consequences of another person's sin. But you will live with the consequences whether you want to or not. Your only choice is whether you will do so in the bondage of bit-

terness or in the freedom of forgiveness.

6. How do you forgive from your heart? You allow God to bring to the surface the mental agony, emotional pain and feelings of hurt toward those who hurt you.

7. Forgiveness is a decision not to use their offense against them.

8. Don't wait to forgive until you feel like forgiving. For now, it is freedom that will be gained, not necessarily a feeling.

Ever since the incident in the Garden of Eden, mankind has played the "blame game" (see Gen. 3:11-13). Pointing the finger at others and refusing to let go of our indignation, though, can be a symptom of a heart more prone to revenge than forgiveness.

That is what forgiveness is always about—innocent ones bearing the consequences for the sins of guilty ones.

Forgiveness is an act of the will whereby we give up our claim to seek revenge for an offense against us. God could have simply chosen to pour out His wrath on us for our sins, but He graciously took it on Himself. That is what forgiveness is always about—innocent ones bearing the consequences for the sins of guilty ones.

Jesus took on Himself the eternal consequences of our sin—spiritual death. In forgiving others from the heart, we choose to accept the temporary consequences of another person's sin. Let's face reality, though; we will bear those consequences whether we like it or not. The only choice we have is whether we will do so in the bondage of bitterness or in the freedom of forgiveness.

I (Rich) was taking a young lady through the Steps to Freedom in Christ. She had just broken up with her boyfriend and I was glad because he was a total jerk. Somewhere along the line he had taken a knife and slashed her on her cheek from her eye to chin. She had a scar there as a permanent reminder of his sin. Apart from expensive plastic surgery (which she could not afford), she would wear that badge of violence the rest of her life. She forgave that man, though, and so was set free from the emotional and spiritual hold he had over her.

A teenager you are counseling might cry out, "But that's not fair!" That is right; it is not fair. It is the reality of life, though, in an imperfect, fallen and unfair world. All of us are living with the consequences of the sins of others. All of us are living with the consequences of Adam's sin—physical death.

Exercising Mercy

Jesus is our model. Even in His glorified state, He has chosen to bear the eternal marks of our sins upon His body—the nail prints upon His hands and feet. The victory of Jesus over sin and Satan was won, but not without cost. We enter into that victory as well through forgiveness.

What is the alternative? To find ourselves tormented by the accuser of the brethren as Matthew 18:21-35 so clearly describes. That parable teaches we are to continue forgiving others, no matter how many times they sin against us. In addition, we are to forgive others as we have been forgiven by God. For no amount of sin against us begins to compare with the seriousness of our sin against God!

Third, God treated us with mercy, knowing we could never repay Him for our crimes against His throne, so we should treat others with mercy as well. If we refuse to forgive, God in His loving discipline will turn us over to the torturers until we learn to forgive.

Satan gains a clear advantage over us when we refuse to forgive (see 2 Cor. 2:10,11) and we give him an opportunity to operate in our lives through our unresolved anger (see Eph. 4:26,27).

God is serious about His people—teenagers included—exercising mercy. Luke 6:36 says, "Be merciful, just as your Father is merciful." Too often we want to exercise justice, but that is God's business. He will "bring every act to judgment, everything which is hidden, whether it is good or evil" (Eccles. 12:14). That is justice, giving people what they deserve.

All of us, however, ought to praise God that He has been merciful and gracious to us in Christ, or we would all be in hell right now. Romans 6:23 says, "For the wages of sin is death, but the free gift [grace] of God is eternal life in Christ Jesus our Lord."

Mercy is withholding judgment and exercising love and kindness instead. Titus 3:4,5 teaches that this is the way God relates to us in Christ: "But when the kindness of God our Savior and His love for mankind appeared, He saved us, not on the basis of deeds which we have done in righteousness, but according to His mercy."

God's justice still had to be served, so Jesus Himself bore the wrath of God in our place.

God, however, goes beyond mercy in forgiving us. He exercises grace. Grace is giving us what we do not deserve. Eternal life, adoption into His family, the gift of the Holy Spirit are just some examples of God's lavish grace (see Eph. 1).

That is why it is an important part of the healing process for teens to pray for God's blessing on those who have hurt them. This is an act of grace and a true indicator of a heart that has extended mercy and forgiven the offender. Luke 6:27,28 puts it this way: "But I say to you who hear, love your enemies, do good to those who hate you, bless those who curse you, pray for those who mistreat you."

It may be dangerous for young people to try to do good face-to-face with those who have abused them, so this should never be attempted without much prayer and the on-site protection of other adults. Teens, however, can always "do good" to those who hate them by praying for them.

To love one's enemies is only possible by the grace of God and the power of the Holy Spirit. Yet forgiving others is an act of love that "does not take into account a wrong suffered" (1 Cor. 13:5). When we love our enemies we show that we are truly Jesus' disciples (see John 13:35) and filled with God Himself, who is love (see 1 John 4:8).

Consider Two Important Errors

Beware of two important errors regarding forgiveness.

The first one says that forgiveness is a process and that many people are not "ready to forgive." According to this teaching, teens would be expected to expose all their painful memories, talk about them and rid themselves of their pain before being able to forgive.

The implication is that we have to heal emotionally in order to forgive, when in actuality the reverse is true. We first make the decision to forgive, and then the emotional healing can take place.

Counselors, even Christian ones influenced by the secular world, may be proponents of this view. They will never be able to lead their patients to resolution because simply sharing painful memories does not bring healing. It will only make the pain worse until forgiveness is exercised.

The second error is more common in the Church. In its extreme form it sounds like this: "You shouldn't feel that way; you just need to forgive." Forgiveness, though, does not involve denying the emotions; it is allowing God to surface them. Any attempt to forgive that bypasses the emotional core will be incomplete and a violation of Scripture, which says to "forgive...from your heart" (Matt. 18:35).

Just before you help young people pray through their lists of people to forgive, encourage them not to rush. Have them stay with each person until they can't think of any more painful memories, and then move on to the next one on the list.

Some people will need to be forgiven for many things (usually close family members), while others may have only committed one offense against the counselee.

The prayer of forgiveness is designed to encourage the young person you are helping to be specific and to get to the emotional core. It goes like this:

Lord, I forgive (name the person) for (say what they did to hurt you) even though it made me feel (share the painful memories or feelings).

It may take young people a little time to get the hang of this process. They may feel a little uncomfortable being specific, thinking they are being mean and judgmental toward those they are forgiving. This can be an especially acute struggle for teens and their parents. They are torn between feelings of love and loyalty and their need to face the pain their parents have caused them. Assure them that they are not condemning the people they forgive, just acknowledging that they were not perfect in some ways.

No parent is perfect and very often the imperfections in a teen's parents are in part a result of the imperfections in their parents' parents. Facing the truth and forgiving Mom and Dad, however, begins to stop the cycle of abuse that has continued from generation to generation.

Rationalizing the Acts of the Perpetrator

Young people may feel as though they deserved the abuse they received. A young anorexic girl came to her dad on the list and said, "I feel like I need to ask him to forgive me." I (Neil) told her, "Maybe you do, but that is not what we are dealing with here. We are dealing with your pain."

Beware of attempts by teens to excuse or rationalize the sin perpetrated against them. I (Rich) was ministering to a young man who had been beaten by his dad. His response was typical: "But I was bad. I didn't do what I was told." I assured him that being physically beaten by a parent is never justified. There is a huge difference between loving discipline and angry, violent punishment.

At first, some of the teens' prayers may be vague and general such as, "Lord, I forgive my mom for what she did to me even though it made me feel bad." That kind of praying won't bring freedom. Encourage young people who pray this way to tell you specifically what was done to them. Ask them how it made them feel at the time. Ask them how it makes them feel now.

Bill approached one of our Freedom in Christ staff at a "Stomping Out the Darkness" youth conference. He said he had attended the leadership portion of the conference held six weeks earlier, and he was struggling with forgiving his father.

That staff member asked Bill to share about his relationship with his dad, and indeed there was much to forgive. He asked Bill if he was ready to forgive his father right then. Bill said, "Yes!"

Bill began praying, "Lord, I forgive Dad for all the things that he said and did to me that have hurt me in so many ways."

The staff member interrupted Bill and said, "Hey, wait a minute.

That's a pretty general prayer you're praying. You need to forgive your dad for specific things. What is the first thing that comes to your mind right now that your dad did to you?"

"He didn't show up to a big football game that I was playing in, and he promised me he would come. He just never showed up and I kept watching for him the whole game."

"Now that's what you need to forgive your dad for," the staff member replied, "as well as any other things that stand out to you like that."

Teens who have been hurt repeatedly by someone close will not necessarily remember everything done to them. The specific incidents that come to mind, though, must be worked out specifically if freedom is to be gained.

Considering Young People's Emotions

For some, forgiving from the heart will be an emotional catharsis, while others will express little or no emotion. We have to allow for a variety of temperaments and for the emotional immaturity of many teenagers. Some (especially boys) are not accustomed to talking about how they feel and so will find it hard to verbalize feelings. When they do, it may be in a very guarded way because they are afraid of baring their hearts, lest they get out of control emotionally.

Many teenage boys believe that being emotional means being weak. Therefore, many will experience a lot of internal resistance to sharing their pain, especially if you as a counselor are a stranger. Some teenage girls may also be hesitant to share their painful memories, especially if they have been betrayed in the past by someone with whom they were once open and honest.

Be gentle and patient. Ask God for wisdom in how to help teens get in touch with their emotional core. Trust Him to express His unconditional love through you, and pray that the young people you help will sense that the freedom appointment is a safe and secure place to be real.

We often hear people say, "I've never told this to anyone before." That is a positive sign the young people feel safe. We must believe and accept without judgment the feelings and perceptions of teen counselees, or they will quickly clam up emotionally.

Nobody is more emotionally inhibited than victims of satanic ritual abuse. They have been programmed that way. They were told, and probably taught through watching the painful torture of others, that if they cried someone would be hurt. I (Neil) have seen tears form in their eyes and roll freely down their cheeks when they renounce the lie that their crying would cause the death or injury of anyone. Until they break that stronghold, they can't forgive from their hearts. Do not think for a minute that Satan does not know that.

Even some young people who had "ordinary" childhoods have learned not to express their emotions, especially negative ones. If the teen you are trying to help is emotionally inhibited, ask, "What happened to you when you were emotionally honest in your home? Do you believe it is wrong or weak to be emotionally honest?"

To be free, the young person must forgive those who trained him or her that way and renounce the lies he or she has been taught concerning the right and wrong way to handle and express emotions. The one who is truly free in Christ will be emotionally free as well.

Help the counselee stay focused on forgiving the offender, and not on just telling the story of the offense. If the young people you are helping start talking to you about what happened, encourage them to tell God. By directing them back to the "model prayer" for forgiveness in the Steps, you can keep moving along. Certainly you do not want to rush them, but neither do you want to take unnecessary time.

Taking Time to Cover All the "Stuff"

Step Three is likely to take the longest time of the seven Steps because it takes time to walk through the pain in a young person's life. The person may look at you in disbelief, saying, "You don't have enough time for me to cover all this stuff!"

Make sure you mean it when you say, "We'll stay here all day and night if we have to."

It is critical that you never start this Step without finishing it. That does not mean other people or incidents might not surface later, but it is imperative you cover what is on that teenager's list completely during the session. The only exception to this rule is if the teenager himself chooses to end the session early or has a prior commitment that is unavoidable. In either case, make yourself available at the first possible time to complete the work together, if the young person desires to do so.

After the young person finishes forgiving each person and before moving on to the next person on the list, have him or her pray the following prayer (it is in Step Three) out loud and from the heart:

> Lord, I choose not to hold any of these things against (name) any longer. I thank You for setting me free from the bondage of my bitterness toward them. I choose now to ask You to bless (name). In Jesus' name. Amen.

Frequently that short prayer may serve to motivate young people to continue praying for a while for that offender, especially if it is a close relative. That is healthy and to be encouraged. Many times teens will take this opportunity to pray for the salvation of a loved one. Feel free to agree with them in prayer, then move on to the next person on the list.

The emotional and spiritual release young people feel upon forgiving others from the heart can range from exuberance to a quiet sense of peace and relief. Those who do a thorough and complete job of forgiving and who reach the emotional core of their pain often cannot believe the burden lifted off themselves.

A "Wow" Forgiveness Experience

Rebecca, a teenager, had come to a conference where I (Rich) was speaking, vowing she would never forgive the neighbor who had sexually abused her for the first six years of her life. She even told her roommates she would never forgive him. About halfway through the conference she decided to come in for a freedom appointment anyway. Coming to Step Three, she continued her solemn vows never to forgive her abuser.

"Do you want to be free, Rebecca?" I asked gently.

"Yes, of course I do," she replied.

"Then you have to forgive. There's no other path to freedom."

At first she continued to refuse to forgive that man, until it slowly dawned on her that finding her freedom was more important than hanging on to her anger and bitterness.

So she prayed, "Father, I forgive my neighbor for abusing me for the first six years of my life, even though it made me feel dirty, lonely, worthless and violated."

Suddenly she leaped out of her chair and started shouting, "Wow!" Her youth pastor and his wife, both of whom loved her like a daughter, looked up from their praying, startled.

Rebecca spent the next couple of minutes bouncing around the room, shouting, "Wow!" She could not believe the change inside her. "Just a couple of minutes ago I was feeling so down, and now I feel such joy! Wow!"

All three of us just reveled in the newfound freedom Rebecca was experiencing through forgiving from the heart. Whenever we take people through this Step, about all we can say at the end is, "Wow!" The Lord never ceases to amaze us with His healing, transforming power. Often the evidence is immediately written all over the face of the counselee!

You may want to make a list of adjectives teens use to describe themselves in this Step and the others. Rebecca used the words "dirty, lonely, worthless and violated." A powerful way of closing the freedom appointment, once all seven Steps are completed, is to give counselees the list of negative labels and have them say, "I renounce the lie that I am (list negative adjectives or labels), because God says...." Then have them recite the biblical truths of their identity in Christ, using the IN CHRIST list at the back of the Steps to Freedom in Christ. Then watch the joy come to their eyes! (See chapter 10 for advice about whether to turn in offenders/abusers to the authorities.)

Seeking Reconciliation

As counselees go through their forgiveness lists, the Lord may bring to their minds people of whom they need to ask forgiveness. That is another issue altogether and is spoken of in Matthew 5:23-26. The

Bible tells us to go to others before we come to Him, so we can seek reconciliation with that person if we know he or she has something against us. Appendix B provides specific instruction for how to do such reconciliatory work.

The important thing to remember is that *if we have hurt someone else*, we need to go to that person first before we go to God. *If we have been hurt by others*, though, we need to forgive them by going first, and in some cases only, to God. Forgiveness must precede reconciliation.

The Bible says, "If possible, so far as it depends on you, be at

> ## *If we have been hurt by others*, we need to forgive them by
> ## ❚❚❚❚❚ going first, and in some cases only, to God. Forgiveness must precede reconciliation.

peace with all men" (Rom. 12:18). Sometimes it does not depend on us. Perhaps the other party is deceased or has moved away to someplace unknown or is unwilling to be reconciled.

Abusers are often unwilling to own up to their sins and seek forgiveness. If they refuse, reconciliation is impossible. Remember, though, the freedom of the abused is never contingent on whether the abuser confesses and repents of his sin or asks forgiveness. Those teens who have been hurt must be willing to forgive from their hearts regardless of what the abuser does or does not do. Otherwise those abused young people will be controlled by their abusers all their lives.

Jesus again is our model of forgiveness. He chose to pray on the cross on behalf of those mocking and crucifying Him, "Father, forgive them, for they do not know what they are doing" (Luke 23:34). Jesus did not wait for his murderers to repent of their sin (they probably *never* did) before forgiving them. We must also forgive as Christ forgave.

After finishing in prayer with the last person on the list, have the counselee pray, asking God to reveal any other people or incidents He would want her to forgive. When you are finally finished with this critical Step, it is time for a break to stretch, use the rest room, get a drink or just walk around a bit before beginning Step Four.

A major portion of the Steps to Freedom has been covered. In normal conditions, you are at or beyond the halfway point in terms of time. Thank the counselee for her courage and commitment to getting right with God and encourage her to hang in there to the end and finish strong.

chapter ten

Resisting Rebellion

Step Four:
Rebellion Versus Submission

Jeremy is an intelligent kid and a Christian. He opened his heart to Christ a couple of years ago and has shown flashes of spiritual hunger. For the most part, though, he remains a spiritual babe, immature in his walk with Christ. He knows basically what he ought to be doing spiritually, but struggles with getting motivated to do it. In the final analysis, he does not seem overly concerned about his spiritual condition and neither does his dad.

That is unfortunate because they should be concerned. Jeremy has developed a habit pattern of manipulation and deception. He has learned how to control his parents so that he can basically do what he wants to do rather than what they tell him to do.

He is what I call a "soft-core rebel." Choosing to defy authority by trickery rather than hard-core defiance or stubborn, passive rebellion, Jeremy is motivated by one driving force in life: to have fun. By his own admission, wriggling his way out from under the constraints of authority is fun. To get his way by deception has become an adrenaline rush, an adventure and a heady challenge that is growing into an addiction.

He makes promises to return home by a certain time when being out with friends, and then wanders in two or three days late, sometimes missing school. Jeremy tells his parents he will be sleeping at a particular buddy's house, and then a phone call from his parents the following morning reveals the truth—he never showed up there.

Jeremy, like many young people, has erroneously concluded that authorities in life rob you of your freedom and pursuit of fun. Therefore, because "having fun" is the ultimate god to be served, anyone—including parents—who stands in the way of worshiping that god must be disobeyed.

Teenagers who show no intellectual imagination or drive when it comes to school work can suddenly rise to genius level when it comes to devising ways of avoiding responsibility and disobeying authority. The possibilities are almost endless, but the following are a few of the more common strategies teens may employ that are indicators of a rebellious spirit. They include:

- Lying about where they are going, what they are doing or with whom they will be associating;
- Claiming ignorance when confronted with poor behavior;
- Deliberately testing the limits of parental authority by breaking rules;
- Stubbornly refusing to submit to or cooperate with authority even after being disciplined;
- Creating confusing stories to explain away misbehavior in order to diminish consequences of rebellion;
- Blaming others in order to play innocent;
- Procrastinating (playing the "waiting game") until the authority figure forgets or gives up;
- Playing one parent against another to get their way;
- Deliberately creating emotional scenes in order to feel a sense of power or control over authorities;
- Engaging in behavior directly contrary to parents' standards.

The list could go on and on. Every teenager has long ago learned how to push the buttons of those in authority over him, especially parents.

One young man expressed to me (Rich) how delighted he was in himself for knowing exactly what to say and how to say it to get a rise out of his dad. To him, it was worth any possible negative consequences he might suffer to gain the satisfaction of having exercised control and power over an adult. He felt that in itself was sufficient reward to make it all worthwhile.

Certain conditions in the household are fertile breeding ground for a rebellious teen to take control. They include the following:

- Parents who are too wrapped up in their own worlds to spend time developing a close relationship with the teen;
- Parents who are so wrapped up in their teen's world that the young person feels smothered, stifled or controlled;
- Major crises (e.g., finances, health problems) with other family members, diverting time and attention from the teen;
- Parental modeling of rebellious behavior toward authority (government, laws, employers, church);
- Tendency of authorities (especially parents) to react to teen's words and lifestyle without patiently allowing the young person to express his opinions and feelings;
- A parental track record (at least from the teen's viewpoint) of being untrustworthy, uncaring or inflexible.

It is no accident that Step Four follows Step Three. This is because it is virtually impossible for a teenager to submit to authority, including God, if that young person is angry with them. Rebellion is often born in the womb of bitterness and resentment. Add to that boiling cauldron of anger and unforgiveness a peer group that considers rebellion against authority "cool," and you have trouble. Adolescence is naturally a healthy time of moving away from parental control anyway, but rebellion is independence that has crossed over the line.

According to 1 Samuel 15:23, "Rebellion is as the sin of divination [witchcraft], and insubordination is as iniquity and idolatry." Defiance against authority places us in the camp of the enemy and subjects us to his influences. We are foolish to pass off a rebellious spirit as an innocent phase a young person is experiencing! Choosing to rebel against God or His human authorities places a teenager in grave spiritual danger.

The warning in Scripture about rebelling against parental authority is a clear and sobering one, as found in Ephesians 6:1-3:

> Children, obey your parents in the Lord, for this is right. Honor your father and mother (which is the first commandment with a promise), that it may be well with you, and that you may live long on the earth.

God's Word promises a great blessing on children who obey and submit to the authority of their parents—a long life under God's blessing.

Is it not safe to say then that the opposite would be true? Those who do not submit to parental authority will not have things go well with them and they will not live long on the earth?

How many teenager problems—such as drug addiction, STDs, occult practices, criminal behavior, suicide and deep emotional pain—are at least in part traceable to rebellion against parents? Only the Lord knows.

Certainly of equal importance is violating the message of Ephesians 6:4, which takes place in far too many homes, even Christian homes. That warning is directed toward parents, especially dads, and declares:

> And, fathers, do not provoke your children to anger; but bring them up in the discipline and instruction of the Lord.

Each person is clearly responsible before God for the choices he or she makes in life. Teenagers are no exception. Without engaging in unhealthy introspection or succumbing to numbing guilt, parents of rebellious teens ought to ask God to reveal any ways they have contributed to the problem by provoking their children to anger.

A change in a young person may be quickened by a change in

parents. That is often the way things operate in the spiritual realm. To exercise spiritual authority, people must be under the authority of God. That includes parents having success in warding off the enemy's attacks on their homes, as well as teenagers winning the spiritual battles in their own lives. A fascinating incident in Scripture makes that point clear.

A Biblical Example

Jesus had just finished teaching the Sermon on the Mount and had moved on to Capernaum when a centurion sent word through some Jewish elders that his slave was deathly ill. The elders strongly encouraged Jesus to grant the centurion his request to heal his servant because that soldier was a good friend of the Jewish people. Jesus agreed to go.

While nearing the soldier's house, some of the centurion's friends brought another message to Jesus from him. It is found in Luke 7:6-8 (*NKJV*):

> "Lord, do not trouble Yourself, for I am not worthy that You should enter under my roof. Therefore I did not even think myself worthy to come to You. But say the word, and my servant will be healed. For I also am a man placed under authority, having soldiers under me. And I say to one, 'Go,' and he goes; and to another, 'Come,' and he comes; and to my servant, 'Do this,' and he does it."

What was Jesus' reaction to the centurion's message? He was amazed at him and announced that he had never seen such faith before, even in Israel! What was it about the soldier's faith that amazed Jesus so much? Certainly his realization that Jesus did not have to be in the presence of the sick slave to heal him, but could do it from afar by saying a word, was pretty amazing. But there was more.

Notice that the centurion compared himself to Jesus in that he, too, (like Jesus) was a man *under* authority. That submission to a higher authority gave the solider (and Jesus) the permission to exercise authority himself!

To what authority was the centurion under submission? To the superior officer over him and ultimately to Caesar. To what authority was Jesus under submission? To the Father. Jesus said it Himself in John 5:19: "Truly, truly, I say to you, the Son can do nothing of Himself, unless it is something He sees the Father doing; for whatever the Father does, these things the Son also does in like manner."

What an astounding concept! Jesus, the eternal God and second person of the Trinity, chose to live on earth in submission to the Father. Why? Certainly not because He had to. After all, He was God; but He chose to submit Himself to the Father to be an example to us of how we should live.

Submitting to God

Leading young people to submit to the human authorities over them—as well as to the ultimate authority, God—is critical. James 4:7 puts it this way: "Submit therefore to God. Resist the devil and he will flee from you."

Can you see why the devil tempts teenagers to rebel against God, parents and other authorities? Rebellion is a trap of Satan, so he can have his way with them. Young people who do not submit to God have no authority to resist the devil. They are wide-open targets for his attacks, basically defenseless against his schemes.

It is critical, therefore, that you pray for the rebellious teenagers you love so as to have their eyes opened and so they will come to their senses and see the spiritual trap into which they are falling. Satan paints a glamorous picture of rebellion, inviting teens to come into that house of pleasures, thrills and power, all the while deceiving them into thinking they are serving themselves. In reality, though, they are being held captive by the devil into doing his will and serving him (see 2 Tim. 2:26).

Denying ourselves is the way of the Cross. Saying no to ourselves and yes to God is the ultimate struggle in life, but the consequences of choosing the alternative could be deadly. Playing God is the biggest mistake we can make.

It seems too much of a sacrifice to many young people to surrender all to God, but what are they really sacrificing? They are sacrificing the lower life to gain the higher life. They are sacrificing the pleasure of things to gain the pleasure of life.

What would young people exchange for love, joy, peace, patience, kindness, goodness, faithfulness, gentleness and self-control? A few minutes of fun or excitement? A new car? A temporary thrill? Approval of peers? Unfortunately, too many Christian young people have been duped into thinking that trade-off will pay off, and have swallowed the lie of the world.

A young person who follows Christ truly sacrifices that which ▮ ▮ ▮ ▮ ▮ is a temporary "fix" to gain that which is eternally satisfying and rewarding.

A young person who follows Christ truly sacrifices that which is a temporary "fix" to gain that which is eternally satisfying and rewarding. Some sacrifice! Learning to trust God means waiting for God to provide our needs in His time and in His way. Rebellious teens do not want to wait. They want gratification now instead of satisfaction later.

Only when teenagers' eyes are opened and they see their weak, limited resources will they discover God's powerful, infinite resources. Surrender to the lordship of Christ then becomes not a negative, stifling concept, but the path to life itself. If young people make Him the Lord of their lives, He also becomes the Lord of their problems. Away from His authority, however, they are wandering on their own, being stalked by their adversary the devil. He prowls around like a roaring lion, seeking to devour them (see 1 Pet. 5:8).

The world system around us fosters a spirit of rebellion. Even Christian young people too often sit in judgment of those who are in positions of authority over them. They go to church and make fun of the choir or worship leader instead of entering into the worship of God. They sit in judgment of the pastor's or youth pastor's message rather than letting the Word of God sit in judgment on their lives.

It is easy to bad-mouth our president (if we disagree with his views), violate traffic laws (if we are in a hurry), laugh at teachers behind their backs and dog it on the athletic field when the coach is not watching.

Submitting to Those in Authority

We are commanded by God, however, to submit to and pray for those who are in authority over us. Romans 13:1,2 says, "Let every person be in subjection to the governing authorities. For there is no authority except from God, and those which exist are established by God. Therefore he who resists authority has opposed the ordinance of God; and they who have opposed will receive condemnation upon themselves."

God's plan is that we yield ourselves to Him and demonstrate this allegiance by being submissive to those He placed in authority over us. We surrender our "right to rule or control" and trust God to work through His established lines of authority for our good.

To be sure, it is a great act of faith for a young person to trust God to work through less than perfect parents, teachers, youth leaders and so on. But that is the way to freedom.

At times, however, the Bible teaches that we need to obey God rather than men. When governing authorities require teens to do something God commands them not to do, or try to prevent them from doing something God requires them to do, they must obey God rather than men. That is what Peter and John did (see Acts 5:29).

Teenagers also are not obligated to obey people who try to exercise authority outside their jurisdictions. An employer or school teacher has no right to tell a young person what she should do in her own home, but can give responsibility and assignments that relate to the job or school. A policeman cannot tell a teen what to believe or where to go to church, but he can tell him to pull over his car.

Daniel's Example

Daniel was the epitome of submission, and his life can be a great example to young people about how to respond to an authority who has overstepped the bounds of his God-given rule.

Daniel was not disrespectful of the king nor of those who were enforcing the king's orders. The king was wrong in wanting Daniel and his friends to eat the king's food, because it violated the Jewish dietary laws given in God's Word. Daniel decided not to defile himself with that forbidden food, so he sought and gained permission from his immediate superior to eat only the food God allowed. Because he was neither defiant nor disrespectful, "God granted Daniel favor and compassion in the sight of the commander of the officials" (Dan. 1:9). Daniel offered a creative alternative that allowed the commander to save face in the sight of the king and also to fulfill the wishes of the king to have wise and healthy servants.

Young people today likewise need to learn to treat those in authority over them respectfully, from the heart and not just with the lips. Though the following Scripture was originally written to slaves, the principle also applies to the relationship between student and teacher, athlete and coach, and employee and employer:

> Slaves, in all things obey those who are your masters on earth, not with external service, as those who merely please men, but with sincerity of heart, fearing the Lord. Whatever you do, do your work heartily, as for the Lord rather than for men; knowing that from the Lord you will receive the reward of the inheritance. It is the Lord Christ whom you serve. For he who does wrong will receive the consequences of the wrong which he has done, and that without partiality (Col. 3:22-25).

Seeing beyond the human authorities in their lives to the God who placed them there provides teens the necessary perspective to joyfully obey.

A New Work Attitude

As a young person, I (Rich) worked as a lifeguard during the summer. Part of the job entailed cleaning the bathrooms when I was not sitting up on the lifeguard stand. Sometime during the day, I could count on some little kid missing the toilet and leaving a smelly mess all over the stall floor. I was ticked off—at the kids, their parents and my boss for making me do that nasty job.

One day I read Colossians 3:22-25 in my morning quiet time before work, and God spoke clearly to me through His Word. I could continue to grumble and complain and displease Him with my attitude or I could submit to my boss. I chose the latter and decided I would clean those bathrooms as if Jesus Himself were coming in next to use them! An incredible change transpired in my attitude. The kids were as messy as ever, but I was able to do the work with sincere joy in my heart.

Commitment to Authority

Another important principle of submission to authority is for young people to be genuinely committed to the success of those over them. Teens must refrain from practices that hinder authorities from carrying out their God-given responsibilities. No person in leadership—and that includes parents—can accomplish much without the loyal support of those under them.

Scripture clearly says that those who rebel do not profit from their rebellion, although they may think they do:

> Obey your leaders, and submit to them; for they keep watch over your souls, as those who will give an account. Let them do this with joy and not with grief, for this would be unprofitable for you (Heb. 13:17).

If a young person's heart is right before God, free from anger and bitterness toward those who are in authority over him, he can feel free to make his request known by being gentle and respectful. If that request is based on a legitimate need, the Lord will often move in that authority's heart to change his mind. That may not happen right away, so a patient trust in God must be exercised by the young person making the plea.

Requests, however, that come from a selfish or greedy heart will probably go unanswered. Rightfully so. Few things turn off a parent more than an ungrateful child who demands more than what is needed.

Daniel's life also provides valuable instruction for young people who must follow their consciences in the face of ungodly leadership. Daniel was willing to be "lion lunch" rather than give in to King Darius's edict not to pray to anyone but him for 30 days. The rest is history.

Do we have the guarantee that the ending will always be happy, as happened to Daniel? No. Joseph, for example, suffered greatly and unjustly in prison for years before being restored to freedom. The injustice of humans never negates the faithfulness of God, however. Much of the book of 1 Peter was written to address the issue of how to live under unjust leadership:

The following is a sample of the wisdom of that book:

> Servants, be submissive to your masters with all respect, not only to those who are good and gentle, but also to those who are unreasonable. For this finds favor, if for the sake of conscience toward God a man bears up under sorrows when suffering unjustly. For what credit is there if, when you sin and are harshly treated, you endure it with patience? But if when you do what is right and suffer for it you patiently endure it, this finds favor with God. For you have been called for this purpose, since Christ also suffered for you, leaving you an example for you to follow in His steps, who committed no sin, nor was any deceit found in His mouth; and while being reviled, He did not revile in return; while suffering, He uttered no threats, but kept entrusting Himself to Him who judges righteously (2:18-23).

What if the authority figure is abusive? Is it being rebellious to turn him in? Absolutely not! It sickens us to hear of Christian leaders who tell battered wives and abused children to go home and be submissive. God has established governing authorities to protect the abused. The heart of God goes out to the weak, defenseless and oppressed.

Turn in the abusers to a higher authority, because they have abdicated their responsibilities to provide for and protect those whom God charged them to watch over. Besides, it is never good for abusers to be allowed to continue their abuse. They are themselves hurting people in need of help. If they are not stopped, they and others will continue to suffer from the cycle of abuse.

Our motive is never to seek revenge, but rather to exercise compassion—both for the abused and the abuser. Both need to find their freedom in Christ, but neither will unless someone intervenes to stop the abuse.

Seeking Protection for Teens

After teens forgive an abusive authority figure, help them set up scriptural boundaries that will stop that cycle of abuse. At times, moving teens to a new school, new church or a new home may be necessary, at least for a while. Steps of this kind may be instituted by child-protection agencies. Otherwise, setting up protective boundaries for teens must be done only after seeking the Lord in prayer, carefully searching God's Word and seeking wise, godly counsel.

A word of caution must be stated here. We are not saying young people are given license to disobey authority simply because that authority is not perfect. If that were the case, nobody would be submissive to anyone but God.

Determining when to reject human authority requires discernment and deep inner conviction based on God's truth that cannot be compromised regardless of the consequences. Teens are acting rebelliously if they refuse to submit simply because they would prefer to do it their own way.

The world system says that teens are missing out on life, liberty and the pursuit of happiness if they are submissive to authority. The Bible tells us those things are found in Christ "who is our life" (Col.

3:4), sets us free (see John 8:36) and promises us the fullness of joy when we obey God (see John 15:10,11).

A Christian young person seeking acceptance, significance, satisfaction and security through the world will be sorely tempted to rebel so as to fit in. Christian young people who know who they are

> **Submission for young people is primarily a relational matter between the creature and the Creator, between the servant and the King, between the child and the Father.**

in Christ and who are living in joyful relationship with their "Abba, Father," however, will trust Him to work through imperfect human authorities, including parents.

Submission to authority, however, is not just a "horizontal," human-to-human issue. Submission for young people is primarily a relational matter between the creature and the Creator, between the servant and the King, between the child and the Father. When teens know it is a privilege and honor to serve the King and walk in a love relationship with their heavenly Father, they won't feel nearly as driven to rebel, manipulate or try to control.

Teens will be able to yield to the lordship of Christ, secure in knowing they can occupy no higher place than the role of a child-servant of God Almighty, the King of kings and Lord of lords.

Areas of Rebellion

God's order is this: "Submit therefore to God. Resist the devil and he will flee from you" (Jas. 4:7). Submitting to God enables young people to resist the devil. The prayer that begins this Step is a commitment to forsake rebellion and choose a submissive spirit, as follows:

Dear heavenly Father,

You have said in the Bible that rebellion is the same thing as witchcraft, and being self-willed is like serving false gods (1 Sam. 15:23). I know that I have disobeyed and rebelled in my heart against You and those You have placed in authority over me. I thank You for Your forgiveness for my rebellion. By the shed blood of the Lord Jesus Christ, I pray that all doors that I opened to evil spirits through my rebellion would now be closed. I pray that You will show me all the ways I have been rebellious. I now choose to adopt a submissive spirit and servant's heart. In Jesus' precious name, I pray. Amen.

When the young people you are helping have finished praying, read the instructional material following the prayer. Then call their attention to the list of possible areas of rebellion, and ask them to place a check by any that apply:

- Civil government (i.e., traffic laws, drinking laws, etc.) (Rom. 13:1-7; 1 Tim. 2:1-4; 1 Pet. 2:13-17);
- Parents, stepparents or legal guardians (Eph. 6:1-3);
- Teachers, coaches and school officials (Rom. 13:1-4);
- Your boss (1 Pet. 2:18-23);
- Husband (1 Pet. 3:1-4) or wife (Eph. 5:21; 1 Pet. 3:7); (Note to Husbands: Take a moment and ask the Lord if your lack of love for your wife could be fostering a rebellious spirit within her. If so, confess that now as a violation of Eph. 5:22,23.)
- Church leaders (pastor, youth pastor, Sunday School teacher) (Heb. 13:17);
- God Himself (Dan. 9:5,9).

It won't be necessary for the counselees to explain the acts of rebellion to you. You have heard their stories and know most of their issues already. The young people you counsel do need to know that rebellion is not just an *act*; it is an *attitude*. God looks at the heart and desires truth in the inner person.

The next prayer is an opportunity for young people to submit these areas of rebellion to God:

Lord, I agree with You that I have been rebellious toward _____. Thank You for forgiving my rebellion. I choose to be submissive and obedient to Your Word. In Jesus' name. Amen.

As suggested in Step Two, the teens you counsel do not have to repeat the prayer for each item. When they come to the blank, they should insert the things that were checked and then complete the prayer.

Be careful, however, that they don't brush off any deep roots of rebellion. This Step may require more counseling to help teens live under authority, especially if there is a history of rebellion against or abuse by authority in their lives.

In the event of ongoing abuse in the life of a teen you are counseling, follow the procedures outlined in chapter 9.

Learning to be assertive and taking a stand against abuse will be difficult for a person who has been passive for years, as learning to be submissive will be for those who have a rebellious nature.

A Young Girl's Testimony

Jackie is a sensitive 15-year-old Christian girl who likes to laugh, have fun and spend time with her daddy. She was set up, though, from an early age to battle with rebellion and sexual promiscuity.

At ages 4 and 5 she was repeatedly molested by her maternal grandfather, and by age 11 had already been involved sexually with a 17-year-old boy in the neighborhood. Jackie had struggled with intense feelings of rebellion toward her mom, feeling as though she just could not trust her. Once her mom divorced her dad, the pain and emptiness in her heart was amplified. She missed her dad and experienced the loneliness of longing for his loving companionship.

When later on she moved in with her dad and stepmom, things started looking up for her. She spent long hours talking with her daddy, drinking in every joyful moment with him that she could.

Then, suddenly her behavior started to change. Claiming she had a heavy homework load, Jackie would eat quickly, dash from the dinner table and retreat to her room to do homework, and talk on the phone.

Guys started calling and she enjoyed the attention from them. At first the conversations were innocent, but soon the talk turned to sexual things. For a month or so, Jackie ran her version of a 900-number service from her room (minus the money). The guys loved the arousal and Jackie loved the attention.

Meanwhile, Jackie's dad and mom were under spiritual attack as well, an attack they failed to recognize at first. Both experienced unusual nightmares, but did not tell each other (until much later). They started bickering with one another about trivial things, which diverted their attention from the real battle.

Jackie's dad would wake up at night sensing an intruder was in the house, but the "prowler" was unseen so it went undetected. The enemy had cunningly maneuvered all his pieces into place, and so things became much worse. Truly a house divided against itself cannot stand.

Eventually, phone talk was not enough for Jackie. She plunged into sexual sin with a couple of the boys, and used her parents' house while they were at work. The rebellion, deception and sexual bondage were intense. Jackie left school early a few times to have sex. She abused the phone privileges given to her. She accepted rides from boys without her parents' knowledge or permission. She also violated the commands of the God she called Father.

Things hit rock bottom for Jackie after a boy convinced her to allow him to videotape their sexual intercourse. That tape was then viewed by a bunch of his friends at a party. Jackie was embarrassed and scared.

Finally, she broke down and confessed it all to her parents. They were angry, of course, but they did not accuse her or badger her. They expressed their love and desire to help. They also cried with her.

What had been the hook to drag Jackie into the rebellion and bondage? Sure, sex was fun and pleasurable at first, but after doing it she would ask herself, *Why did I just do that? That was stupid.* There had to be more to keep bringing her back—and there was.

She admitted, "I wanted the boys to like me and pay attention to me. They said, 'You are pretty,' and that felt good. I didn't want to lose that." So the guys gave her what she felt she needed to get what they wanted. Guys will do that—give "love" to get sex. And girls will do that—give sex to get "love."

It was a set-up job by the enemy. A young girl, sexually abused and deeply hurt from a divorce gave ground to the devil to operate—first in her mind and then in her body. The result? Rebellion, deception, immorality, pain, guilt and tears.

The prodigal daughter had come home, though, having come to her senses. She saw that the devil's bargain was no bargain at all.

Why had Jackie turned away from her rebellion and turned back toward home? Her words show that the Spirit of God, in answer to prayer, was moving powerfully. Her testimony was honest:

"I was feeling just totally, totally guilty. I was just overwhelmed with guilt and I was so sick and tired of lying and hiding and trying to keep everything covered."

Jackie was under conviction, experiencing the godly sorrow that leads to "repentance without regret" (2 Cor. 7:10). What she shared next apparently made the ultimate difference:

"I missed my relationship with daddy. I wanted everything to be good again."

There it is. The open heart and open arms of a daddy were not worth giving up, not even for the attention of all the boys at school.

Now Jackie is learning something even deeper. The open heart and open arms of her heavenly Father are too good to give up, too.

Incidentally, everything *is* good again. Repentance has been complete, and the junk from her past renounced as she went through the Steps to Freedom in Christ. The videotape has been destroyed. The wholesome guidelines her dad and stepmom have instituted are being followed without resistance. Once again a 15-year-old girl spends lots of time talking after dinner with the man she calls "daddy."

chapter eleven

Placing Confidence in God

Step Five:
Pride Versus Humility

Pride is a killer. Proverbs 16:18 says, "Pride goes before destruction, and a haughty spirit before stumbling." Pride is an ugly five-letter word that has a big *I* in the middle. It says, "I don't care what you say anymore, this is my life!" Pride is where all evil began, in the heart of Lucifer.

Scripture says of that fallen angel now called Satan, "But you said in your heart, '*I will* ascend to heaven; *I will* raise my throne above the stars of God, and *I will* sit on the mount of assembly in the recesses of the north. *I will* ascend above the heights of the clouds; *I will* make myself like the Most High.' Nevertheless you will be thrust down to Sheol, to the recesses of the pit" (Isa. 14:13-15, emphasis added).

Up until the devil declared *I will*, there had only been one will in the universe, the will of God. Now everyone born of earthly parents enters this world having a will of their own, one that stands in direct opposition and hostility to God's will.

Hell will be populated with men and angels who refused to bend their will to the will of the King. For eternity, they will say, "My will be done," while in heaven the saints and holy angels shall proclaim, "Thy will be done!"

For now, it is critical that we see the dangerous connection between young people living in pride and the spiritual attack that results. Scripture warns us of that risk in James and in 1 Peter:

> But He gives a greater grace. Therefore it says, "God is opposed to the proud, but gives grace to the humble." Submit therefore to God. Resist the devil and he will flee from you (Jas. 4:6,7).
>
> All of you, clothe yourselves with humility toward one another, for God is opposed to the proud, but gives grace to the humble. Humble yourselves, therefore, under the mighty hand of God, that He may exalt you at the proper time, casting all your anxiety upon Him, because He cares for you. Be of sober spirit, be on the alert. Your adversary, the devil, prowls about like a roaring lion, seeking someone to devour. But resist him, firm in your faith (1 Pet. 5:5-9).

After Jesus had fed the 5,000, He sent the disciples across the Sea of Galilee while He went up to the mountain to pray. In the middle of the sea, the disciples encountered a storm: "And seeing them straining at the oars,...He came to them, walking on the sea; and He intended to pass by them" (Mark 6:48). We believe the Lord always intends to pass by the self-sufficient. Go ahead and row, He will let you struggle until you see your need for help.

The disciples cried out in fear, thinking Jesus was a ghost. Mercifully, Jesus calmed their fears and climbed into their boat. Immediately the wind calmed down and they were able to make it across the sea. The lesson is clear: What we are unable to do in our own strength becomes reality when we humble ourselves, cry out to God for help and allow Jesus to take control.

The only answer the world has for those who are caught in the middle of the storms of life is, "Row harder!" That is the voice of pride. The voice of the devil says, "You can do it by yourself, but if you need a little extra power, I can arrange that...for a price."

God's way is not like that. His word admonishes us:

Trust in the Lord with all your heart, and do not lean

on your own understanding. In all your ways acknowledge Him, and He will make your paths straight (Prov. 3:5,6).

Young people often grow up in families in which self-sufficiency is a way of life. They live by the philosophy that anything can be accomplished by a lot of hard work, human ingenuity and maybe a little luck thrown in for good measure.

To them God says, "I won't interfere with your plans. If you want to try to save yourself, solve your own problems and meet your own needs, you have My permission. But you ultimately will fail, because in the final analysis, you absolutely need Me, and you desperately need others."

Jesus painted the picture in black and white when He said:

I am the vine, you are the branches; he who abides in Me, and I in him, he bears much fruit; for apart from Me you can do nothing (John 15:5).

Pride can sneak up on the best of us. King Uzziah was a godly man who reigned for 52 years (see 2 Chron. 26:3), and "he did right in the sight of the Lord" (v. 4). His accomplishments were exceptional. He built a strong army and fortified the city. "Hence his fame spread afar, for he was marvelously helped until he was strong. But when he became strong, his heart was so proud that he acted corruptly, and he was unfaithful to the Lord his God" (vv. 15,16).

The more Christian young people see God use them and the more they are affirmed in their spirituality by others, the more at risk they are for becoming victims of spiritual pride. More than one Christian leader has fallen when he started receiving glowing accolades. "Therefore let him who thinks he stands take heed lest he fall" (1 Cor. 10:12).

The Stronghold of Pride

Steve was a gifted youth minister—outgoing, fun loving, musically talented and great with kids. He was a real "go-getter," the kind who would storm the gates of hell using a water pistol, if that was all he could find!

On a summer missions project one year, he had a public confrontation with the national director of a Christian organization. His attitude was haughty and totally disrespectful to the older, wiser veteran of the faith. That event seemed to open a Pandora's box of run-ins with authority in which Steve consistently took a stubborn, unbending, confrontational approach.

Unwilling to listen to the godly counsel and warnings of those who loved him and were looking out for his best interests, Steve had to be fired from his job. Unless that stronghold of pride and rebellion is torn down in Steve's life, he will likely spend the rest of his life bouncing from one job to another. He will do well for a while at each place until his leadership gets fed up with his attitude and asks him to move on.

God simply will not bless the life of a proud person—young or old—no matter how gifted he or she might be. Proverbs 18:12 says:

> Before destruction the heart of man is haughty, but humility goes before honor.

What is humility? Is it groveling around in poverty, bemoaning our lowly state? Is it declaring that we are merely the "dirt under the toenail of the little toe of the Body of Christ"? No, that is counterfeit humility that leads only to defeat. Paul said, "Let no one keep defrauding you of your prize by delighting in self-abasement" (Col. 2:18).

Is humility then proclaiming piously that God is everything and we are nothing? No, that is just another version of false humility. Christ did not go to the cross for nothing! He was crucified to establish and build up a fallen humanity. Throughout the New Testament, we are admonished to build up one another, and we are strongly warned against any attempt to tear down each other. How can we then justify tearing down ourselves?

Paul wrote in Romans 12:3:

> For through the grace given to me I say to every man among you not to think more highly of himself than he

ought to think; but to think so as to have sound judgment, as God has allotted to each a measure of faith.

That is not a call to self-abasement; it is a call for sound judgment.
Paul said of himself, "By the grace of God I am what I am, and His
grace toward me did not prove vain; but I labored even more than
all of them, yet not I, but the grace of God with me" (1 Cor. 15:10).

Every Christian teenager is who he or she is because of the grace
of God! To deny that would be to discredit the work Christ accomplished on the cross. For young people to have an inflated view of

▐▐▐▐▐ Humility is confidence properly placed.

themselves or to think they are products of their own doing is to
join the ranks of the deceived millions who have fallen victim to
pride.

Humility is confidence properly placed. Paul's testimony was
that he "put no confidence in the flesh" (Phil. 3:3), although he certainly had the spiritual pedigree to do that if he were so inclined.
True humility knows, "Apart from Me [Christ] you can do nothing"
(John 15:5); but it also affirms, "I can do all things through Him who
strengthens me" (Phil. 4:13). Humility is being "strong in the Lord,
and in the strength of His might" (Eph. 6:10). Pride says with a
smug self-satisfaction, "I did it." True humility says, "I did it only
by the grace of God."

It brings no glory to God, however, for Christian young people to
cower in some corner in unbelief or grovel in the dust of mock
humility. It can be easy for young believers to fall into those errors,
wanting to communicate humility while still enjoying the limelight.
Scripture, however, instructs us to "Let your light shine before men
in such a way that they may see your good works, and glorify your
Father who is in heaven" (Matt. 5:16).

Pretending Humility Through Pride

I (Rich) recall with amusement watching young Christians respond to the sincere appreciation of other believers commenting on their testimony, song or message. "It wasn't me up there, it was Jesus," they would say. That is about as humble sounding a statement pride can utter! A simple "thank you" to the people verbally with a simultaneous "thank you" to God silently is all that is needed.

We all come from a variety of backgrounds, but pride, rebellion and self-will are common to all post-Fall humanity. The whole operation of Satan is ultimately designed to get self-interest recognized as the chief end of man, rather than "to glorify God and enjoy Him forever" (Westminster Shorter Catechism). When Jesus rebuked Peter in Matthew 16, He said, "Get behind Me, Satan! You are a stumbling block to Me; for you are not setting your mind on God's interests, but man's" (v. 23).

Satan is called the "prince of this world" because his philosophy of self-interest rules this world. Self-will or iniquity passes from one generation to the next, and is the chief characteristic of false prophets and teachers.

Peter wrote that they "indulge the flesh in its corrupt desires and despise authority. Daring, self-willed, they do not tremble when they revile angelic majesties" (2 Pet. 2:10). These people operate from independent spirits and won't listen to or answer to anyone. An even more shocking and sobering scenario is given by Jesus in Matthew 7:20-23:

> "So then you will know them by their fruits. Not everyone who says to Me, 'Lord, Lord,' will enter the kingdom of heaven; but he who does the will of My Father who is in heaven. Many will say to Me on that day, 'Lord, Lord, did we not prophesy in Your name, and in Your name cast out demons, and in Your name perform many miracles?' And then I will declare to them, 'I never knew you; depart from Me, you who practice lawlessness [iniquity].'"

Strongholds of pride are not only passed down from one generation to the next, but each new generation will also find its own basis for pride in the world. Young people learn at an early age that they get strokes for how they look physically, perform athletically, achieve academically, excel musically and so on. Apart from the grace of God, however, that area of giftedness, talent or excellence will not only become the basis of self-glorification for children, but will also serve as the primary source of their identity.

Young people who follow that course for living are set up for a great fall, as one day their house built on sand will collapse during a storm of life.

Nothing is wrong with excelling in an area of life and being admired for it if young people are aware it is God who has so gifted them and it is God alone who should be glorified through that area of giftedness.

Too often, however, the significant adults and peer group in a young person's life reinforce the gift without pointing that teen to the Giver.

If, on the other hand, a teenager considers himself "average" or below, he may struggle with poor self-esteem, envy, resentment or depression, erroneously concluding he has been dealt a poor hand in life, having little opportunity for success.

Either through self-exaltation or self-deprecation, the young person's focus is on self and is rooted in pride. The result will be an opening up of himself to a life of trouble, as James 3:13-16 (NIV) warns:

> Who is wise and understanding among you? Let him show it by his good life, by deeds done in the humility that comes from wisdom. But if you harbor bitter envy and selfish ambition in your hearts, do not boast about it or deny the truth. Such "wisdom" does not come down from heaven but is earthly, unspiritual, of the devil. For where you have envy and selfish ambition, there you find disorder and every evil practice.

Incredibly, our society salutes the young person who makes it his goal in life to be a hard-driving entrepreneur, building his own business empire and selfishly pursuing money. Adults will wink at one another, and nod with a smile, thinking "that young man (or woman) is going places!"

The Bible says that teen has missed the boat of what life is all about and has bought into a demonic wisdom born in the womb of pride. Those who live in such a way can be counted on to stop at no evil practice to attain their goals.

How do you spot godly wisdom born of humility? It shows up not by what a young person says, but by what he does:

> But the wisdom that comes from heaven is first of all pure, then peace-loving, considerate, submissive, full of mercy and good fruit, impartial and sincere. Peacemakers who sow in peace raise a harvest of righteousness (vv. 17,18, *NIV*).

True humility brings a sweetness and gentleness to a young person's soul that is magnetically attractive. Unfortunately, it is a rare commodity in a society that glorifies self and congratulates the "self-made man (or woman)." This "deification of the super-star" mentality has invaded the Church as well, and we should know better. For true greatness we should be looking to the hill of calvary rather than to Capitol Hill or the Hollywood hills, as Jesus clearly taught in Matthew 20:25-28:

> "You know that the rulers of the Gentiles lord it over them, and their great men exercise authority over them. It is not so among you, but whoever wishes to become great among you shall be your servant, and whoever wishes to be first among you shall be your slave; just as the Son of Man did not come to be served, but to serve, and to give His life a ransom for many."

Peter heard what Jesus had said about true greatness, but he had to learn the hard way. After eating the Passover meal with Jesus on the night of His betrayal, Jesus said to Peter, "Simon, Simon, behold, Satan has demanded permission to sift you like wheat; but I have prayed for you, that your faith may not fail; and you, when once you have turned again, strengthen your brothers" (Luke 22:31,32). Notice that Jesus did not say He would stop Satan from sifting Peter like wheat. He just said He would pray for him, and afterward Peter was to help others.

What right did Satan have to demand permission of God? The previous context reveals that a dispute had arisen among the apostles regarding who was the greatest (see v. 24). Such pride can coex-

> ▌▌▌▌▌ **A proper sense of self-worth for Christian young people comes from recognizing and appropriating the biblical truth that they are loved and valued by their heavenly Father.**

ist with the best of intentions, for Peter had said, "Lord, with You I am ready to go both to prison and to death!" (v. 33). Peter's boasting was shown to be the fleshly braggadocio it was when hours later he ignored Jesus' admonition to keep watching and praying to avoid temptation.

Truly, Peter's spirit was willing but his flesh was weak. Leaning on himself rather than on God's strength in prayer, later on that night he denied the Lord three times.

A proper sense of self-worth for Christian young people comes from recognizing and appropriating the biblical truth that they are loved and valued by their heavenly Father. Their value is not based upon their own merit, but on the fact that they are His precious children for whom Christ was willing to die. Every teenager in Christ is blessed with every spiritual blessing in the heavenly places, chosen by God, holy and blameless before Him, predestined to adoption as sons, having redemption, the forgiveness of sins, with the riches of His grace lavished upon them! (see Eph. 1:3-14).

Checking Areas of Pride

As you take teens through Step Five, you should find the transition generally smooth, because you have already dealt with pride from the standpoint of control and rebellion in Step Four. These two Steps are closely linked (as are Steps Three and Four) because the source of a rebellious spirit can be pride as well as bitterness.

To introduce this Step, simply read or paraphrase the material preceding the opening prayer. Then have the young person you are helping pray out loud as follows:

> Dear heavenly Father,
> You have said that pride goes before destruction and an arrogant spirit before stumbling (Prov. 16:18). I confess that I have been thinking mainly of myself and not of others. I have not denied myself, picked up my cross daily and followed You (Matt. 16:24). And as a result, I have given ground to the enemy in my life. I have believed that I could be successful by living according to my own power and resources.
> I now confess that I have sinned against You by placing my will before Yours and by centering my life around myself instead of You. I renounce my pride and my selfishness and close any doors I've opened in my life or physical body to the enemies of the Lord Jesus Christ. I choose to rely on the Holy Spirit's power and guidance so that I can do Your will.
> I give my heart to You and stand against all of Satan's attacks. I ask You to show me how to live for others. I now choose to make others more important than me and to make You the most important Person of all in my life (Matt. 6:33; Rom. 12:10). Please show me specifically now the ways in which I have lived pridefully. I ask this in the name of my Lord Jesus Christ. Amen.

After praying this prayer, the teen then has the opportunity to check areas of pride that may be present in his or her life. You can have the young people you help look over the following list and check them by themselves. I (Rich) have found it helpful to read each area of pride out loud one by one, giving a brief explanation if necessary, and having the counselee check them as I proceed.

The areas in which pride can show up in a young person's life include the following, but this is not an exhaustive list. Be sensitive to the Holy Spirit's leading to bring to mind other areas in the counselee's life.

- I have a stronger desire to do my will than God's will.
- I rely on my own strengths and abilities rather than on God's.
- I too often think my ideas are better than other people's ideas.
- I want to control how others act rather than develop self-control.
- I sometimes consider myself more important than others.
- I have a tendency to think I don't need other people.
- I find it difficult to admit when I am wrong.
- I am more likely to be a people pleaser than a God pleaser.
- I am overly concerned about getting credit for doing good things.
- I often think I am more humble than others.
- I often think I am smarter than my parents.
- I often feel my needs are more important than other people's needs.
- I consider myself better than others because of my academic, artistic or athletic abilities and accomplishments.
- Other _____

Examples of areas not covered in this list might be things such as racial or ethnic pride, denomination or church pride, and gender pride. Certainly nothing is wrong with being glad for one's race, ethnic background, church, denomination or gender, but when we believe we are superior to others who are different from ourselves, we become guilty of the most divisive pride.

The teaching of the apostle Paul makes it clear that our primary identity is now found in Christ, and that all other characteristics are secondary to that unifying truth:

> For you are all sons of God through faith in Christ Jesus. For all of you who were baptized into Christ have clothed yourselves with Christ. There is neither Jew nor Greek, there is neither slave nor free man, there is neither male nor female; for you are all one in Christ Jesus (Gal. 3:26-28).

For each issue that surfaces in the lives of the young people you counsel, have them pray through the prayer of confession. As suggested in Step Four, they may pray through the prayer just once, filling in the blank with each and every item they checked. Encourage them to feel the freedom to add to the prayer of confession if they feel the need to do so. If selfishness and bigotry have been major issues in their lives, they may need to express their godly sorrow in their own words in addition to the following prayer:

> Lord, I agree I have been prideful in the area of _____. Thank You for forgiving me for this pridefulness. I choose to humble myself and place all my confidence in You. Amen.

A Humbling Cleansing Process

When I (Rich) was a kid, our family had a dog named Sam. He was a purebred mutt, loyal, lovable but cocky. He refused to stay in the yard so we had to keep him chained up in the backyard most of the time. I remember one time when Sam was in the house. My brother was walking out the garage door and Sam saw his chance to escape, so he bolted out before we could grab him.

While loose, that dog was a pain in the neck to everyone in the neighborhood. He would bark at pedestrians, try to bite the shoes of bike riders and stand defiantly in the middle of the road, daring cars to pass. The more we would run after him to catch him and bring him home, the farther away he would run. Evading his master's grasp was like a game to him.

Normally when Sam was loose, he would stay in sight of our house, strutting around as though he owned the place, but this time was different. He was gone a long time and we were starting to get worried.

Suddenly he appeared, running up the street straight toward our house. We figured he was thirsty because he had been gone so long, so we moved his water dish near the door to lure him in. We need not have bothered because he blew right by the dish and ran into the house.

Then we smelled it. Sam had been skunked! What ensued was mass hysteria as two adults and two kids frantically tried to grab the stinky dog before the whole house stunk of skunk.

My mom finally grabbed him and hauled him out to the garage where she soaked him with tomato juice to get out the odor.

What a humbling thing for such a macho dog! To get skunked was bad enough, but to be washed in tomato juice had to have been the ultimate humiliation. It was necessary, though, for him to go through that cleansing process to get out of the garage and come into the house again.

Pride goes before destruction. Before honor comes humility. These are principles of life that every young person needs to learn. Some learn the easy way, by reading and obeying God's Word. Sure they have their battles with pride, but they are minor skirmishes from which they learn.

Others are like Sam. They enjoy the thrill of being on their own, daring the world to stop them from doing what they want. They do enough spiritually (they think) to keep God "off their backs," but in reality they are playing the church game. Scripture says, "God is not mocked; for whatever a man sows, this he will also reap. For the one who sows to his own flesh shall from the flesh reap corruption, but the one who sows to the Spirit shall from the Spirit reap eternal life" (Gal. 6:7,8).

For them, the "big one" is coming. The day they hit the brick wall. The day they get skunked. It will not be pleasant for them, nor for those who love them. All will suffer.

So what is our role? To be waiting with an open door when the prodigals come running home so that God can wash them and cleanse them. Not with tomato juice this time, but with the precious blood of the unblemished and spotless lamb of God, Jesus Christ.

chapter twelve

Breaking the Chains

Step Six:
Bondage Versus Freedom

Imagine for a moment that you are one of God's holy angels and can see the spiritual battle raging for the souls of the young people around you. You focus in on a Christian teen named Danny who has just discovered how to access pornography on the Internet. He is sitting at his desk preparing to turn on his PC. Outside his bedroom door lurks a dark angel, intensely interested in the battle going on in that young man's mind.

Brilliantly disguised as an angel of light, this demon suggests to Danny that he go ahead and sneak a peek. *Aw c'mon, just a quick look won't hurt. It's what you really want anyway. No one will ever know. It'll be over before you know it and your curiosity will be satisfied. All your friends have been talking about how cool it is. You'll miss out and be left out if you don't.*

The Spirit of God inside Danny sends an immediate warning to his mind and offers a way of escape. His eyes glance upward to the place where he can click his mouse and shut down the computer. Also inside of him, though, is a strong appetite for sex, food and other things preprogrammed to act independently of God. Danny's flesh wants to be gratified and so his mind begins to rationalize, countering the Spirit of God's prompting. *What's wrong with looking at this stuff anyway? They're only pictures. I'm not doing anything to hurt anybody. After all, God created me with these desires. Why would He get angry if I did what came naturally?*

The battle for Danny's mind is intense. He is experiencing what Galatians 5:17 says: "For the flesh sets its desire against the Spirit, and the Spirit against the flesh; for these are in opposition to one another." Instead he chooses to ignore God's escape route by failing to take "every thought captive to the obedience of Christ" (2 Cor. 10:5).

At first, the pornographic images on his computer screen are a delight to his eyes, and his body responds in an explosion of ecstatic feelings. The pleasure is short lived, though, because "each one is tempted when he is carried away and enticed by his own lust. Then when lust has conceived, it gives birth to sin; and when sin is accomplished it brings forth death" (Jas. 1:14,15).

A little while later Danny feels awful. The dark angel takes advantage of the open door and moves from the role of tempter to the role of accuser. *You're in big trouble now. Your parents and Christian friends are going to find out what you've done. You call yourself a Christian? You watched that filthy stuff and now you'll be messed up for the rest of your life!*

His conscience overcome by guilt, Danny cries out to God, "Lord, please forgive me, I'll never do it again!" Two days later, however, Danny is feeling bored and a little lonely so he sins again, which precipitates another cry for forgiveness. As the downward spiral of "sin, confess, sin, confess, and sin again" continues, Danny begins to give up and give in to the growing compulsion to lust. Deep down he wants to stop, but he just can't.

One day while Danny is absorbed in the images on his monitor, a Christian friend enters his room unnoticed. Instead of acting as a minister of reconciliation, he joins with the unseen accuser, heaping more guilt on him.

"You're sick!" he shouts at him as Danny whirls his head around in horror. "How can you do that and call yourself a Christian? I'm telling your parents! You'd better confess it and beg God to forgive you!"

Little does Danny's friend know that he is already forgiven by God and that he has confessed his sin a hundred times before. His friend's merciless and insensitive attack will only drive Danny to greater depths of despair and lustful behavior as he wallows in the self-pity of rejection.

The end result? The world, the flesh and the devil have brought another precious young saint down to defeat. Unfortunately, scenes similar to this are being played out in the lives of our Christian young people daily. How do we help teens break this cycle of defeat? Is confession enough?

To confess means to agree with God or to "walk in the light as He Himself is in the light" (1 John 1:7). It is the critical first step in the process of repentance. We must agree with God about our sin and face the truth, but that alone will not overcome sin's entrapment.

Young people who have genuinely confessed their sins have submitted to God, but they have not yet resisted the devil (see Jas. 4:7).

Complete repentance means to submit to God, resist the devil, and close the door. Romans 13:14 puts it this way: "But put on the Lord Jesus Christ, and make no provision for the flesh in regard to its lusts."

The door will be closed when all the bondage has been broken and the mental strongholds have been torn down. Every time sin becomes a habit, the one in bondage has believed the devil's lies concerning that sin. To be set free, young people need to renounce those lies and choose to believe God's truth.

Acceptance of Self

Step Six is intended to break the bondage of fleshly sin and tear down any mental strongholds of deception that have been built. After that, the process of renewing the counselee's mind can begin so that his or her life can be transformed (see Rom. 12:1,2).

What is the biblical way to respond to someone caught in sin? How can we avoid the same tragic error Danny's friend committed in our story?

Several issues are critical to understand. First, Christian young people in bondage are still "children of God" (John 1:12) and new creations in Christ (see 2 Cor. 5:17). They are supposed to consider themselves "to be dead to sin, but alive to God in Christ Jesus"

(Rom. 6:11), but they seldom do. Their self-perceptions are extremely negative and they are largely ignorant of their identity in Christ.

Some will say of themselves "I'm evil" or "I'm no good." We must remind them of the truth of God's Word, which says, "You're not evil. You are a forgiven child of God." They may counter, "But I just hate myself," to which we must respond, "But God loves you, therefore you can accept yourself."

These teens have been cruelly victimized by the accuser of the brethren. We become deeply troubled when we see self-righteous and legalistic "Christians" go after a brother or sister in Christ. Why are we joining ranks with the enemy's condemning thoughts when Romans 8:1 says, "There is therefore now no condemnation for those who are in Christ Jesus"?

Why are we counting their trespasses against them when even Jesus doesn't (see 2 Cor. 5:19)? What sickness lies within us that delights in exposing the sins of others when Scripture says, "Hatred stirs up strife, but love covers all transgressions" (Prov. 10:12)?

Confessing and Renouncing

Josh walked into his freedom appointment looking about three inches shorter than his six-foot two-inch frame. It was obvious he was loaded down with a burden of guilt from which he felt there was little hope of escape.

Though still only a teenager, Josh had been battling lustful thoughts toward girls for nearly 10 years. It had all started when as a young boy he had slept with his sister. While together, he had spotted her navel and that had elicited a sexual response in him.

From that time on, Josh could not look at a girl's navel without having sexual fantasies about her. He was convinced he was a "bad person" and all this was happening because something about him was unusually evil.

To make matters worse, Josh had also believed the devil's lie that for him to be free, he would have to go back to each and every girl for whom he had lusted and personally ask her for forgiveness. Believing this was God's voice speaking to him, the sheer impossibility of that task drove him even deeper into despair and sexual bondage. He could not even begin to remember all the girls, not to mention the futility of trying to contact all of them.

He was also afraid God would not reveal all the names to him and hence he forever would be just one step away from freedom. He was in bondage to the lie that there would always be one more thing he had do to be completely free.

Once Josh confessed and renounced the wrongful use of his eyes as an instrument of unrighteousness, he began to perk up. Then he renounced the lies he had believed and affirmed the truth that his forgiveness was a matter between him and God, not him and all the girls.

He came to realize that freedom was a matter of appropriating what Christ had done for him at calvary, not an impossible "work" he needed to perform. Then the smile came back. Josh knew he was free.

Our ministry is one of reconciliation, not condemnation. Had Josh been rebuked by the encourager during his freedom appointment, he probably would have lost the little bit of hope he still had.

After Paul's teaching about walking by the Spirit in Galatians 5, the first practical application that follows is:

> Let us not become boastful, challenging one another, envying one another. Brethren, even if a man is caught in any trespass, you who are spiritual, restore such a one in a spirit of gentleness; each one looking to yourself, lest you too be tempted (Gal. 5:26—6:1).

Reconciliation and Restoration

The ministry of a spiritual Christian is to be reconciliation and restoration. We are to "bear one another's burdens" (Gal. 6:2), not add to them. If that is not your motive in confronting another person caught in sin, it is best that you do nothing at all.

Young people caught in addictive and immoral patterns of behavior are already being subjected to some of the cruelest harassment by the enemy. First, Satan tempts them to sin, then he mercilessly condemns them for sinning, attacking their sense of worth.

If you are working with those who are in bondage to sex, alcohol or drugs, we strongly recommend you read Neil's books *A Way of Escape* (or the youth version coauthored with Dave Park, *Purity Under Pressure*) and *Freedom from Addiction.*

These books provide the biblical basis for breaking the bondage and tearing down the strongholds of sex and substance abuse, and they include many illustrations and practical applications.

Sincere Christian teens who are struggling and failing to break free from habitual sins often question their salvation. They wonder if they really are children of God, new creatures in Christ, in whom the Holy Spirit dwells. Many think they have committed the unpardonable sin and have lost hope. By the time they have finished walking through Step Six, most have regained their assurance of salvation as the "Spirit Himself bears witness" with their spirit that they are "children of God" (Rom. 8:16).

Many times young people will confess that they have never told anyone of their dark, secret sins before. They may have been trapped in tormenting guilt from abortion, homosexual tendencies, molestation or incest for years. To survive, they attempted to cope by living a lie and remaining in denial, refusing to admit the gravity of their sins and the power those sins had over them. Frequently, close family members and friends have been totally unaware of the young people's problems.

Some have been so discouraged that they have simply resigned themselves to living in bondage, trying to hang on until the rapture and hoping somehow God will accept them into heaven in spite of themselves. In desperation, many ask the question Paul raised: "Who will set me free from the body of this death?" (Rom. 7:24). Paul answered his own question in the next verse: "Thanks be to God through Jesus Christ our Lord!"

There is hope and a way of escape for the person who is willing to face the truth and walk in the light.

These young people do not need and cannot handle any more condemnation. Most really want to be free, hating the pathetic condition they are in. They long to be released from bondage, but are terribly afraid of being rejected or embarrassed.

Because of that fear, you will find that this Step is the most difficult for teens to be totally honest about, especially when it comes to sexual sin. Sinning sexually is a sin against one's own body (see 1 Cor. 6:18) and so it carries with it an incredible amount of shame.

It is important not to communicate shock, surprise or revulsion when young people confess their sins of the flesh to you. Make sure you do not react with a judgmental attitude or they will clam up.

After coming to terms with one sexual sin after another, one person said, "Oh, I forgot you're here. What do you think of me?"

I (Neil) replied, "I love you for what you have just shared."

What a relief it was for her to discover that she had finally found a safe place where she could deal with hidden, shameful sins with-

> **Young people must be inwardly submitting to God while they ▮ ▮ ▮ ▮ ▮ are outwardly confessing sin, renouncing lies and choosing truth.**

out the fear of rejection. What a joy it is to see the hope in people's faces when they begin to understand that resolution is possible, and they no longer have to be mastered by sin.

It is important to remind young people as they are going through the Steps that they are not just uttering "magic" words. They must be inwardly submitting to God while they are outwardly confessing sin, renouncing lies and choosing truth.

Confessing Habitual Sins

Introduce this Step by simply reading the introductory material preceding the opening prayer. The counselee should then pray the following prayer out loud:

> Dear heavenly Father,
> You have told us to put on the Lord Jesus Christ and make no provision for the flesh in regard to its lust

(Rom. 13:14). I agree that I have given in to sinful desires that wage war against my soul (1 Pet. 2:11).

I thank You that in Christ my sins are forgiven, but I have broken Your holy law and given the devil an opportunity to wage war in my body (Rom. 6:12,13; Jas. 4:1; 1 Pet. 5:8).

I come before Your presence now to admit these sins and to seek Your cleansing (1 John 1:9) that I may be freed from the bondage of sin. I now ask You to reveal to my mind the ways that I have broken Your moral law and grieved the Holy Spirit. In Jesus' precious name, I pray. Amen.

The purpose here is to allow the Holy Spirit to bring to the counselee's mind areas of habitual sin as well as other specific unconfessed sins. Young people will often have a good idea of what they need to confess, but in some cases they will need help in pinpointing areas of sin in their lives. Direct their attention to the list of deeds of the flesh found in Step Six after the opening prayer. They should put a check mark by any area the Spirit of God puts His finger on and then use the prayer of confession following the list to confront each issue.

In some cases, encouragers have found it helpful to go to Scriptures such as Galatians 5:19-21 to see what God says is sin. Questions such as, "Are there any issues in your life that you have been too ashamed to admit to God or me so far?" can be helpful in encouraging teens to be honest.

They need to know that God is "able to judge the thoughts and intentions of the heart. And there is no creature hidden from His sight, but all things are open and laid bare to the eyes of Him with whom we have to do" (Heb. 4:12,13). God knows all about us, yet He loves us in spite of our sins. He is not out to get us; He is out to restore us. But we need to "walk in the light as He Himself is in the light" to have "the blood of Jesus cleanse us from all sin" (1 John 1:7).

The next area covered in Step Six is bondage from sexual sin. Scripture places this area of sin in its own category, as 1 Corinthians 6:15-20 points out:

Do you not know that your bodies are members of Christ? Shall I then take away the members of Christ and make them members of a harlot? May it never be! Or do you not know that the one who joins himself to a harlot is one body with her? For He says, "The two will become one flesh." But the one who joins himself to the Lord is one spirit with Him. Flee immorality. Every other sin that a man commits is outside the body, but the immoral man sins against his own body. Or do you not know that your body is a temple of the Holy Spirit who is in you, whom you have from God, and that you are not your own? For you have been bought with a price: therefore glorify God in your body.

It is the responsibility of Christian teens not to let sin reign in their mortal bodies and not to obey its lusts (see Rom. 6:12). How do young people avoid this trap?

By not "presenting the members of your body to sin as instruments of unrighteousness; but present yourselves to God as those alive from the dead, and your members as instruments of righteousness to God" (v. 13).

An instrument is a neutral object. It can be used for good or evil. It is like a tool. A hammer can be used to drive nails into the wood frame of a house under construction or it can be used to smash a window in a burglary attempt. In the same way, the parts of our bodies can be used for good or evil.

When we use our bodies for sexual intercourse in marriage, we are using them as instruments of righteousness, pleasing to God. Sexual activity outside of marriage, though, is wrong. In no way can a young person commit a sexual sin and not use his or her body as an instrument of unrighteousness.

We have learned that helping teens accomplish complete repentance requires that they pray and ask the Lord to reveal every sexual use of their bodies as instruments of unrighteousness. Then they must renounce every one of those occasions the Lord brings to their minds.

The positive side of the exercise is that once the sexual sin is confessed, young people can then present their bodies again as "a living and holy sacrifice, acceptable to God" (Rom. 12:1,2).

When sex outside of marriage takes place, an unholy bonding also results. The young person has become one flesh with his or her partner. This is one reason a teenage guy and girl who should have broken up long ago still hang on to each other. They have bonded sexually and become one flesh so that the thought and act of breaking up can be extremely traumatic.

Tragically, this bonding also takes place even in the case of incest or rape. As unfair as that is, it is still reality.

What happened cannot be changed, but young people can be free from that unholy bonding by forgiving the one who molested them and renouncing the unrighteous use of their bodies by the offender.

Forgiving Sexual Abuse

Recently, I (Rich) was conducting one of our "Breaking the Chains" conferences. After taking the group through the Steps to Freedom in Christ, at least four or five young ladies shared that they had been sexually abused, but that Christ had set them free. Then Sharon came forward. In her womb, she was carrying the child of the man who had raped her, and yet the joy of the Lord beamed through her tears as she testified of the freedom Jesus had given her.

That freedom came by the grace of God as Sharon was able to forgive her rapist. Then she renounced his criminal violation of her body, having used the temple of the Holy Spirit as an instrument of his unrighteousness. Courageously, she chose to carry that precious child in her womb to term, and now is mother to a beautiful baby girl. That is true freedom!

We have observed that if there is voluntary cooperation with the sexual abuser, the victim usually becomes sexually active, apparently looking for affirmation. If that sexual abuse is against his or her will, the individual usually shuts down sexually.

We are warned emphatically in Scripture to "abstain from fleshly lusts, which wage war against the soul" (1 Pet. 2:11). Giving in to sexual temptation, even once, can be self-destructive. It is like declaring civil war against your own soul.

God and Satan both know our weakness to sexual passions. Satan plays on the weakness, but God provides the way of escape. His Word, in 1 Corinthians 10:13 affirms that there is always a way out:

> No temptation has overtaken you but such as is common to man; and God is faithful, who will not allow you to be tempted beyond what you are able, but with the temptation will provide the way of escape also, that you may be able to endure it.

Young people who believe it is impossible for them to resist the "urge to merge" are deceived. The way is open to escape sexual temptation to any and all who wish to find the way out. The way is open for freedom from past sexual sins to any and all who are willing to bring their sin into the light.

Many young people will feel an acute shame when faced with the reality of having to own up to their sexual sins. Excuses such as, "That would be too embarrassing to share," "You'll think I'm a terrible person" or "I can't even remember a lot of them. I was stoned most of the time" are common.

Try encouraging them by saying something such as the following:

> Nothing you share is going to cause me to think less of you. There is no condemnation here in this room. I'm only interested in helping you find your freedom. The Lord wants you to be free, and that is the reason He is bringing these experiences to mind. There will be no benefit to you to hide anything at this point, so be sure to be totally honest about every sexual sin from your past or present. We don't know the specific deeds that have kept you in bondage, so we need to be very thorough here. We can't change what you've done, but wouldn't you love to be able to walk out of this appointment with all that behind you?

We do not want to put any stumbling block in the path of a young person seeking freedom, so sensitivity needs to be exercised. At times, I (Rich) have told a teenage girl at this portion of the Steps that I will be glad to leave the room while she renounces her sexual sins. I make sure the prayer partner (a woman) is willing and able to handle this short section on her own and I leave the room and pray until they inform me the work has been done.

Usually, by the time we get to this point in the Steps to Freedom in Christ, a strong bond of trust has already been established, so the teenage girl has no problem with my staying through this section. At times, however, my leaving has helped a counselee be more open and honest about her past. That is the bottom line.

As encouragers, we must make sure our own hearts are pure and that we are not seeking to fulfill our own fleshly curiosities by listening to the stories of others' sexual sins. That is nothing but voyeurism.

Confession and Freedom from Sexual Sins

The stories of victory over sin are the really fun ones to hear anyway, and it is our privilege to hear the testimonies of young people whom Jesus has set free in a powerful way. One such story is about Joseph.

He was the first one to come to the front of the meeting room after the whole youth conference had gone through the Steps to Freedom in Christ.

To be honest, it was kind of refreshing to see a popular, football-playing jock cry so openly. It was hard to tell if he was crying more from remorse, relief or joy. Confessing his sexual sin with his girlfriend and the torment he had felt as a result of hiding it all, Joseph pulled no punches.

Later on he wrote a letter to me and filled me in on the history of his relationship gone sour:

> In the summer of 1994 I met this girl, and by the fall we began seeing each other. Eventually we ended up going steady. Everything was going along fine in our relationship until around Thanksgiving, when kissing just wasn't enough. At first we just started messing around (touching) and by Christmas it grew to more than just messing around. We decided that we would never have sex, though (Yeah right).

Joseph went on to admit that the Holy Spirit's conviction was strong, but he chose to shut out the Lord's warning signals and plunged ahead.

I thought I could resist sex, but one day I couldn't. It was Saturday, April 1, when we had sex for the first time.

I can't help but be a little amused at the irony of that statement. They first committed the sin of fornication on April Fool's Day. How appropriate! They had been fooling themselves for a long time that sexual intercourse would never happen!

Soon after this sin, the word got out and Joseph's youth pastor, parents and brother all found out. They told him he needed to give up the sexual sin and break up with the girl. That was God's second warning.

■ ■ ■ ■ ■ **Nothing—no matter how enticing, exhilarating or exciting—is worth more than a clear conscience and peace of mind.**

Instead of humbling himself and admitting his wrongdoing, Joseph hardened his heart and rebelled even more. His rebellion turned out to be an expressway into even more sexual sin.

God, in His mercy, however, wonderfully intervened in Joseph's life and brought him to the end of himself. That was when he came to the conference. During the Steps, he found freedom from his guilt and shame. Obedient to what God had showed him, he went home and broke off that destructive relationship.

This story, unlike too many others, has a happy ending, as Joseph concludes his story:

Now I am able to face God as a child of God with a clear conscience rather than as a no-good teen who lost his virginity.

God also gave me the freedom and liberty to speak openly about my past with my friends, both saved and non-Christians. Now as I look back...I can say only one thing: It sure feels good to be a brand-new man.

Hindsight is always 20/20 and never more so than when you look back on sin from the perspective of freedom from bondage. Indeed, nothing—no matter how enticing, exhilarating or exciting—is worth more than a clear conscience and peace of mind. To be able to look at yourself in the mirror without guilt and shame and to walk through the day without the fear of some skeleton in the closet being discovered; *that* is ecstasy!

As you come to the place of helping young people face any and all sexual sin in their lives, read the paragraph in Step Six about sexual sin to the counselees. Within that paragraph is a list of sexual sins in which they may have participated. Some may be surprised at what is included there because they have not had a biblical understanding of what is right and wrong.

Provide a brief explanation if necessary, then make sure they understand the issue of unholy bonding that takes place through sexual sin. Then ask them to pray:

> Lord, I ask You to reveal to my mind every sexual use of my body as an instrument of unrighteousness. In Jesus' precious name, I pray. Amen.

Then help the person to begin by reading to them, "As the Lord brings to your mind every sexual use of your body, whether it was done to you (i.e., rape, incest, or any sexual abuse) or willingly by you, renounce every occasion." They should use the following prayer:

> Lord, I renounce (name the specific use of your body) with (name the person involved) and I ask You to break that sinful bond with (name).

The counselees should pray that prayer separately for each person and/or activity God brings to mind. For example, they might pray, "Lord, I renounce having sex with Jerry and I ask you to break that sinful bond with Jerry" or "Lord, I renounce the sexual abuse by my uncle and I ask you to break that sinful bond with him."

If the teens you are helping cannot remember the names of the abusers, they can say "that guy in the bar" or "the blond in St. Louis" or "that person whose face I see in my mind." God is certainly aware of the identity of the person and that is all that matters.

In the case of sexual sin done alone, such as looking at pornography or habitual masturbation, the prayer would be modified to, "Lord, I renounce masturbation and I ask You to break that sinful bond."

You do not want to usurp the Holy Spirit's leading in the counselee's life, but if you sense some things are being kept hidden you might need to probe a bit. Gently ask, "Is there anything else in the sexual area that you are not sharing now because you feel ashamed? If so, remember that the devil works in the darkness and he wants us to keep things hidden so he can use them against us. God wants us to walk in the light so we can be free."

If needed, you can ask if they have had involvement with any of the following:

- Arousing foreplay (heavy kissing, petting, mutual masturbation);
- Premarital sex (oral, anal or vaginal);
- Homosexual or bisexual behavior;
- Pornography (books, magazines, movies, videos, 900 calls, Internet);
- Sexual perversions and compulsions (uncontrollable sex drive, sexual fantasies, sex devices, sex with animals (bestiality), sadomasochism, transvestitism, voyeurism);
- Pedophilia (sexual preoccupation with children);
- Rape (including date rape);
- Abuse of them as a child or incest (molestation);
- Abortion;
- Sexual spirits (incubi and succubi).

Because of the intense shame of these things, you may not ever know if the counselee has been totally open and honest with you or not. You can only do your best to pray for and seek to cultivate an atmosphere of safety and security. Beyond that, you must trust that "it is God who is at work" in them "both to will and to work for His good pleasure" (Phil. 2:13).

Some teen counselees will protest that they have already confessed these things to God or may complain about having to dredge up things that may have happened years before. Gently explain that in the area of habitual sexual sin and sexual abuse, James 5:16 must be followed: "Confess your sins to one another, and pray for one another, so that you may be healed. The effective prayer of a righteous man can accomplish much."

Explain that your desire is for their healing, and that you and the prayer partner want to be able to pray effectively for them. Mention that silent confession is fine as far as God is concerned, but we must resist the devil out loud by renouncing the uses of our bodies as instruments of unrighteousness.

Although most young people struggle with talking about these personal matters at all, occasionally you will run into a teen who seems to enjoy sharing them. Gently control that tendency by saying, "You don't need to give that kind of graphic detail. All we need for you to do is name the sin, not describe it." If they persist, encourage them to make the following renunciation: "Lord, I renounce the practice of retelling the details of my past sexual experiences for the purpose of self-arousal, arousing others or feeling proud of my exploits. I affirm that my body is the temple of the Holy Spirit and that You, Lord, want my entire body and mind to be clean."

As the confession proceeds, you may become aware of lies the counselees have believed.

A young girl was told she was "special" by her abuser. After being sexually molested as a child, she became sexually promiscuous. At the freedom session, she was encouraged to say: "I renounce the lie that I need to give my body to someone sexually in order to be accepted and special. I announce the truth that I am already accepted by God in Christ and special because Jesus died for me."

Victims of molestation as children or teens often feel dirty and guilty for what was done to them and may experience feelings of revulsion toward legitimate sexual relationships in marriage. The following renunciation can help: "I renounce the lie that I am evil or dirty as a result of being molested. Thank You, Lord, that You know I was young and that I needed love and acceptance. I receive Your forgiveness for any way in which I may have cooperated and I choose to forgive myself. I accept the truth that sex within marriage is good and clean and a wonderful gift from You."

Teens who have given in to sexual perversions would benefit from saying: "I renounce all of the ways that Satan has twisted my view of sex as a result of my past experiences with (name them). I announce the truth that I don't have to continue to be a victim of those past experiences, but that I can now walk in the newness of life that is mine in Christ. You, Lord, make all things new and so I ask You to renew my mind and transform my life into Your image. I trust You to set me free to enjoy sex and my sexuality in the way You intended."

When they have finished exposing all the sexual issues the Lord has brought to mind, ask them to pray the following prayer out loud. Encourage them to pray through it slowly and think about the wonderful cleansing that has taken place in their bodies through the grace of God:

> Lord, I renounce all these uses of my body as an instrument of unrighteousness, and ask You to break all bondages Satan has brought into my life through that involvement. I admit my participation. Lord, I choose to present my eyes, my mouth, my mind, my hands and feet, my whole body to You as instruments of righteousness. I now present my body to You as a living sacrifice, holy and acceptable unto You, and I choose to reserve the sexual use of my body for marriage only (Heb. 13:4).
>
> I reject the lie of Satan that my body is not clean or that it is dirty or in any way unacceptable to You as a result of my past sexual experiences. Lord, I thank You that You have totally cleansed and forgiven me, and

that You love me just as I am. Therefore, I can accept myself and my body as cleansed in Your eyes. In Jesus' name. Amen.

Addressing Specific Issues

The last part of Step Six focuses on "Special Prayers for Specific Needs." By this time, you probably have a good idea which of the following areas need to be specifically addressed, but one or more issues may have remained hidden up until now.

Begin by saying something like, "We are going to take a look at some other areas of fleshly sin that can be a source of real bondage to teens. Don't think I am accusing you of anything as I ask you if you have struggled with these things. I ask everyone who goes through the Steps, just to be on the safe side."

One by one, gently ask them if they have struggled with each area, and encourage them to pray the prayer out loud for each one that has been a problem, either presently or in the past.

The following information is for your benefit and, in most cases, does not need to be shared with the counselee. It is designed to provide some insight for you about why a young person might struggle with these areas of sin.

Homosexuality

Homosexual desires or behavior can have its roots in childhood. They may have been homosexually molested as children. They may have "always" felt different sexually and perhaps believed the lie that God created them "homosexual." They may not have received the affirmation they needed as a male or female early in life (especially by a loving father) and so have a lot of gender identity confusion. For example, a lack of affirmation as a male can cause a lonely, young boy to crave attention from an older man. That longing can become eroticized at puberty and homosexual urges in that adolescent can become intense.

Whatever the root issue(s), we want to help them realize the existence of homosexual behavior, but God created us male and female in His image (see Gen. 1:27) to relate properly to both the opposite sex and one's own gender. These teens may be very frightened and may feel intense guilt and sadness. They need to be reminded they are loved and accepted in Christ and He can restore and heal them.

Abortion

God entrusts parents, even teen parents, with the lives of the children they conceive. He expects them to assume responsibility for the care and protection of those children. Most women have remorse about abortions they have had and many have grieved for years without comfort.

Many will have had serious struggles with suicidal thoughts.

Some teenage girls need to forgive the person (parent, boyfriend) who convinced them to get the abortion. Forgiving themselves is almost always an issue. Once they do so they often feel a tremendous release and making the choice to entrust that child to God may be a tearful and meaningful experience.

Teenage boys who have played any part in an abortion need to pray the prayer as well. If they paid for the abortion or fathered the child and did not try to prevent the abortion, they are guilty of sin.

Suicidal Tendencies

This includes attempts at suicide as well as suicidal thoughts. Suicide is the devil's final solution to escape the pain of life, but he is a thief who comes to steal, kill and destroy. Teens must make the decision to choose life in Christ who said that He came to give us life and life abundantly (see John 10:10).

As stated earlier in the book, you have a legal obligation to contact any teen's immediate family if he or she confesses to presently having suicidal thoughts or plans. Real liberty from these struggles may indeed be gained during the freedom appointment, but freedom must be maintained, and the life of the counselee protected. Involving family members and the church in a suicidal young person's life can help ensure that complete recovery takes place.

Eating Disorders or Cutting on Yourself

Young people (usually girls) who struggle in this area have developed a stronghold of acceptance based on physical appearance or performance. They also may be desperately trying to maintain control of one area of their lives in their otherwise out-of-control existences. In addition, purging the body of food or waste through vomiting or taking laxatives as well as intentionally cutting one's body are counterfeit attempts at cleansing oneself of evil.

Counselees need to be affirmed that they are accepted unconditionally in Christ and that cleansing only comes through the shed blood of the Lord Jesus Christ.

Although much resolution can take place during the Steps to Freedom in Christ, ongoing counseling to establish them in their identity in Christ and to give them time to renew their minds may be necessary as well.

Many are aware of the battle going on for their minds and after finding their freedom will exclaim, "It's incredible how many lies I've believed!" They should be encouraged to specifically renounce all the secret, hidden things associated with their behavior (e.g., wearing ankle weights to appear heavier, flushing food down the toilet, feeding food to a pet, excessive exercising) in addition to praying through the generic prayer in this section.

Substance Abuse

Teens often resort to the use of alcohol, tobacco, food, prescription or street drugs out of curiosity, to find pleasure, to escape painful circumstances or to try to cope with life. For whatever reason, these misuses and abuses of substances must be renounced. They may also need to renounce their misuse of time, money and energy on these things.

In the case of illegal or addictive substances in their possession, young people should be encouraged to destroy or dispose of them when they leave the appointment. The use of prescription drugs, however, should not be discontinued without a physician's approval. Teens who have abused prescription medications should be urged to tell their doctors and parents of their problem.

Young people who have had a serious problem with alcoholism or drug abuse will likely need further counseling to continue to choose truth and walk in freedom. They will also need assistance in getting back into the mainstream of society, learning to live responsibly at home, in school or on the job. The local church is called by God to be a source of support for teens in recovery, so young people need assistance in being plugged in there.

Drivenness and Perfectionism

Teenagers today often struggle with the terrible burden of trying desperately to please others (drivenness) or themselves (perfectionism) by their performance. Young people who bear these yokes of slavery are rarely able to rest, relax or feel satisfied.

They are often obsessed with a consuming need to stay busy, work harder or longer hours and get everything "just right." They need to renounce the driving mechanism behind their impossible goals, which is the lie that their happiness stems from pleasing others or themselves by what they do.

By affirming that they are already accepted, significant and secure in Christ, they can be set free from this crushing and cruel load they carry.

After praying through all the "Special Prayers for Special Needs" that apply to them, encourage the counselees to pray:

> I now confess these sins to You and claim through the blood of the Lord Jesus Christ my forgiveness and cleansing. I cancel all ground that evil spirits have gained through my willful involvement in sin. I ask this in the wonderful name of my Lord and Savior, Jesus Christ. Amen.

Practicing Spiritual Discipline

We do not want to leave young people mistakenly believing that once they have gone through this Step they will never struggle with these areas of fleshly sin again. Working through these issues will provide teens with a fresh start, however, so they are no longer dragged down by the chains of past sins.

Breaking those chains through confession, repentance and renunciation frees them to make the choice to walk in the Spirit rather than in the flesh. Spiritual disciplines need to be practiced, however, to maintain freedom.

Some may need ongoing help to solidify the gains they have made. This does not minimize the freedom they will have gained here, however. Mountains of anger, guilt, condemnation and hopelessness will be replaced with resolution, joy and freedom. It is one thing to get free; it is quite another to stay free. This is particularly true in the sexual and other addictive areas.

If the young people have addressed deep issues in this Step, you need to alert them to the fact that the enemy delights in tempting people in their areas of weakness, trying to entice them back into bondage again. Remind them that they are not helpless victims, powerless to resist the temptations. They are children of the living God and when they submit to Him and resist the devil, he will flee from them.

Ask teens if they have a friend to whom they can be accountable and on whom they can count for prayer support. In reality, all of us need to be part of a fellowship group for regular encouragement and prayer support. Once again, we absolutely need God and we desperately need one another.

A Story of Recovery

We close this chapter by sharing the wonderful testimony of a 17-year-old recovering from bulimia, from anger toward a perfectionistic dad and from the trauma of an attempted gang rape.

Dear Rich,

It is incredible what God has done in my heart! There is freedom in Jesus! Helping me forgive those guys who tried to rape me. To have a deeper understanding of what Jesus did on the cross! Being set free from the fear and guilt-misery I was in.

To forgive and be loosed from all bitterness and resentment toward my Dad. Sometimes a surge of anger toward him comes, but the Lord reminds me that it is all paid for and that both my Dad and I have been washed in Jesus' blood.

To know that in Jesus I have victory over the bulimia, and by faith know that instead of the thornbush the cypress is coming up and instead of the nettle the myrtle is coming up, and that it is a memorial to the Lord, an everlasting sign that will not be cut off!

It is such a fight and such a war! Sometimes I do feel as though I am losing, but I'm not.

You cannot imagine how clean, forgiven, refreshed and beautiful I feel inside! I have so much joy, I feel like exploding!

Thank you for being like an older brother and just a friend! It is so beautiful what God has done in my life.

Worthy is the Lamb who was slain to receive power, glory and honor! It's kind of funny because sometimes I feel like I could cry, and cry, and cry, but there is also a deep joy! I guess that is part of the healing process.

Family Matters

Step Seven:
Curses Versus Blessings

This final Step to freedom focuses on the sins passed down from one generation to the next, and the direct spiritual attacks that come from the enemy. This is a critical turning point for young people who come from dysfunctional families or families involved in cults and the occult.

By going through this Step, teens will be able to break the final links of bondage that have chained them to their pasts. This, however, is an active, not passive, process of choosing to accept themselves as new creations in Christ and take their places in the family of God.

After a conference, I (Neil) noticed one of my students sitting rather dazed in his chair.

"Are you all right?" I asked.

"Yes," he responded.

"You look rather perplexed. What happened when you went through this Step?" I asked.

"I had to literally hang on to my chair to keep from running out of here," he said. It turned out his mother was a psychic.

As that case illustrates, some interference from the enemy can be expected in this last Step, especially if cult or occult experiences have been present in that young person's family heritage.

An ex-Mormon I (Neil) was helping suddenly stopped in the middle of the declaration in total fear.

"What's going on in your mind?" I asked.

She cried out, "You mean you don't see him there?"

"Who?" I asked.

"My father, standing right there," she said, pointing her finger at the space beside me.

I did not bother to look because I knew I would not see anything. Does that mean I doubted what she saw was real? No, not at all. It was real all right, but the problem was not in the room. It was in her mind.

"Tell me about your father," I continued.

"I'm responsible for my father," she said.

I told her that was a lie. We have a responsibility *to* one another, but not *for* one another. So she renounced the lie and continued reading the declaration. This time her "grandmother" showed up!

Clearly, these were not actual appearances of deceased relatives. They were counterfeit manifestations by an impostor demon. The story of the rich man and Lazarus in Luke 16:19-31 clearly teaches that the spirits of the dead do not return to visit the earth. The dead are either in hell or in the presence of Christ and no travel is allowed between those places of eternity and earth.

Every Christian is a new creation in Christ, "the old things passed away" and the new things have come (2 Cor. 5:17). We have been given everything we need for "life and godliness" (2 Pet. 1:3). But unless we consciously choose to walk in the newness of life we have in Christ, we will simply continue to walk according to our flesh, bound to the past.

Many Christians, however, do not take an active stand by faith in their new identity. They acquiesce to their old positions in Adam, rather than according to their new standing in Christ. Acquiescence is passively giving in or accepting something quietly without protesting. Ground that is not actively taken from Satan's greedy control will remain under his jurisdiction.

A Case of Genetics, Environment and Spirituality

Why are young people, even Christian ones, so prone to continue in the sins of the fathers, and how are those sins passed down? The cycle of abuse, for example, is one of the more attested social phenomena. Is it passed on genetically, environmentally, or spiritually? The answer, we believe, is yes! All the above.

Genetics
First, it is true that teens can be genetically predisposed to certain strengths and weaknesses. Athletic ability, for example, is an example of a strength that clearly is a genetic trait. In addition, it is well accepted that some people are more prone to becoming alcoholics than are others. They are not born alcoholics, but they can more easily become addicted to alcohol than other teens if they choose to drink as a means of partying or coping.

Similarly, some boys have higher levels of testosterone than do others. This is a genetically inherited trait. They will develop beards by the time they are 14 years old, while others won't have full beards until they are 21. Having lower levels of the male hormone does not make a boy a homosexual, but it may make him more vulnerable to it. In addition, boys who develop later may experience more teasing, and that could easily affect their self-perceptions. That reality brings us to the second factor, our environment.

Environment
The environment in which we were raised is the biggest contributor to our development. Values and attitudes are caught more than taught. If a teen is raised in a home in which Mom and Dad watch porno movies and read pornographic magazines, he is going to see it as a normal part of life. Later on, Dad may hand condoms to the boy and encourage him to "sow his wild oats." Clearly, that young man is going to struggle with lust more than one who comes from a moral home atmosphere.

The environment in which young people grow up includes their friends (or lack of them), neighborhood, schools, parents (stepparents or guardians), churches (or absence of them) and so on.

Spirituality
The third factor is spiritual. In giving the Ten Commandments, God said:

"You shall not make for yourself an idol, or any likeness of what is in heaven above or on the earth beneath
or in the water under the earth. You shall not worship
them or serve them; for I, the Lord your God, am a jealous God, visiting the iniquity of the fathers on the children, on the third and the fourth generations of those
who hate Me, but showing lovingkindness to thousands, to those who love Me and keep My commandments" (Exod. 20:4-6).

One Family's Experience

Bill and Sarah were at the end of their rope with their daughter
Melissa. She lived in fear and as a result the whole house was dis-
rupted, and tired. Her parents and brother were irritated and worn
out from Melissa playing musical beds at night because she was
afraid to sleep alone.

Bill's eloquent testimony of what happened to Melissa is helpful,
especially coming from a parent. All three factors we just discussed
can be picked up as you read the story:

*Scripture plainly teaches that God has a plan for every believer's life for
that person's welfare. It is equally evident that the enemy has a counterplan.
With this thought in mind, it can safely be said that from the outset Melissa
was targeted for trauma and fingered for fear. She entered this world fighting for her life, being delivered by emergency C-section. Two weeks later she
stopped eating and paid the first of many visits to the hospital.*

*Because of a weak immune system and other abnormalities, her first five
years were a blur of pokes, prods and surgeries. Melissa faced each ordeal as
bravely as could be expected, but always there was an undercurrent of fear.*

*In fact, fear-producing circumstances seemed to be magnetically attract-
ed to her. There was the attack by a dog and the neighbor who shared a little too freely about the "ghost" in her house.*

*Melissa's kindergarten teacher, in presenting the plan of salvation, told
the class that if they didn't receive Jesus, demons might get them. This only
caused her to associate Jesus with fear instead of freedom.*

*For a time, Melissa had an imaginary friend. One day this "friend" told
my wife, Sarah, that Melissa was dead. The imaginary friend had spoken*

through Melissa's mouth. This scared the living daylights out of Sarah, especially as a few minutes later a swing hit Melissa in the head, causing her to bleed profusely. Obviously, the "imaginary" friend wasn't so imaginary after all!

An exhaustive list of Melissa's negative experiences would make for exhausting reading, but the cumulative effect of them was a child dominated by fear...most notably the fear of being alone and the fear of going to sleep.

We knew enough to address the issue on spiritual grounds and even led Melissa through the Steps to Freedom in Christ, but the fear remained entrenched. As everyone must before meaningful change can occur, we became desperate.

You correctly discerned the need to devote the brunt of your counseling time to addressing and having us renounce the fear element in Sarah and me. Sin began with a tree and wherever we see its fruit, we can nearly always trace its roots to prior generations.

[Note: After working with Bill and Sarah and their fears, we had Melissa renounce her fears as well. She was reluctant to share them at first, but with some gentle prodding and reminders from Mom and Dad, she finally dealt with them.]

Certainly, in our case, with the roots destroyed, the fruit soon began to wither. When we left your place, I was confident Sarah and I had made significant strides. However, I was less than optimistic, okay unbelieving, where Melissa was concerned. Before our vacation week ended, though, she showed signs of improvement and even evidenced an interest in spiritual things.

I would love to boast of an absolute victory, but most honestly assess Melissa today as a recovering phobic. Just as time and trauma made her who she became, so now time and the truth are helping her become who she already is in Christ.

There were some tough times of putting our feet down as parents, too, realizing that we had given in too much. When we first returned from vacation, there were several nights of sheer torment when we forced Melissa to remain in her room come what may. No telling what the neighbors thought about all that screaming. Her will began to yield after about a week, at which point her mind began to renew. And we all began to get some sleep.

On occasion, we still find it necessary to have Melissa renounce (again) certain fears. We pray with her each night before bedtime and she always asks to read the "bedtime prayer" in the back of the Steps. She knows that what she's reading is the truth and is making the daily choice to believe it. Isn't this, after all, our walk in the Spirit in a nutshell?

Thank you for being willing to perform your role in the Body of Christ for the benefit of a family of strangers. Melissa was a puzzle with a missing piece. God sovereignly knew whose hand He had placed it in.

Scriptural Guidance to Genetics

Some Christian leaders respond negatively to the teaching that believers can inherit spiritual problems from their ancestors.

> Young people are not guilty for their parents' sins; but because ♦♦♦♦♦ of their ancestors' sin, they are vulnerable to the same areas of weakness.

Let us respond by saying that young people are not guilty for their parents' sins; but because of their ancestors' sins, they are vulnerable to the same areas of weakness. Consider Jeremiah 32:17,18, emphasis added:

> "Ah Lord God! Behold, Thou hast made the heavens and the earth by Thy great power and by Thine outstretched arm! Nothing is too difficult for Thee, who showest lovingkindness to thousands, but repayest the iniquity of fathers *into the bosom* of their children after them, O great and mighty God. The Lord of hosts is His name."

Whatever is being passed down intergenerationally is clearly not because of the environment (according to Jeremiah), because it occurs in the bosom of the children. That could make it a genetic factor for those who insist upon a natural explanation for everything, but we do not think so.

Leviticus 26:38-42 offers more valuable insight:

> "But you will perish among the nations, and your enemies' land will consume you. So those of you who may be left will rot away because of their iniquity in the lands of your enemies; and also because of the iniquities of their forefathers they will rot away with them. If they confess their iniquity and the iniquity of their forefathers, in their unfaithfulness which they committed against Me, and also in their acting with hostility against Me—...then I will remember My covenant with Jacob."

If the problems of the people were just a problem of bad genes, confessing their sins would not have cured them. Certainly confessing the sins of the fathers would have no affect on the present generation genetically!

A New Focus on Ancestors

A story I (Neil) saw recently on television is a modern-day illustration of this. A high school girl in a small hamlet in southern Germany decided to do a report on the role her town played in World War II. She had always been told that her town had resisted Hitler and that the Catholic church had taught its people not to even pray for him.

What she discovered in the local library was just the opposite. The town had acquiesced to Hitler's regime. Her report brought quick disclaimers from town leaders as well as warnings not to dig up any more dirt. She felt betrayed by her ancestors and so decided to do more extensive research.

The whole town eventually turned against her when she reported her findings. Her husband left her, her family deserted her and she was finally run out of town.

Is it any wonder white supremacy has risen again in Germany? Complete repentance never occurred. They covered it up. Some also deny that the Holocaust even took place! Truly those who will not face the sins of the fathers are doomed to repeat them.

Some may still protest the need to do this because we are new creatures in Christ, and Jesus paid the penalty for all our sins. Indeed He did, but when we were born again, were our minds instantly transformed? We believe as strongly as anyone that our new position in Christ has had a profound effect on our being. Because we are new creatures in Christ, we can actively choose to confess and renounce the sins of our ancestors and stop the cycle of sin and abuse. That is the final step in the process of repentance.

The Cure for Curses

Curses are blasphemous pronouncements, oaths or swearing intended to bring injury to another person. This is more common in Third World countries, but it is also present in North America because of the upsurge in occult activity, witchcraft, New Age practices and satanism.

A major purpose of satanic worship is to summon and send demons out to curse targeted people. If the young people you counsel have ever been abruptly awakened at a certain time of the night, say 3:00 A.M., or if they have suffered nighttime panic attacks, they may have been targeted.

In addition, predictions given by a medium, or even things unwisely said or done by a parent, may be *used* by Satan as a curse on a person's life. One teenage boy had struggled for eight years with his sense of worth because at age seven his dad had divorced his mom. As he was moving out of the house he angrily shouted at the boy, "Go ahead, stay with your mom! I never wanted you as a son anyway!"

Although those hateful words may have been meant more for his mom than for him, that teenager had been severely damaged by them. He was able to break that curse's hold on his life by affirming his true identity in Christ and his new relationship with his heavenly Father who loves him, wants him and will never leave him.

Another man, well into middle age, had been haunted all his life by the cruel words of his father as he raped him as a boy. His dad had snarled, "I'm going to fix you so that no one will ever want you!" This man found wonderful release from that awful curse through renouncing it and claiming the truth that God the Father wanted him so much that He sent His Son to die for him!

Playing games such as the Ouija board or Magic Eight Ball also can cause messages to be imprinted on a young person's mind so they act like a curse or assignment. That person, either consciously or unconsciously, can feel helplessly bound to that "prophetic" message.

If the Lord brings specific curses to mind during this Step, have the counselees renounce them specifically. If not, the general renunciation will suffice. Christ is ultimately their defense and as they come under His authority and protection, they will be able to break any and all links to the bondage of generational sins and curses. They do not have to be the victims of their past anymore.

Renouncing Ancestors' Sins

Begin this Step by reading the introductory paragraph (or by paraphrasing it if you are familiar with the principles and Scripture). Then ask the counselee to pray the following prayer:

> Dear heavenly Father,
> I ask You to reveal to my mind all the sins of my ancestors that are being passed down through family lines. I want to be free from those influences and walk in my new identity as a child of God. Amen.

Then give the teens you are helping some time to jot down the things the Lord brings to mind. Feel free to have the young person you are counseling glance back at the list of non-Christian practices in Step One, the fear list in Step Two and the habitual sins and special needs lists in Step Six. Those will help them pinpoint likely areas of generational sin. If you as an encourager think the counselee is obviously overlooking some areas, feel free to suggest them. Let him or her decide, though, which ones need to be specifically renounced.

Those specific generational sins will be renounced during the upcoming Declaration.

Before having them read through the Declaration and praying the Prayer that follows, share the information just prior to those exercises in Step Seven.

The Declaration is as follows:

> I here and now reject and disown all the sins of my ancestors. I specifically renounce the sins of (list here the areas of family sin the Lord revealed to you). As one who has been delivered from the domain of darkness and placed into the kingdom of God's Son, I cancel out all demonic working that was passed down to me from my family. As one who is crucified and raised with Jesus Christ and who sits with Him in heavenly places, I renounce all satanic assignments that are directed toward me and my ministry. I cancel out every curse that Satan and his workers have put on me. I announce to Satan and all his forces that Christ became a curse for me (Gal. 3:13) when He died for my sins on the cross. I reject any and every way in which Satan may claim ownership of me.
>
> I belong to the Lord Jesus Christ who purchased me with His own blood. I reject all the blood sacrifices whereby Satan may claim ownership of me. I declare myself to be eternally and completely signed over and committed to the Lord Jesus Christ. By the authority that I have in Jesus Christ, I now command every spiritual enemy of the Lord Jesus Christ to leave my presence. I commit myself to my heavenly Father to do His will from this day forward.

The Prayer is as follows:

> Dear heavenly Father,
> I come to You as Your child, purchased by tne blood

of the Lord Jesus Christ. You are the Lord of the universe and the Lord of my life. I submit my body to You as an instrument of righteousness, a living sacrifice, that I may glorify You in my body. I ask You to fill me with Your Holy Spirit to lead and empower me to know and do Your will. I commit myself to the renewing of my mind in order to prove that Your will is good, perfect and acceptable for me. All this I do in the name and authority of the Lord Jesus Christ. Amen.

The young person has just completed a fierce and thorough moral inventory. The effect on some teens is dramatic. They look different. They are living examples of Psalm 34:5: "They looked to Him and were radiant, and their faces shall never be ashamed."

The peace that passes all understanding is what God wants ● ● ● ● ● to give each one of His children. That peace will guard our hearts and minds in Christ Jesus.

Many counselees feel a deep sense of joy and relief while others feel totally wiped out. Some combination of exhilaration and exhaustion is common.

We usually have teens close their eyes and share with us what is going on in their minds. Many experience a peace and quietness they have never felt before.

One lady said, "My mind is quiet. Usually there are racing thoughts. In fact, this is the first time I can ever remember it being quiet inside my head!" This woman was well up in her fifties and had never experienced peace of mind! That peace that passes all understanding is what God wants to give each one of His children. That peace will guard our hearts and minds in Christ Jesus (see Phil. 4:7).

Gaining Complete Resolution

For some, the joyful emotions come later. One young man I (Rich) took through the Steps was driving home after the freedom appointment and could not wait to make it to his house. He called my pastor to tell him how excited he was. "My emotions just kicked in!" he shouted over the phone. "I've been driving down the road singing praises to God and lifting my hands to Him!" I certainly hope he kept one hand on the steering wheel!

It is important to give counselees some immediate follow-up so they can know what to expect, how to handle it, as well as suggestions for continued growth and freedom maintenance. That will be the subject of the next and final chapter of this book.

If the teens you counsel do not sense complete resolution after finishing Step Seven, encourage them to pray and ask the Lord to reveal what is still keeping them in bondage. Allow them to sit quietly for a few minutes. Then ask something like, "What is the *first thing* that came to your mind?"

Frequently we have seen God bring to mind something specific that still needed to be addressed.

Once in a while a young person will say, "It is almost completely quiet, but there are voices way off in the distance," or "I hear laughing in the background." You can help him or her learn to walk in Christ's authority by leading the teen to say, "In the name of the Lord Jesus Christ, I command you to leave my presence. I am a child of God and the evil one cannot touch me."

If the teens have indeed been faithful to deal with everything the Lord has revealed to them, they will usually exclaim, "It's quiet!" The exception could be if you happen to be working with a severe case of satanic ritual abuse (SRA). Once again, for more information on working with victims of SRA, consult Neil's books *Helping Others Find Freedom in Christ* and *Released from Bondage*.

If the young person had difficulty working through a particular Step, you may want to go back and work through it again. This is particularly true of the Statement of Truth in Step Two. Many who experienced difficulty reading through it the first time are amazed at the ease with which they can do it the second time. That concrete example of change can be a great encouragement to a teen who may be wondering if anything really happened.

Young people who live by their feelings and who have developed a passive mental state (and that's a lot of teens today!) are the most difficult to work with. They are also the ones who will struggle the most with maintaining their freedom.

They struggle with assuming responsibility for their own thoughts, having developed the habit of going with the flow of whatever passes through their minds. Some genuinely have A.D.D. and can be helped by proper medication, while others are just mentally lazy.

In either case, developing mental discipline to learn to take "every thought captive to the obedience of Christ" (2 Cor. 10:5) will be the critical factor in determining their freedom maintenance.

Maintaining Freedom

Having young people journal their thoughts and emotions each day, then sitting down with them (as parent or youth leader) and evaluating their journal entries can be a great help. Encourage teens to compare their thoughts and feelings with the truth of God's Word. Look up Scripture together and ask them if what they are thinking or feeling is true. Included in the back of this book is a beginning glossary of Bible verses that present truth to counteract many of the most common adolescent struggles. You can add to it as the Lord directs you to other Scripture passages.

Encourage them to renounce any lies they have believed. Helping them memorize the truth of God's Word will then give them ammunition against future spiritual attacks.

Some further counseling concerning the music, reading material, TV programs, movies, video and computer games these young people are involved with will most likely be necessary. Do not be judgmental, but rather provide Christian teens with material to read, listen to and watch that is youth oriented, and that promotes biblical values and teaches them to think.

Four 40-day youth devotionals, *Extreme Faith, Reality Check, Ultimate Love* and *Awesome God* have been developed by Freedom in Christ authors to act as follow-up to the Steps to Freedom in Christ.

In addition, a copy of the IN CHRIST list should be taped to the back of their journals. That list of scriptural truths will be of great help to teens who struggle with feelings of inadequacy, worthlessness, helplessness and rejection.

Before ending the freedom appointment you can encourage a doubting teen by sharing something like the following:

> We know that God answers prayer. If you were honest and did not hide anything as we went through the Steps, then I believe God has answered your prayers today and many of your personal and spiritual conflicts have been resolved.
>
> When you leave today, don't listen to your feelings if they tell you that nothing happened. That is one of Satan's most common tricks. Choose to believe what God says is true. Remember that the battle is for your mind. The more you fill your mind with God's Word, the stronger you'll become. Think about how much God loves you and how powerful He is.
>
> Don't get bogged down with what didn't happen. You have faced and dealt with a lot today. There may still be more to deal with, but God will bring those things to the surface at the right time. For now, take every thought captive to the obedience of Christ and ignore any doubt, fear or anxiety that pops into your head. It is the truth that has set you free and it is the truth that will continue to keep you free.

John said he had no greater joy than to hear of his children walking in the truth (see 3 John 4). Whether the teens you help are your own children or your "spiritual children," you, too, will experience that incomparable joy as you see them "submit to God and resist the devil."

A Story of Hope

We close this chapter with the story of Julie, a girl who hit rock bottom. By God's grace, she looked up from the bottom and took hold of the Rock. She was already on the road to recovery when she came to one of our conferences during which she went through the Steps to Freedom in Christ. God did a major work in her life. She found her freedom, and she is sticking with Jesus. She wrote the following letter to me (Rich) so I could pass it on to parents and teens who need hope.

Dear Mr. Miller,

I wanted to write you and share a little bit of my testimony of the great things God has done in my life.

When I was 12 years old I started "rebelling" and not caring about the world or anyone in it. I got into drugs and then stealing from my parents to keep up my habit. During all this pain I was putting my family, friends and God through, I started dating a drug dealer.

I was already on probation for forgery and assault with a deadly weapon. I decided that I'd go and get into some more trouble. I dropped out of school and two months later I got put in jail. My boyfriend came to jail a few weeks later for intent to sell cocaine. I got out of jail 81 days later, but I decided to move in with him and help him traffic crack cocaine.

Five months later I was arrested and put in a women's state prison at age 16. When I got out I wasn't on parole, so I moved back in with my boyfriend.

God started showing me the pain I was putting everybody and myself through. I've now been drug free for over a year! I told my mother that I wanted a change in my life. She picked me up and all of my stuff and took me to a youth home to learn discipline through God's eyes.

Two weeks later I found out that I was pregnant, so I moved into a group home for pregnant mothers.

Now I live for God and only God. I went back to school and I made the A,B honor roll. And my mother can actually look me in the eyes and tell me that she's proud of me.

I was so mad at the world. Now Christ has shown me that I was the one holding myself in bondage. I want everyone to know that God loves you no matter what you've done and it's never too late to start over and become a child of God. God will forgive you for whatever has happened in the past, but we have to forgive ourselves.

God is my best friend now and I want everyone to know it!

Wrapping Up

S tephanie looked like a rag doll, but her eyes revealed the truth of her newfound freedom. She had just completed a marathon session through the Steps to Freedom in Christ and was experiencing tremendous resolution.

"I'm exhausted!" she said.

"You should be," I (Neil) responded. "You have just emerged from an incredible war, and you won. Congratulations."

"Thanks," she said, "but what will I do next week if I have a problem? You will be out of town!"

Many counselees think they can't make it without their encourager or helper.

I asked Stephanie, "What did I actually do? You were the one who did all the work, and it was God who set you free."

Even the best of parents and youth leaders have limited time and resources, but God doesn't. Young people can call on Him 24 hours a day, seven days a week for the rest of their lives. "God is our refuge and strength, a very present help in trouble. Therefore we will not fear" (Ps. 46:1,2). "Trust in Him at all times, O people; pour out your heart before Him; God is a refuge for us" (62:8).

We do not want the teens we counsel to be dependent upon us; we want them to be dependent upon God. He is their deliverer. He is the Wonderful Counselor, not us. He alone can set them free and give them the grace to continue on. Walking through the Steps to Freedom in Christ does not only resolve present and past conflicts, but it also teaches and trains them how to stand and resolve issues that will surface later.

What can you expect by the end of the freedom appointment? How will the young person feel? How much freedom can we realistically expect to be gained? Will he or she continue on and walk in freedom?

Clearly, no set answer to these questions can be found. The human heart is far too complex and too many variables exist to state categorically what will or will not happen. The young people you take through the Steps will have differing life experiences, problems, personalities, biblical knowledge, spiritual maturity and levels of commitment. The one constant is our faithful and gracious God who does hear and answer prayer.

The chances of teens getting hurt emotionally or spiritually by going through the Steps are minimal, unless you lose control in the session. Stay on track, stick to the script of the Steps to Freedom, and stay away from controversial issues. If you let the young person draw you into an argument, or let the devil set the agenda, you could go down a thousand unprofitable rabbit trails.

By God's grace, every young person you take through the Steps will have made some spiritual progress in walking with God. If they were honest and thorough, they will have done a complete housecleaning. Often they say things such as, "I feel like such a burden has been lifted off me" or "I can't remember when I've felt so clean inside."

Some teens may feel a little let down because they don't experience dramatic changes the way others do. They may have unrealistic expectations, thinking everything will be perfect after they go through these Steps.

It is not a good idea to make any promises beforehand of what will happen in the session. We have no way of knowing. God may choose to wait until later to surface certain issues, so you should never promise a total resolution. We can give a teen hope, but don't give him or her *false* hope.

Joyous Moments After the Appointment

One young man named James came in for a freedom appointment. He was extremely discouraged with his relationship with God. He admitted that he was not even sure if he believed "this Christian stuff" anymore. He was willing, though, to give it one more chance.

Having grown up in an extremely legalistic church, James did not have a healthy view of God at all. His "God" was so angry, controlling and judgmental that it is no wonder he decided to look elsewhere for spiritual reality. Following the "free spirit" of his dad, James dove into Taoism, Buddhism and a number of other "isms," looking for answers. His spiritual journey also took him into the realm of the occult and white magic.

When he read through the "Statement of Truth" in Step Two, he was really reading "by faith." Not certain if all the doctrinal statements were true, he faithfully continued on anyway. God blessed his commitment to know the truth.

At the end of the sessions, James could not believe how clean he felt. He knew something significant had occurred. What had really happened in his life did not dawn on him, however, until he called me a few days later on the phone.

"Rich, this is really wild. I was at work the other day preparing to eat my lunch and I found myself saying "grace" out loud! I hadn't done that for years.

"But that isn't the end of it. I was working later on and suddenly I started singing praise and worship songs that I didn't even know I'd remembered. And not only that, I was lifting up my hands, too!"

I laughed because I knew where James worked. He had recently joined the Marines out of high school and so I had this humorous picture in my mind of this rough, tough leatherneck humbly praising God.

James laughed, too, and continued, "Once I realized what I was doing, I looked around real quick to see if anybody saw me. Then I ran around to the back of the building and finished my worship service there!

"But that's still not all. Later on, my boss was ragging on me about something and I was getting a little angry. Usually I mouth off and then feel bad about it later. This time I kept my mouth shut. Can you believe what's happened to me?"

My mind immediately flashed to Ephesians 5:19-21, the result of being filled with the Holy Spirit:

> Speaking to one another in psalms and hymns and spiritual songs, singing and making melody with your heart to the Lord; always giving thanks for all things in the name of our Lord Jesus Christ to God, even the Father; and be subject to one another in the fear of Christ.

"James," I said excitedly, "you have just given the most wonderful three-point sermon illustration of being filled with the Holy Spirit that I have ever heard!"

Issues for After the Steps

Young people who are on medications may ask you whether they need them anymore. Unless you are that teen's doctor, do not give medical advice. If young people feel they are cured of the condition requiring medication, they can be encouraged to talk to their parents and doctor. Then a wise decision can be made.

Teens can develop a tolerance to certain prescription drugs, and they could have serious side effects if they go off too suddenly.

It would be helpful for you to buy an inexpensive "pill book" at a bookstore. That book will tell you the names of prescription drugs, their uses and side effects.

It is possible that some young people will come back after going through the Steps and say they are still not free. That can happen for several possible reasons. They include the following:

1. Teens who take themselves through the Steps can easily skip over items, rationalizing their sin. It is hard to be complete and objective doing it by themselves, especially if some major issues in their lives need

resolving. The most common area in which we need help is forgiveness. Going through Step Three again with an encourager is often very helpful.

We do not want to give the wrong impression, however. It is possible to work through the Steps and find freedom on your own. We have received letters from people around the world whom Christ has set free just from reading the books and taking themselves through the Steps.

2. Young people may need some more help even after having gone through the Steps with an encourager and prayer partner. If you know the issue that is still troubling them, go back to the appropriate Step (usually the first, third or sixth), and make sure the issues involved are clearly understood. If you have any doubts, it won't do any harm to go through all the Steps again.

One teenage girl went through the Steps to Freedom in Christ with a personal encourager and began the process of forgiving the man who had molested her. She was not done, though. She went to a two-day training of youth leaders (although she herself was still in high school), but missed going through the group Steps at the end of the first day. On the morning of the second day, during the sharing time, she admitted to the whole group that she was hearing voices, struggling with intense anger and was having a terrible time sitting through the teaching sessions.

Mercifully, a group of godly women gathered around her to pray for her to find freedom. Later on that day, she went through the Steps a second time, involving a different ministry team. By that time, she was ready to do business with God. She confessed her bitterness and truly forgave from the heart those who had hurt her. As a result, the Lord set her free from an eating disorder that had started after the molestation.

If you are having any difficulty identifying a specific issue to resolve, it is generally best to go back and review all of Steps One,

Three and Six. Those are the areas that most often require another layer to be removed. Some renouncing and forgiving may need to be done, but usually an identity issue is associated with one of those Steps.

Somewhere the teens may still be believing a lie. We will often go back to the concept of the identity chart and work through the troubling issues with them, identifying the lies they have believed. By repudiating the lies and choosing to cling to the truth of God's Word, freedom usually comes.

A Thank-You Letter

After pinpointing the identity issues that needed to be resolved, one person wrote:

Thank you so much for taking me through the Steps to Freedom yesterday. It really helped me to get an objective view of where the battle line is in my life. I knew that what I believed about my identity was out of alignment with the truth, but I just couldn't practically apply it to my life by myself.

When I had gone through the Steps by myself a few years ago, I had such a radical freedom experience. I really thought I could maintain it myself forever, and I planned to. But I didn't realize that I still hadn't dealt with some of the real underlying emotions. I had certainly gotten in touch with my hurt and anger during times of forgiveness before, but I hadn't realized how it had affected my core identity. Because I felt rejected and unworthy, I believed that I needed to "perform" in order to be accepted.

Thanks for your acceptance and love. It helped me to be real and transparent about my struggles with others. It was important for my own growth, but also in the ability to help others. I have more honest compassion for others now. It is amazing that going through the Steps allowed me to share all my skeletons in only a few hours. In all my years of Christian counseling, I had only started to approach talking about the really painful things. During the Steps, it all comes out and gets resolved with no guilt or remorse.

I've already started looking up Scriptures to counter all the lies I believed about myself. Thanks especially for seeing in me something of value worth devoting time to. I've spent my entire life trying to act like everything was all right and trying to figure out how to do the right thing so I wouldn't get in trouble or be rejected. Now I just want to be the person God wants me to be, and let the doing come naturally.

Awareness of Future Doubts

Many young people will have won major battles by going through the Steps, but they need to know that other battles will come. They will walk out the door with the rest of their lives to live. They will certainly face more conflicts ahead, but they will be more winnable, having broken the bondage in their lives and having gained a greater sense of God's presence and power.

There will never be a time (this side of heaven) when we ▮ ▮ ▮ ▮ ▮ don't need to submit to God, resist the devil and put on the full armor of God.

Remind the teens you counsel that they may hear a little voice in their heads saying, "I'm back!" or "It didn't work!" The battle goes on and they need to be aware of that. There will never be a time (this side of heaven) when we don't need to submit to God, resist the devil and put on the full armor of God (see Eph. 6:10-20; Jas. 4:7). By going through the Steps, however, young people should be more aware of who the enemy is, what his weapons and strategies are and how they can stand against him.

To maintain freedom, teens must continue doing what they started doing by going through the Steps: renounce lies, choose truth, confess sin, forgive offenders and so on. They should take their thoughts, reading material, music, entertainment and conversations through the grid of Philippians 4:8, focusing their minds only on things that are true, right, pure and pleasing to God.

Working on "Old Business" and "New Business"

A teenage girl came up to one of our staff members at a youth conference and asked if she could go through the Steps to Freedom in Christ. As the appointment began, the girl shared that she had gone through the Steps a year and a half earlier with another Freedom in Christ staff member.

Although things went great for about a year, recently she had been struggling with nightmares and hearing voices. Within an hour and a half, she was able to resolve the issues in her life and again rejoice in her freedom in Christ.

As it turned out, this teenage girl had both "old business" and "new business" to resolve. During her first freedom appointment, her girlfriend had sat in as prayer partner. Some forgiveness issues between them were therefore glossed over. During her second time through the Steps, she forgave her friend. That was the "old business."

The "new business" involved hanging around her old friends again and allowing them to have a negative influence on her thoughts and actions. That involvement seemed to precipitate the return of the nightmares and voices.

Teens must assume responsibility for their minds and lives and choose to take "every thought captive to the obedience of Christ (2 Cor. 10:5). Most of your counselees will be able to do this if they sincerely desire to walk with Christ. If their commitment to God is wishy-washy, they are likely to fall back into the same bondage again.

Encourage them to seek friends who love them, who understand spiritual conflicts and who will pray for them when the battle gets intense. These can be relatives, godly friends or church leadership. Every Christian teen needs at least one friend who will stand with him or her in this way.

Prepare Counselee for Aftercare

Follow-up begins in the appointment itself as you prepare the counselee for what lies ahead. Read the sections entitled "Something to Remember" and "Maintaining Your Freedom" (located right after

Step Seven) to the counselee, emphasizing any of the points you feel are particularly applicable to him or her.

In addition, here are a few key suggestions that have helped young people in the past. Be careful not to overwhelm the teens you counsel with a huge list of "to-do's" when they go home; they need just a few practical helps to start with.

1. Encourage them to read through the Steps again when they go home. Suggest that they read through the "Statement of Truth" in Step Two and IN CHRIST pages out loud each day for the next two weeks, as well as the "Daily Prayer" (in the morning) and "Bedtime Prayer" (at night). Those prayers are found in the back of the Steps. All these tools will help them continue to renew their minds and choose truth.

2. Encourage them to identify a person with whom they could regularly meet for prayer. If a group of young people is studying *Busting Free*, *Stomping Out the Darkness* or *The Bondage Breaker Youth Edition*, help them get involved in that group. If not, make sure they have a copy of *Stomping Out the Darkness* and *The Bondage Breaker Youth Edition*, and encourage them to read those books on their own if they have not already done so.

3. Encourage them in the areas where they are weak, and let them know that you will be praying for them. You will want to pray for them before the end of the freedom appointment, lifting up those weak areas to the Lord. Remind them that other areas in their lives may surface, but they do not ever need to be afraid of the truth. Tell them it is okay to look back through the Steps to be reminded of how to handle future conflicts. the Steps to Freedom in Christ is a resource they can utilize their whole lives in helping themselves and others find and maintain spiritual freedom.

4. In some cases, the young people you counsel will need help beyond what you can give them. Parents can seek help in finding appropriate professional help by con-

sulting their pastor. A word of caution: professional counselors should be wise, Bible-believing Christians who will not scoff at or seek to undo that which was accomplished during the freedom appointment. Parents should exercise prayerful discernment when choosing professional help for their children and should avoid self-help groups that view teens as merely products of their past rather than new creations in Christ.

5. Before closing the session in prayer, ask the young people you are counseling to read aloud the IN CHRIST list at the end of the Steps. Before you do, though, this would be an excellent time to explain the list you may have made while they were praying through their forgiveness list in Step Three.

During the forgiveness process, you may have written a list of words they used to describe the pain in their lives. They may have used terms such as "victim," "rejected," "unwanted" and so on to describe themselves, and those terms may have become labels of a false identity and self-perception.

Before reading through the IN CHRIST statements of truth, hand them the list of negative terms you compiled from their statements about themselves. You could call this list the "OLD ME" list. Then ask them to make the following renunciation, filling in the blanks with all the items on the "OLD ME" list:

> I renounce the lie that I am (a) (list the "OLD ME" items). Those items represent false labels of how I once viewed myself or how others viewed me. I now reject those lies and choose to believe only the truth about me as God sees me.

Then immediately move into reading through the IN CHRIST list. What a powerful contrast that will be, as teens—perhaps for the first time in their lives—understand how their powerful, all-wise, loving heavenly Father views them.

This can be a particularly moving time for teens who are adopted. Because of the God-ordained search for identity teens go through, the teenage years are often the time when adopted children long to meet their birth parents. How intense that yearning is varies from child to child.

Sometimes, however, the desire to be united with their birth parents is evidence of a misplaced identity on the part of adopted children.

Finding a New Identity

One of our staff members had a freedom appointment with a high-school-age young lady who was intent on finding her birth parents. It was obvious that her longing went beyond the natural curiosity any young person might feel in her situation. She was determined to meet her birth parents and make that connection or else!

> **We cannot overemphasize the liberating and life-transforming power of knowing and believing one's identity in Christ.**

As the appointment progressed, it became clear that her quest to find her real mom and dad was actually a search for identity. She had come to believe the lie that she could never know who she was until she met them. In her life she had always felt unwanted. Although she knew her adoptive parents loved her very much, she felt as though they only adopted her because they could not have any children of their own.

Somehow she had found ways to pay off government officials to gain access to privileged information about her real parents. Fortunately, she came to see that was not the right thing to do.

She renounced the lies that nobody wanted her and that she was a "nobody" until she found her birth parents. Next she chose to believe the truths of her new identity in Christ. Then she was able to relax. The drivenness was gone. She was able to rejoice that first and foremost she was a child of God, a part of His family and that she could call her heavenly Father "daddy."

She still had the desire to meet her birth parents, but it was no longer that all-consuming goal in her life. She would no longer be *driven* by insecurity; she could be *led* by the Spirit of God.

Aftercare Discipleship

We cannot overemphasize the liberating and life-transforming power of knowing and believing one's identity in Christ. This is true for all people, but is particularly powerful for adolescents who are searching for solid answers to the question "Who am I?"

Before you close the freedom appointment in prayer, have the counselees close their eyes and relax. Then ask them, "What's going on in your mind right now?"

This is often a deeply moving moment. You may hear comments such as: "It's peaceful, and the voices are gone," "It's quiet and I feel like my mind is my own," or "It's light, and I feel free."

Some will just feel tired, and that is perfectly all right. Chances are, later on their emotions will "kick in" and they will experience the joy of the Lord.

Many Christians have said that after going through the Steps to Freedom in Christ, they felt just as they did when they first received Christ. Could it be because they have returned to their first love? Naturally, a strong desire on the part of sincere followers of Christ will be to want to maintain that freedom. As happens with new believers, these renewed Christian teens need a place where they can be spiritually nurtured. We cannot overemphasize the value of a small-group discipleship experience to establish young people in truth and freedom.

Teenagers are normally gregarious, social creatures anyway who enjoy being part of a group. For many who have struggled with feelings of worthlessness and inadequacy, they may have always felt as if they were misfits who did not belong anywhere.

Properly conducted, small groups offer safe environments in which young people feel love and acceptance, receive nurture and encouragement, and can mature in their faith. The maturity of the leader, and the willingness of the participants to grow spiritually are key factors in the value of such a group.

Our ministry has prepared materials that can be used for youth groups of this kind.

The study guides for *Stomping Out the Darkness* and *The Bondage Breaker Youth Edition* offer a question-and-answer format in which each teen in the group has a workbook and comes to the small-group session ready to discuss the insights gained.

Busting Free is a curriculum guide for the youth leader of a small-group study, Sunday School class or youth group. This curriculum reviews the content of both *Stomping Out the Darkness* and *The Bondage Breaker Youth Edition* and can easily be used in a 13-week or 26-week format.

Because it is a leader's guide, only one copy of *Busting Free* is necessary. The book contains pages that can be duplicated and distributed to every member of the group. It is of optimum benefit, however, if each member has a copy of both *Stomping Out the Darkness* and *The Bondage Breaker Youth Edition*. Then the teens can read ahead each week and be better prepared for the discussion time.

The sheer magnitude of the needs of our Christian youth would overwhelm any single individual in the average church or community. If the Lord lays on your heart a desire to start a "freedom ministry" for youth, we encourage you to purchase Tom McGee and Neil's *Helping Others Find Freedom in Christ Training Manual & Study Guide*. An extensive section in that book shows how to develop such a church-based community ministry. It is drawn largely from the experiences of the Crystal Evangelical Free Church in the Minneapolis-St. Paul area, and will provide important principles and guidelines for an effective "freedom ministry" wherever you live.

Whether you are coming to understand your own freedom in Christ or seeking to help young people do likewise, know that ups and downs will always be a part of life. Proverbs 24:16 says, "For a righteous man falls seven times, and rises again." Falling is inevitable this side of heaven. The question is, Will you get up each time you fall?

The Race

We share the following poetic story as a conclusion to this book. This insightful work is just slightly adapted from Dee Groberg's *The Race*. May it help give you the strength to fight the good fight, finish the course and keep the faith, knowing that in the future there is laid up for you the crown of righteousness, which the Lord, the righteous Judge will award you (see 2 Tim. 4:7,8).

"Quit! Give up, you're beaten," they shout and plead,
"There's just too much against you now; this time you can't
   succeed."
And as I start to hang my head in front of failure's face,
My downward fall is broken by the memory of a race.
And hope refills my weakened will as I recall that scene,
For just the thought of that short race rejuvenates my being.
A children's race, young boys, young men; now I remember well.
Excitement, sure, but also fear; it wasn't hard to tell.
They all lined up so full of hope; each thought to win that race
Or tie for first, or if not that, at least take second place.
And fathers watched from off the side, each cheering for his son,
And each boy hoped to show his dad that he would be the one.
The whistle blew and off they went, young hearts and hopes of
   fire
To win, to be the hero there, was each young boy's desire.
And one boy in particular, his dad was in the crowd,
Was running near the lead and thought, "My dad will be so
   proud."
But as he speeded down the field across a shallow dip,
The little boy who thought to win, lost his step and slipped.
Trying hard to catch himself, his hands flew out to brace
And mid the laughter of the crowd, he fell flat on his face.
So down he fell and with him hope; he couldn't win it now.
Embarrassed, sad, he only wished to disappear somehow.
But as he fell his dad stood up and showed his anxious face,
Which to the boy so clearly said, "Get up and win that race!"
He quickly rose, no damage done, behind a bit that's all,

And ran with all his mind and might to make up for his fall.
So anxious to restore himself to catch up and to win,
His mind went faster than his legs, he slipped and fell again.
He wished that he had quit before with only one disgrace.
"I'm hopeless as a runner now, I shouldn't try to race."
But, in the laughing crowd he searched and found his father's
    face,
That steady look that said again, "Get up and win that race."
So, up he jumped to try again, ten yards behind the last.
"If I'm to gain those yards," he thought, "I've got to run real fast!"
Exceeding everything he had, he regained eight or ten,
But trying so hard to catch the lead, he slipped and fell...again.
Defeat!! He lay there silently, a tear dropped from his eye.
There's no sense running anymore, three strikes I'm out—Why
    try?
The will to rise has disappeared, all hope had fled away,
So far behind, so error prone, loser all the way.
"I've lost, so what's the use?" he thought, "I'll live with my
    disgrace."
But then he thought about his dad, who soon he'd have to face.
"Get up," an echo sounded low, "Get up and take your place.
You were not meant for failure here, get up and win the race."
With borrowed will, "Get up," he said, "You haven't lost at all,
For winning's nothing more than this—to rise each time you fall."
So up he rose to win once more, and with a new commit,
He resolved that win or lose, at least he wouldn't quit.
So far behind the others now, the most he'd ever been.
Still he gave it all he had and ran as though to win.
Three times he'd fallen stumbling, three times he'd rose again
Too far behind to hope to win, he still ran to the end.
They cheered the winning runner as he crossed, first place,
Head high and proud and happy; no falling, no disgrace.
But, when the fallen youngster crossed the line, last place,
The crowd gave him the greater cheer for finishing the race.
And even though he came in last, with head bowed low,
    unproud;
You would have thought he won the race, to listen to the crowd.

And to his dad he sadly said, "I didn't do so well."
"To me you won," his father said, "You rose each time you fell."
And now when things seem dark and hard and difficult to face.
The memory of that little boy helps me in my own race.
For all of life is like that race, with ups and downs and all,
And all you have to do to win is rise each time you fall.
"Quit! Give up, you're beaten" they still shout in my face
But another voice within me says, "Get up and win the race."

We have the joy and privilege of running the race together, not competing against one another, but locking arms and armor so that we can cross the finish line and win—*together*.

> Therefore, since we have so great a cloud of witnesses surrounding us, let us also lay aside every encumbrance, and the sin which so easily entangles us, and let us run with endurance the race that is set before us, fixing our eyes on Jesus, the author and perfecter of faith, who for the joy set before Him endured the cross, despising the shame, and has sat down at the right hand of the throne of God (Heb. 12:1,2).

footnotes

Introduction

1. "Adolescent Chemical Use," *Search Institute Source* II, no. 1 (January 1986): 1. (As cited in Walt Mueller's book *Understanding Today's Youth Culture*, p. 284).
2. L. D. Johnston, quoted by Lawrence Wallack and Kitty Corbett in "Illicit Drug, Tobacco, and Alcohol Use Among Youth: Trends and Promising Approaches in Prevention" in *Youth and Drugs: Society's Mixed Message*. (Rockville, Md.: Office for Substance Abuse Prevention, 1990), p. 7. (As cited in Mueller, p. 277.)
3. "More Teens Turning to Cigarettes, Drugs" *Los Angeles Times* (December 15, 1995).
4. "Drug Use Down, Suicide Up for High Achievers," *Group* (February 1989): 15. (As cited in Mueller, p. 301.)
5. Neil Anderson and Steve Russo, *The Seduction of Our Children* (Eugene, Oreg.: Harvest House Publishers, 1991), p. 35.
6. Ibid.

Chapter One

1. Walt Mueller, *Understanding Today's Youth Culture* (Wheaton, Ill.: Tyndale House Publishers, Inc., 1994), p. 15.
2. Les Parrott III, *Helping the Struggling Adolescent* (Grand Rapids: Zondervan Publishing House, 1993), p. 15.
3. Ibid.

Chapter Two

1. "What Parents Don't Know," *Parents & Teenagers* (February/March 1989): 2. (As cited in Mueller, p. 47.)

2. Robert Laurent, *Keeping Your Teen in Touch with God* (Colorado Springs: David C. Cook, 1988), p. 86. (As cited in Mueller, p. 188.)
3. Ibid. (As cited in Mueller, p. 189.)
4. "Keeping kids safe or scaring them to death?" *USA Today* (August 21, 1995).
5. Ibid.
6. Ibid.
7. Anderson and Russo, *The Seduction of Our Children*, p. 130.
8. Adapted from *Raising Healthy Teenagers*, a workshop for parents sponsored by Young Life, p. 9.
9. Ibid.
10. Fred Green, "What Parents Could Have Done" *Pulpit Helps* (November 1987): 19. (As cited in Mueller, p. 343.)
11. Anderson and Russo, *The Seduction of Our Children*, p. 171.
12. Adapted from *Raising Healthy Teenagers*, p. 29.

Chapter Four

1. *Spiritual Conflicts and Counseling Youth*, Freedom in Christ Youth Ministries seminar workbook, pp. 13, 14.

Chapter Seven

1. *Webster's New World Dictionary of the American Language, College Edition* (New York: World Publishing Company, 1968), p. 1232.
2. W. E. Vine, *Vine's Expository Dictionary of Old and New Testament Words, Reference Library Edition*, Vol. 3 (Iowa Falls, Iowa: World Bible Publishers, 1981), p. 279.

Appendices

Please Note: Permission to copy appendices A through G is granted for individual counseling and church use only.

Youth Edition of the Steps to Freedom in Christ

Preface

It is our deep belief that the finished work of Jesus Christ and the presence of God in our lives are the only means by which we can solve personal and spiritual problems. Christ in us is our only hope (see Col. 1:27) and He alone can meet our deepest needs of life—acceptance, identity, security and significance. These Steps are not based on just another counseling technique. They are an encounter with God. He is the Wonderful Counselor. He is the One who helps us see our sin, confess it and turn our backs on it. He grants this repentance that leads to a knowledge of the truth that sets us free (see 2 Tim. 2:24-26).

The Steps to Freedom in Christ do not set you free. *Who* sets you free is Christ, and *what* sets you free is your response to Him in repentance and faith. These steps are just a tool to help you submit to God and resist the devil (see Jas. 4:7). Then you can start living a fruitful life by recognizing who you are in Christ, spending time with Him and becoming the person He created you to be. Many Christians will be able to work through these steps on their own and discover the wonderful freedom that Christ purchased for them on the cross. Then they will experience the peace of God that surpasses all understanding, and it shall guard their hearts and their minds (see Phil. 4:7).

The chances of that happening and the possibility of maintaining that freedom will be greatly increased if you first read *Stomping Out the Darkness* and *The Bondage Breaker: Youth Edition*. Many Christians in our Western world need to understand the reality of the spiritual world and our relationship to it. Some can't read these books or even the Bible with understanding because of the battle that is going on for their minds. They may need the help of someone who has been trained to take them through the Steps to Freedom in Christ. The theological and practical process of taking others through the Steps to Freedom in Christ is explained in the book *Helping Others Find Freedom in Christ*, and the study guide that accompanies it.

It would be best if everyone had a pastor, youth pastor or counselor who would help them go through this process because it is simply applying the wisdom of James 5:16, "Therefore, confess your sins to one another, and pray for one another, so that you may be healed. The effective prayer of a righteous man can accomplish much." Another person can prayerfully support you.

Spiritual freedom is meant for every Christian, young or old. Being "free in Christ" is to have the desire and power to worship God and do His will. It is to know God's truth, believe God's truth and live according to God's truth. It is to walk with God in the power of the Holy Spirit and to experience a life of love, joy and peace. It is not a life of perfection, but progress! All these qualities may not be yours now, but they are meant for everyone who is in Christ.

If you have received Christ as your Savior, He has already set you free through His victory over sin and death on the cross. However, experiencing our freedom in Christ through repentance and faith, and maintaining our life of freedom in Christ are two different issues. It was for freedom that Christ set us free, but we have been warned not to return to a yoke of slavery that is legalism in this context (see Gal. 5:1) or to turn our freedom into an opportunity for the flesh (see Gal. 5:13). Establishing people free in Christ makes it possible for them to walk by faith according to what God says is true and live by the power of the Holy Spirit and not carry out the desires of the flesh (see Gal. 5:16). The true Christian life avoids both legalism and license. But if freedom is not a constant reality for you, it may be because you do not understand how Christ can help you deal with the pain of your past or the problems of your present life. As one who knows Christ, it is your responsibility to do whatever is needed to maintain a right relationship with God and others. Your eternal life is not at stake; you are safe and secure in Christ. But your daily victory is at stake if you fail to understand who you are in Christ and live according to that truth.

We have great news for you! You are not a helpless victim caught between two nearly equal but opposite heavenly superpowers, God and Satan. Only God is all-powerful, always present and all-knowing. Sometimes, however, the presence and power of sin and evil in our lives can seem more real to us than the presence and power of God. But that is part of Satan's tricky lie. Satan is a deceiver, and he wants you to think he is stronger than he really is. But he is also a defeated enemy, and you are in Christ, the victor. Understanding who God is and who you are in Christ are the two most important factors in determining your daily victory over sin and Satan. The greatest causes of spiritual defeat are false beliefs about God, not understanding who you are as a child of God, and making Satan out to be as powerful and present as God is.

The battle is for your mind. You may experience nagging thoughts such as *this isn't going to work* or *God doesn't love me*. These thoughts are lies, implanted in your mind by deceiving spirits. If you believe them, you will really struggle as you work through these Steps. These opposing thoughts can control you only if you believe them.

If you are working through these Steps by yourself, don't pay attention to any lying or threatening thoughts in your mind. If you are working through the Steps with a youth pastor, pastor or counselor (which we strongly recommend), then share any opposing thoughts with that person. Whenever you uncover a lie and choose to believe the truth, the power of Satan is broken.

You must cooperate with the person who is trying to help you. Do this by sharing what is going on inside your mind. If you experience any physical discomfort (e.g., headache, nausea, tightness in the throat, etc.), don't be alarmed. Just tell the person you are with so he or she can pray for you.

As believers in Christ, we can pray with authority to stop any interference by Satan. The following prayer and declaration will get you started. All prayers and declarations throughout the Steps should be read out loud.

Prayer

Dear heavenly Father,

We know that You are always here and present in our lives. You are the only all-knowing, all-powerful, ever-present God. We desperately need You, because without Jesus we can do nothing. We believe the Bible because it tells us what is really true. We refuse to believe the lies of Satan. We stand in the truth that all authority in heaven and on earth has been given to the resurrected Christ. Because we are in Christ, we share His authority in order to make followers of Jesus and set captives free. We ask You to protect our thoughts and minds and lead us into all truth. We choose to submit to the Holy Spirit. Please reveal to our minds everything You want to deal with today. We ask for and trust in Your wisdom. We pray for Your complete protection over us. In Jesus' name. Amen.

Declaration

In the name and the authority of the Lord Jesus Christ, we command Satan and all evil spirits to let go of (name) in order that (name) can be free to know and choose to do the will of God. As children of God, seated with Christ in the heavenlies, we agree that every enemy of the Lord Jesus Christ be bound to silence. We say to Satan and all of his evil workers that you cannot inflict any pain or in any way stop or hinder God's will from being done today in (name)'s life.

The following seven Steps are designed to help you be free from your past. You will cover the areas where Satan most often takes advantage of us and where strongholds have been built. Christ purchased your victory when He shed His blood for you on the cross. You will experience your freedom when you make the choice to believe, confess, forgive, renounce and forsake. No one can do that for you. The battle for your mind can only be won as you personally choose truth.

As you go through these Steps to Freedom in Christ, remember that Satan cannot read your mind, thus he won't obey your thoughts. Only God knows what you are thinking. As you go through each Step, it is important that you submit to God inwardly and resist the devil by reading out loud each prayer—verbally renouncing, forgiving, confessing, etc.

You are going to be taking a thorough look at your life in order to get radically right with God. If it turns out that you have another kind of problem (not covered in these Steps) that is negatively affecting your life, you will have lost nothing. If you are open and honest during this time, you will greatly benefit anyway by becoming right with God and close to Him again.

May the Lord greatly touch your life during this time. He will give you the strength to make it through. It is essential that you work through *all* seven Steps, so don't allow yourself to become discouraged and give up. Remember, the freedom that Christ purchased for all believers on the cross is meant for you!

Step 1
Counterfeit Versus Real

The first Step toward experiencing your freedom in Christ is to renounce (to reject and turn your back on all past, present and future involvement with) any participation in satanic-inspired occult practices, things done in secret and non-Christian religions. You must renounce any activity or group that denies Jesus Christ, offers directions through any source other than the absolute authority of the written Word of God, or requires secret initiations, ceremonies, promises or pacts (covenants). Begin with the following prayer:

> Dear heavenly Father,
> I ask You to guard my heart and my mind and to reveal to me anything I have done or anyone has done to me that is spiritually wrong. Reveal to my mind any and all involvement I have knowingly or unknowingly had with cult or occult practices, and/or false teachers. I ask this in Jesus' name. Amen.

Even if you took part in something as a game or as a joke, you need to renounce it. Satan will try to take advantage of anything he can in our lives. Even if you just stood by and watched others do it, you need to renounce it. Even if you did it just once and had no idea it was evil, still you need to renounce it. You want to remove any and every possible foothold of Satan in your life.

Non-Christian Spiritual Experiences Checklist

(Please check all those that apply to you.)

☐ Out of body experience
(astral projection)

☐ Bloody Mary

☐ Table lifting or body lifting
(light as a feather)

☐ Magic Eight Ball

☐ Using spells or curses

☐ Mental control of others

☐ Automatic writing

☐ Spirit guide(s)

☐ Fortune-telling

☐ Tarot cards

☐ Palm reading/tea leaves

☐ Astrology/horoscopes

☐ Hypnosis

☐ Seances

☐ Black or white magic
(Dungeons and Dragons or other
fantasy role-playing games such as
"Magic," etc.)

☐ Video or computer games involving
occult powers or cruel violence

☐ Blood pacts or cutting yourself on
purpose

☐ Objects of worship/good luck
charms

☐ Superstitions

☐ Sexual spirits

☐ Mormonism (Latter-Day Saints)

☐ New Age

☐ New Age medicine (use of crystals)

☐ Masons

☐ Christian Science

☐ Science of the Mind

☐ Science of Creative Intelligence

☐ The Way International

☐ Unification Church (Moonies)

☐ The Forum (EST)

☐ Church of the Living Word

☐ Children of God (Children of Love)

☐ Scientology

☐ Unitarianism

☐ Roy Masters

☐ Silva Mind Control

☐ Transcendental Meditation (TM)

☐ Yoga

☐ Chants/Mantras

☐ Hare Krishna

☐ Bahaism

☐ Spirit worship

☐ Idols: rock stars, actors/actresses,
sports heroes, etc.

☐ Islam

☐ Muslim/Black Muslim

☐ Martial Arts (involving Eastern
mysticism, meditation or devotion
to sensei)

☐ Buddhism (including Zen)

☐ Rosicrucianism

☐ Hinduism

☐ Other_____
_____

(Note: This is not a complete list. If you have any doubts about an activity not included here, renounce your involvement in it. If it has come to mind here, trust that the Lord wants you to renounce it.)

(List those that especially glorified Satan, caused fear or nightmares, or were gruesomely violent.)

Anti-Christian Movies	Anti-Christian Music
_____	_____
_____	_____

Anti-Christian TV Shows or Video Games	Anti-Christian Books, Magazines and Comics
_____	_____
_____	_____

1. Have you ever heard or seen or felt an evil spiritual being in your room?
2. Do you or have you had an imaginary friend, spirit guide or angel offering you guidance and companionship?
3. Have you ever heard voices in your head or had repeating negative, nagging thoughts such as _I'm dumb, I'm ugly, Nobody loves me, I can't do anything right,_ etc. as if a conversation were going on in your head? Explain.
4. Have you ever consulted a medium, spiritist or channeler?
5. What other spiritual experiences have you had that would be considered out of the ordinary (contact with aliens, etc.)?
6. Have you ever been involved in satanic worship of any kind or attended a concert where Satan was the focus?
7. Have you ever made a vow or pact?

Once you have completed the checklist, confess and renounce each item you were involved in by praying aloud the following prayer (repeat the prayer separately for each item on your list):

> Lord, I confess that I have participated in _____. I renounce any and all influence and involvement with_____, and thank You that in Christ I am forgiven.

If you have been involved in any satanic ritual or heavy occult activity, you need to say aloud the following special renunciations and affirmations. Read across the page, renouncing the first item in the column under Kingdom of Darkness, and then affirming the first truth in the column under Kingdom of Light. Continue down the entire list in that manner.

Kingdom of Darkness	Kingdom of Light
1. I renounce ever signing my name over to Satan or having my name signed over to Satan by someone else.	1. I announce that my name is now written in the Lamb's Book of Life.
2. I renounce any ceremony where I was wed to Satan.	2. I announce that I am the Bride of Christ.
3. I renounce any and all covenants, agreements or promises that I made with Satan.	3. I announce that I am in a new covenant with Jesus Christ alone.
4. I renounce all satanic assignments for my life, including duties, marriage and children.	4. I announce and commit myself to know and do only the will of God and I accept only His guidance for my life.
5. I renounce all spirit guides assigned to me.	5. I announce and accept only the leading of the Holy Spirit.
6. I renounce ever giving of my blood in the service of Satan.	6. I trust only in the shed blood of my Lord Jesus Christ.
7. I renounce ever eating flesh or drinking blood in satanic worship.	7. By faith I partake in Communion that represents the flesh and the blood of the Lord Jesus.
8. I renounce all guardians and satanist parents that were assigned to me.	8. I announce that God is my heavenly Father and the Holy Spirit is my guardian by whom I am sealed.
9. I renounce any baptism whereby I am identified with Satan.	9. I announce that I have been baptized into Christ Jesus and my identity is now in Him.
10. I renounce every sacrifice made on my behalf by which Satan may claim ownership of me.	10. I announce that only the sacrifice of Christ has any claim on me. I belong to Him. I have been purchased by the blood of the Lamb.

All satanic rituals, covenants (promises) and assignments must be specifically renounced as the Lord brings them to your mind. Some people who have been subjected to Satanic Ritual Abuse (SRA) develop multiple personalities (alters) to cope with their pain. In this case, you need someone who understands spiritual conflicts to help you maintain control and not be deceived into false memories. You can continue to walk through these Steps to Freedom in Christ to resolve all that you are aware of. Only Jesus can bind up the brokenhearted, set captives free and make us whole.

Step 2
Deception Versus Truth

God's Word is true, and we need to accept the truth deep in our hearts (see Ps. 51:6). What God says is true whether we feel it is true or not! Jesus is the truth (see John 14:6), the Holy Spirit is the Spirit of truth (see John 16:13) and the Word of God is truth (see John 17:11). We ought to speak the truth in love (see Eph. 4:15). The believer in Christ has no business deceiving others in any way, whether by lying, exaggerating, telling little lies or stretching the truth. Satan is the father of lies (see John 8:44) and he seeks to keep people in bondage through deception (see 2 Tim. 2:26; Rev. 12:9), but it is the truth in Jesus that sets us free (see John 8:32-36).

We will find real joy and freedom when we stop living a lie and walk openly in the truth. King David wrote, after confessing his sin, "How blessed is the man...in whose spirit there is no deceit" (Ps. 32:2).

How can we find the strength to walk in the light (see 1 John 1:7-9)? When we are sure God loves and accepts us, we can be free to own up to our sin, face reality and not run or hide from painful circumstances.

Start this step by praying the following prayer out loud. Don't let any opposing thoughts, such as *This is a waste of time* or *I wish I could believe this stuff but I just can't*, keep you from praying and choosing the truth. Belief is a choice. If you choose to believe what you feel, then Satan, the "father of lies," will keep you in bondage. We must choose to believe what God says, regardless of what our feelings might say. Even if you have a hard time doing so, pray the following prayer:

> Dear heavenly Father,
> I know You want me to face the truth, being honest with You. I know that choosing to believe the truth will set me free. I have been deceived by Satan and I have deceived myself. I thought I could hide from You, but You see everything and still love me. I pray in the name of the Lord Jesus Christ, asking You to rebuke all of Satan's demons that are deceiving me. By faith I have received You into my life and I am now seated

with Christ in the heavenlies (Eph. 2:6). I acknowledge that I have the responsibility to submit to you and the authority to resist the devil, and when I do, he will flee from me (Jas. 4:7).

I have trusted Jesus alone to save me, so I am your forgiven child. Because You accept me just as I am in Christ, I can be free to face my sin. I ask for the Holy Spirit to guide me into all truth. I ask You to "Search me, O God, and know my heart; try me and know my anxious thoughts; and see if there be any hurtful way in me, and lead me in the everlasting way" (Ps. 139:23,24). In the name of Jesus, I pray. Amen.

Satan, "the god of this world" (2 Cor. 4:4), seeks to deceive us in many ways. Just as he did with Eve, so the devil tries to convince us to rely on ourselves and to try to get our needs met through the world around us, rather than trusting in the provision of our Father in heaven.

Ways you can be deceived by the world:

△ Believing that accumulating money and possessions will bring happiness (see Matt. 13:22; 1 Tim. 6:10).

△ Believing that eating food and drinking alcohol without restraint will make me happy (see Prov. 20:1; 23:19-21).

△ Believing that a sexy, attractive body and personality will get me what I want or need (see Prov. 31:10; 1 Pet. 3:3,4).

△ Believing that gratifying sexual lust will bring true fulfillment (see Eph. 4:22; 1 Pet. 2:11).

△ Believing that I can sin and get away with it and not have it affect my heart and character (see Heb. 3:12,13).

△ Believing that my needs cannot be totally taken care of by God (see 2 Cor. 11:2-4,13-15).

△ Believing that I am important and strong and I can do whatever I want and no one can touch me! (see Prov. 16:18; Obad. 1:3; 1 Pet. 5:5).

Use the following prayer of confession for each item on the previous list that you have believed. Pray through each item separately.

> Lord, I confess that I have been deceived by
> _____. I thank You for Your forgiveness and
> I commit myself to only believing Your truth. Amen.

It is important to know that in addition to being deceived by the world, false teachers and deceiving spirits, you can also fool yourself. Now that you are alive in Christ, forgiven and totally accepted, you don't need to live a lie or defend yourself the way you used to. Christ is now your truth and defense.

Ways you can deceive yourself:

- ☐ Hearing God's Word but not doing it (see Jas. 1:22; 4:7).
- ☐ Saying I have no sin (see 1 John 1:8).
- ☐ Thinking I am something I'm not (see Gal. 6:3).
- ☐ Thinking I am wise in the things of the world (see 1 Cor. 3:18,19).
- ☐ Thinking I can be a good Christian and still hurt others by what I say (see Jas. 1:22).
- ☐ Thinking my secret sin will only hurt me but will not hurt others (such as pornography, voyeurism, hatred) (see Exod. 20:4,5).

Use the following prayer of confession for each item on the previous list that you have believed. Pray through each item separately.

> Lord, I confess that I have deceived myself by
> _____. I thank You for Your forgiveness and
> commit myself to believing Your truth.

Wrong ways of defending yourself:

- ☐ Refusing to face the bad things that have happened to me (denial of reality).

☐ Escaping from the real world by daydreaming, TV, movies, computer or video games, music, etc. (fantasy).
☐ Withdrawing from people to avoid rejection (emotional insulation).
☐ Reverting (going back) to a less threatening time of life (regression).
☐ Taking out frustrations on others (displaced anger).
☐ Blaming others for my problems (projection).
☐ Making excuses for poor behavior (rationalization).

Use the following prayer of confession for each item on the previous list in which you have participated. Pray through each item separately.

> Lord, I confess that I have defended myself wrongly by
> _____. I thank You for Your forgiveness and commit myself to trusting in You to defend and protect me.

Sometimes we are greatly hindered from walking by faith in our Father God because of lies we have believed about Him. We are to have a healthy fear of God (awe of His holiness, power and presence), but we are not to be afraid of Him. Romans 8:15 says, "For you have not received a spirit of slavery leading to fear again, but you have received a spirit of adoption as sons by which we cry out, 'Abba! Father!'" The following exercise will help break the chains of those lies and enable you to begin to experience that intimate "Abba, Father" relationship with Him.

Work your way down the following list, one by one, left to right. Begin each one with the statement at the top of that list. Read through the list aloud.

I renounce the lie that my heavenly Father is...
1. distant or disinterested.
2. insensitive or uncaring.
3. stern or demanding.
4. passive or cold.
5. absent or too busy for me.

6. never satisfied with what I do, impatient or angry.
7. mean, cruel or abusive.
8. trying to take all the fun out of life.
9. controlling or manipulative.
10. condemning or unforgiving.
11. nit-picking, nagging or perfectionistic.

I accept the truth that my heavenly Father is...
1. intimate and involved (Psalm 139:1-18).
2. kind and compassionate (Psalm 103:8-14).
3. accepting and filled with joy and love (Zephaniah 3:17; Romans 15:7).
4. warm and affectionate (Isaiah 40:11; Hosea 11:3,4).
5. always with me and eager to spend time with me (Jeremiah 31:20; Ezekiel 34:11-16; Hebrews 13:5).
6. patient, slow to anger and pleased with me in Christ (Exodus 34:6; 2 Peter 3:9).
7. loving, gentle and protective of me (Psalm 18:2; Isaiah 42:3; Jeremiah 31:3).
8. trustworthy. He wants to give me a full life. His will is good, perfect and acceptable for me (Lamentations 3:22,23; John 10:10; Romans 12:1,2).
9. full of grace and mercy, and He gives me freedom to fail (Luke 15:11-16; Hebrews 4:15,16).
10. tenderhearted and forgiving. His heart and arms are always open to me (Psalm 130:1-4; Luke 15:17-24).
11. committed to my growth and proud of me as His growing child (Romans 8:28,29; 2 Corinthians 7:4; Hebrews 12:5-11).

A central part of walking in the truth and rejecting deception is to deal with the fears that plague our lives. First Peter 5:8 says that our enemy, the devil, prowls around like a roaring lion, seeking people to devour. Just as a lion's roar strikes terror into the hearts of those who hear it, so Satan uses fear to try to paralyze Christians. His intimidation tactics are designed to rob us of faith in God and drive us to try to get our needs met through the world or the flesh.

Fear weakens us, causes us to be self-centered and clouds our minds so that all we can think about is the thing that frightens us. But fear can only control us if we let it.

God, however, does not want us to be mastered by anything, including fear (see 1 Cor. 6:12). Jesus Christ is to be our only Master (see John 13:13; 2 Tim. 2:21). In order to begin to experience freedom from the bondage of fear and to be able to walk by faith in God, pray the following prayer from your heart:

> Dear heavenly Father,
>
> I confess to You that I have listened to the devil's roar and have allowed fear to master me. I have not always walked by faith in You, but instead have focused on my feelings and circumstances (2 Cor. 4:16-18; 5:7). I thank You for forgiving me for my unbelief.
>
> Right now I renounce the spirit of fear and affirm the truth that You have not given me a spirit of fear but of power, love and a sound mind (2 Tim. 1:7).
>
> Lord, please reveal to my mind now all the fears that have been controlling me so that I can renounce them and be free to walk by faith in You.
>
> I thank You for the freedom You give me to walk by faith and not by fear. In Jesus' powerful name, I pray. Amen.

The following list may help you recognize some of the fears the devil has used to keep you from walking by faith. Check the ones that apply to your life. Write down any others the Spirit of God brings to your mind. Then, one by one, renounce those fears aloud, using the suggested renunciation following the list.

- ☐ Fear of death
- ☐ Fear of Satan
- ☐ Fear of failure
- ☐ Fear of rejection by people
- ☐ Fear of disapproval
- ☐ Fear of financial problems

- ☐ Fear of never getting married
- ☐ Fear of becoming homosexual
- ☐ Fear of the death of a loved one
- ☐ Fear of being a hopeless case
- ☐ Fear of losing my salvation
- ☐ Fear of having committed the unpardonable sin
- ☐ Fear of not being loved by God
- ☐ Fear of never being able to love or be loved by anyone
- ☐ Fear of embarrassment
- ☐ Fear of being victimized
- ☐ Fear of marriage
- ☐ Fear of divorce
- ☐ Fear of going crazy
- ☐ Fear of pain
- ☐ Other specific fears that come to mind now

> I renounce the fear of (name of the fear) because God has not given me a spirit of fear. I choose to live by faith in God, who has promised to protect me and meet all my needs as I walk by faith in Him (Ps. 27:1; Matt. 6:33,34).

After you have finished renouncing all the specific fears you have allowed to control you, pray the following prayer from your heart:

> Dear heavenly Father,
> I thank You that You are trustworthy. I choose to believe You, even when my feelings and circumstances tell me to fear. You have told me not to fear, for You are with me; not to anxiously look about me, for You are my God. You will strengthen me, help me and surely uphold me with Your righteous right hand (Isa. 41:10). I pray this with faith in the name of Jesus, my Master. Amen.

Choosing the truth may be difficult if you have been living a lie and have been deceived for some time. The Christian needs only one defense, Jesus. Knowing that you are completely forgiven and accepted as God's child sets you free to face reality and declare your total dependence upon Him.

Faith is the biblical response to the truth, and believing the truth is a choice we can all make. If you say, "I want to believe God, but I just can't," you are being deceived. Of course you can believe God because what God says is always true!

Faith is something you decide to do, whether or not you feel like doing it. Believing the truth doesn't make it true, however. **It's true; therefore, we believe it.**

The New Age movement twists the truth by saying we create reality through what we believe. We can't create reality with our minds. We face reality with our minds. Simply "having faith" is not the key issue here. It's what or who you believe in that makes the difference. You see, everybody believes in something and everybody lives according to what he or she believes. The question is: Is the object of your faith trustworthy? If what you believe is not true, then how you live will not be right.

For centuries, Christians have known that it is important to tell others what they believe. Read aloud the following Statement of Truth, thinking about the words as you read them. Read it every day for several weeks. This will help you renew your mind and replace with the truth any lies you have believed.

Statement of Truth

1. I believe there is only one true and living God (Exod. 20:2,3) who is the Father, Son and Holy Spirit. He is worthy of all honor, praise and glory. I believe that He made all things and holds all things together (Col. 1:16,17).

2. I recognize Jesus Christ as the Messiah, the Word who became flesh and lived with us (John 1:1,14). I believe He came to destroy the works of Satan (1 John 3:8), that He disarmed the rulers and authorities and made a public display of them, having triumphed over them (Col. 2:15).

3. I believe that God showed His love for me by having Jesus die for me, even though I was sinful (Rom. 5:8). I believe that God rescued me from the dark power of Satan and brought me into the kingdom of His Son, who forgives my sins and sets me free (Col. 1:13,14).

4. I believe I am spiritually strong because Jesus is my strength. I have authority to stand against Satan because I am God's child (1 John 3:1-3). I believe that I was saved by the grace of God through faith, that it was a gift and not the result of any works of mine (Eph. 2:8,9).

5. I choose to be strong in the Lord and in the strength of His might (Eph. 6:10). I put no confidence in the flesh (Phil. 3:3) because my weapons of spiritual battle are not of the flesh, but are powerful through God for tearing down Satan's strongholds (2 Cor. 10:4). I put on the whole armor of God (Eph. 6:10-20), and I resolve to stand firm in my faith and resist the evil one (1 Pet. 5:8,9).

6. I believe that apart from Christ I can do nothing (John 15:5), yet I can do all things through Him who strengthens me (Phil. 4:13). Therefore, I choose to rely totally on Christ. I choose to abide in Christ in order to bear much fruit and glorify the Lord (John 15:8). I announce to Satan that Jesus is my Lord (1 Cor. 12:3), and I reject any counterfeit gifts or works of Satan in my life.

7. I believe that the truth will set me free (John 8:32). I stand against Satan's lies by taking every thought captive in obedience to Christ (2 Cor. 10:5). I believe that the Bible is the only reliable guide for my life (2 Tim. 3:15,16). I choose to speak the truth in love (Eph. 4:15).

8. I choose to present my body as an instrument of righteousness, a living and holy sacrifice, and to renew my mind with God's Word (Rom. 6:13; 12:1,2). I put off the old self with its evil practices and put on the new self (Col. 3:9,10). I am a new creation in Christ (2 Cor. 5:17).

9. I trust my heavenly Father to direct my life and give me power to live by the Holy Spirit (Eph. 5:18), so that He

can guide me into all truth (John 16:13). I believe He will give me strength to live above sin and not carry out the desires of my flesh. I crucify the flesh, choose to be led by the Holy Spirit and obey Him (Gal. 5:16,24).

10. I renounce all selfish goals and choose the greatest goal of love (1 Tim. 1:5). I choose to obey the two greatest commandments to love the Lord my God with all my heart, soul and mind and to love my neighbor as myself (Matt. 22:37-39).

11. I believe that Jesus has all authority in heaven and on earth (Matt. 28:18) and that He rules over everything (Col. 2:10). I believe that Satan and his demons have been defeated by Christ and are subject to me because I am a member of Christ's Body (Eph. 1:19,20; 2:6). So I obey the command to submit to God and to resist the devil (Jas. 4:7) and I command Satan, by the power and authority of the Lord Jesus Christ, to leave my presence.

Step 3
Bitterness Versus Forgiveness

When you fail to forgive those who hurt you, you become a wide-open target for Satan. God commands us to forgive others as we have been forgiven (see Eph. 4:32). You need to obey this command so that Satan can't take advantage of you (see 2 Cor. 2:10,11). Christians are to forgive others and show them mercy because our heavenly Father has shown mercy to us (see Luke 6:36). Ask God to bring to your mind the names of those people you need to forgive by praying the following prayer out loud. (Remember to let this prayer come from your heart as well as your mouth!)

> Dear heavenly Father,
> I thank You for Your great kindness and patience, which has led me to turn from my sins (Rom. 2:4). I know I have not always been completely kind, patient and loving toward those who have hurt me. I have had bad thoughts and feelings toward them. I ask You to bring to my mind all the people I need to forgive (Matt. 18:35). I ask You to bring to the surface all my painful memories so I can choose to forgive these people from my heart. I pray this in the precious name of Jesus who has forgiven me and who will heal me from my hurts. Amen.

On a sheet of paper, make a list of the people who come to your mind. At this point, don't question whether you need to forgive a certain person or not. If a name comes to your mind, write it down.

Finally, write "myself" at the bottom of the list. Forgiving yourself means accepting God's cleansing and forgiveness. Also write "thoughts against God." We sometimes harbor angry thoughts toward God.

We can expect or even demand that He act in a certain way in our lives and when He doesn't do what we want in the way we want, we can get angry. Those feelings can become a wall between us and God, and even though we don't actually need to forgive

Him, because He is perfect, we do need to let those feelings go.

Before you begin working through the process of forgiving the people on your list, stop and consider what real forgiveness is and what it is not.

Forgiveness is not forgetting. People who want to forget all their pain before they get around to forgiving someone usually find they cannot. God commands us to forgive now. Confusion sometimes arises because Scripture says that God "will remember [our sins] no more" (see Heb. 10:17). But God knows everything and can't "forget" as if He had no memory of our sin. His promise is that He will never use our past against us (see Ps. 103:10). The key issue is this: We may not be able to forget our past, but we can be free from it by forgiving others. When we bring up the past and use it against others, we are showing that we have not yet forgiven them (see Mark 11:25).

Forgiveness is a choice, a decision of the will. Because God requires us to forgive, it is something we can do. Forgiveness seems hard because it pulls against our sense of what is right and fair. We naturally want revenge for the things we have suffered. But we are told by God never to take our own revenge (see Rom. 12:19). You might be thinking, *Why should I let them off the hook?* And that is exactly the problem! As long as you do not forgive, you are still hooked to those who hurt you! You are still chained to your past. **By forgiving, you let them off your hook, but they are not off God's hook.** We must trust Him to deal with the other person justly, fairly and mercifully, something we cannot do.

You say, "But you don't understand how much this person hurt me!" But until you let go of your hate and anger, they will continue to be able to hurt you. You finally stop the pain by forgiving them. **You forgive for your sake, so that you can be free. Forgiveness is mainly an issue of obedience between you and God. God wants you to be free; this is the only way.**

Forgiveness is agreeing to live with the consequences of another person's sin. Forgiveness costs you something. You choose to pay the price for the evil you forgive. **But you will live with the consequences whether you want to or not. Your only choice is whether you will do so in the bondage of bitterness or in the freedom of forgiveness.**

Of course, Jesus took the eternal consequences of all sin upon Himself. "God made Him who had no sin to be sin for us, so that in Him we might become the righteousness of God" (2 Cor. 5:21, *NIV*). We need, however, to accept the temporary consequences of what was done to us. But no one truly forgives without suffering the pain of another's sin. That can seem unfair and we wonder, *where is the justice?* It is found at the Cross, which makes forgiveness legally and morally right. As those who crucified Jesus mocked and jeered, Jesus prayed, "Father, forgive them, for they do not know what they are doing" (Luke 23:34).

How do you forgive from your heart? You allow God to bring to the surface the mental agony, emotional pain and feelings of hate toward those who hurt you. If your forgiveness does not reach down to the emotional core of your life, it will be incomplete. Too often we try to bury the pain inside us, making it hard to get in touch with how we really feel. Though we may not know how to or even want to bring our feelings to the surface, God does. Let God bring the pain to the surface so He can deal with it. This is where God's gentle healing process begins.

Forgiveness is the decision not to use their offense against them. It is not unusual for us to remember a past, hurtful event and find the anger and hate we felt returning. It is tempting to bring up the issue with those who hurt us in order to make them feel bad. But we must choose to take that thought of revenge captive to the obedience of Christ, and choose to maintain forgiveness.

This doesn't mean you must continue to put up with the future sins of others. God does not tolerate sin and neither should you. Nor should you put yourself in the position of being continually abused and hurt by the sins of others. You need to take a stand against sin while continuing to forgive those who hurt you.

Don't wait to forgive until you feel like forgiving. You will never get there. Your emotions will begin to heal once you have obeyed God's command to forgive. Satan will have lost his power over you in that area and God's healing touch will take over. **For now, freedom will be gained, not necessarily a feeling.**

As you pray, God may bring to mind painful memories you had totally forgotten. Let Him do this, even if it hurts. God wants you to be free; forgiving these people is the only way. Don't try to excuse the offender's behavior, even if it is someone close to you.

Remember, forgiveness is dealing with your own pain and leaving the other person to deal with God. Good feelings will follow in time. Freeing yourself from the past is the critical issue right now.

Don't say, "Lord, please help me to forgive." He is already helping you and will be with you all the way through the process. Don't say, "Lord, I want to forgive," because that bypasses the hard choice we have to make. Say, "Lord, I forgive." As you move down your list, stay with each individual until you are sure you have dealt with all the remembered pain, everything the person did that hurt you and how it made you feel (rejected, unloved, unworthy, dirty, etc.). It's time to begin. For each person on your list, pray aloud:

Start:

> Lord, I forgive (name the person) for (say what they did to hurt you) even though it made me feel (share the painful memories or feelings).

Once you have dealt with every offense that has come to your mind and you have honestly expressed how that person hurt you, conclude by praying:

Finish:

> Lord, I choose not to hold any of these things against (name) any longer. I thank You for setting me free from the bondage of my bitterness toward them. I choose now to ask You to bless (name). In Jesus' name. Amen.

Step 4
Rebellion Versus Submission

We live in rebellious times. Often young people today don't respect people that God has placed in authority over them. You may have a problem living in submission to authority. You can easily be deceived into thinking that those in authority over you are robbing you of your freedom. In reality, however, God has placed them there for your protection.

Rebelling against God and His authorities is serious business. It gives Satan an opportunity to attack you. Submission is the only solution. God requires more of you, however, than just the outward appearance of submission. He wants you to sincerely submit to your authorities (especially parents) from the heart. Your commanding general, the Lord Jesus Christ, is telling you to "get into ranks and follow Me!" He promises that He will not lead you into temptation, but will deliver you from evil (see Matt. 6:13).

The Bible makes it clear that we have two main responsibilities toward those in authority over us: to pray for them and to submit to them. Pray the following prayer out loud from your heart:

> Dear heavenly Father,
>
> You have said in the Bible that rebellion is the same thing as witchcraft, and being self-willed is like serving false gods (1 Sam. 15:23). I know that I have disobeyed and rebelled in my heart against You and those You have placed in authority over me. I thank You for Your forgiveness for my rebellion. By the shed blood of the Lord Jesus Christ, I pray that all doors that I opened to evil spirits through my rebellion would now be closed. I pray that You will show me all the ways I have been rebellious. I now choose to adopt a submissive spirit and servant's heart. In Jesus' precious name, I pray. Amen.

Being under authority is an act of faith! By submitting, we are trusting God to work through His lines of authority.

At times parents, teachers, employers and others may abuse their authority and break the laws that are ordained by God for the protection of innocent people. In those cases, you need to seek help from a *higher authority* for your protection. The laws in your state may require you to report such abuse to the police or other protective agencies. If there is continuing abuse (physical, mental, emotional or sexual), at home or anywhere else, counseling may be needed to change the situation. If someone abuses their authority by asking you to break God's law or compromise yourself, you need to obey God rather than man (see Acts 4:19,20).

We are told to submit to one another as equals in Christ (see Eph. 5:21). In addition, however, God uses specific lines of authority to protect us and give order to our daily lives.

- ☐ Civil government (i.e., traffic laws, drinking laws, etc.) (see Rom. 13:1-7; 1 Tim. 2:1-4; 1 Pet. 2:13-17).
- ☐ Parents, stepparents or legal guardians (see Eph. 6:1-3).
- ☐ Teachers, coaches and school officials (see Rom. 13:1-4).
- ☐ Your boss (see 1 Pet. 2:18-23).
- ☐ Husband (see 1 Pet. 3:1-4) or wife (see Eph. 5:21; 1 Pet. 3:7).
- ☐ Church leaders (pastor, youth pastor, Sunday School teacher (see Heb. 13:17).
- ☐ God Himself (see Dan. 9:5,9).

Examine each of the seven areas of authority listed and confess to the Lord those times you have not respected these positions or submitted to them, by praying:

> Lord, I agree with You that I have been rebellious toward _____. Thank You for forgiving my rebellion. I choose to be submissive and obedient to your Word. In Jesus' name. Amen.

Step 5
Pride Versus Humility

Pride is a killer. Pride says, "I can do it! I can get myself out of this mess without God or anyone else's help." Oh no we can't! We absolutely need God and we desperately need each other. Paul wrote: "We worship in the Spirit of God and glory in Christ Jesus and put no confidence in the flesh" (Phil. 3:3).

Humility is confidence properly placed in God. We are to be "strong in the Lord and in the strength of His might" (Eph. 6:10). James 4:6-10 and 1 Peter 5:1-10 tell us that spiritual problems will follow when we are proud. Use the following prayer to express your commitment to live humbly before God:

> Dear heavenly Father,
> You have said that pride goes before destruction and an arrogant spirit before stumbling (Prov. 16:18). I confess that I have been thinking mainly of myself and not of others. I have not denied myself, picked up my cross daily and followed You (Matt. 16:24). And as a result, I have given ground to the enemy in my life. I have believed that I could be successful by living according to my own power and resources.
> I now confess that I have sinned against You by placing my will before Yours and by centering my life around myself instead of You. I renounce my pride and my selfishness and close any doors I've opened in my life or physical body to the enemies of the Lord Jesus Christ. I choose to rely on the Holy Spirit's power and guidance so that I can do Your will.
> I give my heart to You and stand against all of Satan's attacks. I ask You to show me how to live for others. I now choose to make others more important than me and to make You the most important Person of all in my life (Matt. 6:33; Rom. 12:10). Please show me specifically now the ways in which I have lived pridefully. I ask this in the name of my Lord Jesus Christ. Amen.

Having made that commitment in prayer, now allow God to show you any specific areas of your life where you have been prideful, such as:

- ☐ I have a stronger desire to do my will than God's will.
- ☐ I rely on my own strengths and abilities rather than on God's.
- ☐ I too often think my ideas are better than other people's ideas.
- ☐ I want to control how others act rather than develop self-control.
- ☐ I sometimes consider myself more important than others.
- ☐ I have a tendency to think I don't need other people.
- ☐ I find it difficult to admit when I am wrong.
- ☐ I am more likely to be a people-pleaser than a God-pleaser.
- ☐ I am overly concerned about getting credit for doing good things.
- ☐ I often think I am more humble than others.
- ☐ I often think I am smarter than my parents.
- ☐ I often think my needs are more important than other people's needs.
- ☐ I consider myself better than others because of my academic, artistic or athletic abilities and accomplishments.
- ☐ Other _____

For each of these areas that has been true in your life, pray out loud:

> Lord, I agree I have been prideful in the area of _____. Thank You for forgiving me for this pridefulness. I choose to humble myself and place all my confidence in You. Amen.

Step 6
Bondage Versus Freedom

The next Step to Freedom deals with the sins that have become habits in your life. If you have been caught in the vicious cycle of "sin-confess-sin-confess," realize that the road to victory is "sin-confess-**resist**" (see Jas. 4:7). Habitual sin often requires help from a trusted brother or sister in Christ. James 5:16 says, "Confess your sins to one another, and pray for one another, so that you may be healed. The effective prayer of a righteous man can accomplish much." Seek out a stronger Christian who will lift you up in prayer and hold you accountable in your areas of weakness.

Sometimes the assurance of 1 John 1:9 is sufficient: "If we confess our sins, He is faithful and righteous to forgive us our sins and to cleanse us from all unrighteousness."

Remember, confession is not saying "I'm sorry"; it is openly admitting "I did it." Whether you need the help of others or just the accountability of God, pray the following prayer out loud:

> Dear heavenly Father,
> You have told us to put on the Lord Jesus Christ and make no provision for the flesh in regard to its lust (Rom. 13:14). I agree that I have given in to sinful desires that wage war against my soul (1 Pet. 2:11).
> I thank You that in Christ my sins are forgiven, but I have broken Your holy law and given the devil an opportunity to wage war in my body (Rom. 6:12,13; Jas. 4:1; 1 Pet. 5:8).
> I come before Your presence now to admit these sins and to seek Your cleansing (1 John 1:9) that I may be freed from the bondage of sin. I now ask You to reveal to my mind the ways that I have broken Your moral law and grieved the Holy Spirit. In Jesus' precious name, I pray. Amen.

Many kinds of habitual sins can control us. The following list contains some of the more common sins of the flesh. Look through the list and ask the Holy Spirit to reveal to your mind which ones from the past or the present you need to confess. He may bring to mind others that are not here. For each one God reveals, pray the following prayer of confession from the heart. Note: sexual sins, eating disorders, substance abuse, abortion, suicidal tendencies and perfectionism will be dealt with later.

- ☐ stealing (shoplifting)
- ☐ lying
- ☐ fighting
- ☐ quarreling/arguing
- ☐ hatred
- ☐ jealousy, envy
- ☐ anger
- ☐ complaining and criticism
- ☐ impure thoughts
- ☐ eagerness for lustful pleasure
- ☐ cheating
- ☐ gossip/slander
- ☐ procrastination (putting things off)
- ☐ swearing
- ☐ greed/materialism
- ☐ apathy/laziness
- ☐ other_____

> Lord, I admit that I have committed the sin of _____. I thank You for Your forgiveness and cleansing. I turn away from this sin and turn to You, Lord. Strengthen me by Your Holy Spirit to obey You. In Jesus' name. Amen.

It is our responsibility to take control of sin in our bodies. We must not use our bodies or someone else's as instruments of unrighteousness (see Rom. 6:12,13). If you are or have been struggling with sexual sins (such as pornography, masturbation, heavy petting, heavy kissing, oral sex, same-sex relationships, voyeurism, phone sex or sexual intercourse), pray as follows:

Lord, I ask You to reveal to my mind every sexual use of my body as an instrument of unrighteousness. In Jesus' precious name, I pray. Amen.

As the Lord brings to your mind every sexual use of your body, whether it was done to you (i.e., rape, incest or any sexual abuse) or willingly by you, renounce every occasion:

Lord, I renounce (name the specific use of your body) with (name the person involved) and I ask You to break that sinful bond with (name).

After you have completed this exercise, commit your body to the Lord by praying out loud from your heart:

Lord, I renounce all these uses of my body as an instrument of unrighteousness, and ask You to break all bondages Satan has brought into my life through that involvement. I admit my participation. Lord, I choose to present my eyes, my mouth, my mind, my hands and feet, my whole body to You as instruments of righteousness. I now present my body to You as a living sacrifice, holy and acceptable unto You, and I choose to reserve the sexual use of my body for marriage only (Heb. 13:4).

I reject the lie of Satan that my body is not clean or that it is dirty or in any way unacceptable to You as a result of my past sexual experiences. Lord, I thank You that You have totally cleansed and forgiven me, and that You love me just as I am. Therefore, I can accept myself and my body as cleansed in Your eyes. In Jesus' name. Amen.

Special Prayers for Specific Needs

Homosexuality

Lord, I renounce the lie that You have created me or anyone else to be homosexual, and I agree that You clearly forbid homosexual behavior. I accept myself as a child of God and declare that You created me a man (or a woman). I renounce all homosexual thoughts, urges or drives, as well as any bondages of Satan, that have perverted my relationships with others. I announce that I am free to relate to the opposite sex and my own sex in the way that You intended. In Jesus' name. Amen.

Abortion

Note to men: Just as mothers are called to be responsible for the life God has entrusted to them, so, too, the father shares in this responsibility. If you have failed to fulfill your role as a father, pray the following prayer:

Lord, I confess that I was not a proper guardian of the life You entrusted to me and I admit that as sin. I choose to accept your forgiveness, and I now commit that child to You for Your care for all eternity. In Jesus' name. Amen.

Suicidal Tendencies

Lord, I renounce suicidal thoughts and any attempts I have made to take my own life or in any way injure myself. I renounce the lie that life is hopeless and that I can find peace and freedom by taking my own life. Satan is a thief, and he comes to steal, kill and destroy. I choose life in Christ who said He came to give me life and to give it to the full. I choose to accept Your forgiveness and to believe that there is always hope in Christ. In Jesus' name. Amen.

Eating Disorders or Cutting on Yourself

Lord, I renounce the lie that my value as a person is dependent upon my physical beauty, my weight or size. I renounce cutting myself, vomiting or using laxatives, or starving myself as a means of cleansing myself of evil or altering my appearance. I announce that only the blood of the Lord Jesus Christ cleanses me from sin.

I accept the reality that there may be sin present in me due to the lies I have believed and the wrongful use of my body, but I renounce the lie that I am evil or that any part of my body is evil. My body is the temple of the Holy Spirit and I belong to God. I am totally accepted by God in Christ just as I am. In Jesus' name. Amen.

Substance Abuse

Lord, I confess that I have misused substances (alcohol, tobacco, food, prescription or street drugs) for the purpose of pleasure, to escape reality or to cope with difficult problems. I confess that I have abused my body and programmed my mind in a harmful way. I have not allowed Your Holy Spirit to guide me. I ask Your forgiveness, and I reject any satanic connection or influence in my life because of my misuse of drugs or food. I cast my cares onto Christ who loves me, and I commit myself to no longer give in to substance abuse, but instead to allow the Holy Spirit to lead and empower me. In Jesus' name. Amen.

Drivenness and Perfectionism

Lord, I renounce the lie that my self-worth is dependent on my ability to perform. I announce the truth that my identity and sense of worth is found in who I am as Your child. I renounce seeking the approval and acceptance of other people and I choose to believe that I am already approved and accepted in Christ because of His death and resurrection for me. I choose to believe the truth that I have been saved, not by deeds that I have done, but according to Your mercy. I choose to believe that I am no longer under the curse of the law, because Jesus became a curse for me. I receive the free gift of life in Christ and choose to abide in Him. I renounce striving for perfection by living under the law. By Your grace, heavenly Father, I choose from this day forward to walk by faith according to what You said is true, by the power of the Holy Spirit.

After you have confessed all known sin, say:

I now confess these sins to You and claim through the blood of the Lord Jesus Christ my forgiveness and cleansing. I cancel all ground that evil spirits have gained through my willful involvement in sin. I ask this in the wonderful name of my Lord and Savior, Jesus Christ. Amen.

Step 7
Curses Versus Blessings

The last Step to Freedom is to renounce the sins of your ancestors and any curses that may have been placed on you. In giving the Ten Commandments, God said, "You shall not make for yourself an idol, or any likeness of what is in heaven above or on the earth beneath or in the water under the earth. You shall not worship them or serve them; for I, the Lord your God, am a jealous God, visiting the iniquity of the fathers on the children, on the third and the fourth generations of those who hate Me" (Exod. 20:4,5).

Ask the Lord to show you specifically what sins are characteristic of your family by praying the following prayer. Then list those sins in the space provided following the prayer:

> Dear heavenly Father,
> I ask You to reveal to my mind all the sins of my ancestors that are being passed down through family lines. I want to be free from those influences and walk in my new identity as a child of God. Amen.

As the Lord brings those areas of family sins to your mind, list them in the space provided. You will be specifically renouncing them later in this Step.

1. _____
2. _____
3. _____
4. _____

Demonic or familiar spirits can be passed on from one generation to the next if you don't renounce the sins of your ancestors and claim your new spiritual heritage in Christ. *You are not guilty for the sin of any ancestor,* but because of their sin, Satan may have gained access to your family.

Some problems, of course, are hereditary or acquired from an immoral environment. But other problems can be the result of generational sin. All three conditions can contribute toward causing someone to struggle with a particular sin.

In addition, deceived and evil people may try to curse you or satanic groups may try to target you. You have all the authority and protection you need in Christ to stand against such curses. In order to walk free from the sins of your ancestors and any demonic influences, read the following declaration and pray the following prayer out loud. Let the words come from your heart as you remember the authority you have in Christ Jesus.

Declaration

I here and now reject and disown all the sins of my ancestors. I specifically renounce the sins of (list here the areas of family sin the Lord revealed to you). As one who has been delivered from the domain of darkness and placed into the kingdom of God's Son, I cancel out all demonic working that was passed down to me from my family. As one who is crucified and raised with Jesus Christ and who sits with Him in heavenly places, I renounce all satanic assignments that are directed toward me and my ministry. I cancel out every curse that Satan and his workers have put on me. I announce to Satan and all his forces that Christ became a curse for me (Gal. 3:13) when He died for my sins on the cross. I reject any and every way in which Satan may claim ownership of me.

I belong to the Lord Jesus Christ who purchased me with His own blood. I reject all the blood sacrifices whereby Satan may claim ownership of me. I declare myself to be eternally and completely signed over and committed to the Lord Jesus Christ. By the authority that I have in Jesus Christ, I now command every spiritual enemy of the Lord Jesus Christ to leave my presence. I commit myself to my heavenly Father to do His will from this day forward.

Prayer

Dear heavenly Father,

I come to You as Your child, purchased by the blood of the Lord Jesus Christ. You are the Lord of the universe and the Lord of my life. I submit my body to You as an instrument of righteousness, a living sacrifice, that I may glorify You in my body. I ask You to fill me with Your Holy Spirit to lead and empower me to know and do Your will. I commit myself to the renewing of my mind in order to prove that Your will is good, perfect and acceptable for me. All this I do in the name and authority of the Lord Jesus Christ. Amen.

Something to Remember

Once you have gone through these seven Steps, you may find demonic influences attempting to gain control of your mind again, days or even months later. One person shared that she heard a spirit say to her mind "I'm back" two days after she had been set free. "No you're not!" she proclaimed aloud. The attack stopped immediately.

The devil is attracted to sin the same way flies are attracted to garbage. Get rid of the garbage and the flies will depart for smellier places. In the same way, walk in the truth, confessing all sin and forgiving those who hurt you, and the devil will have no place in your life to set up shop.

Realize that one victory does not mean the battles are over. Freedom must be maintained. After completing the Steps, one happy girl asked, "Will I always be like this?" I told her that she would stay free as long as she remained in right relationship with God. "Even if you slip and fall," I encouraged, "you know how to get right with God again."

One victim of incredible abuse shared this illustration: "It's like being forced to play a game with an ugly stranger in my own home. I kept losing and wanted to quit, but the ugly stranger wouldn't let me. Finally I called the police (a higher authority), and they came and escorted the stranger out. He knocked on the door, trying to regain entry, but this time I recognized his voice and didn't let him in."

What a beautiful illustration of gaining freedom in Christ. We call upon Jesus, the final and most powerful authority, and He escorts the powers of darkness out of our lives.

Maintaining Your Freedom

Freedom must be maintained. We cannot emphasize that point enough. You have won a very important battle in an ongoing war. Freedom will remain yours as long as you keep choosing truth and standing firm in the strength of the Lord. If new memories should surface, if you become aware of "lies" you have believed, or other non-Christian experiences you have had, renounce them and choose the truth. If you realize that there are some other people you need to forgive, Step Three will remind you of what to do. Most people have found it helpful to walk through the Steps to Freedom in Christ again. As you do, read the instructions carefully.

We recommend that you read the book *Stomping Out the Darkness* to strengthen your understanding of your identity in Christ. *The Bondage Breaker Youth Edition* will help you overcome spiritual problems. If you struggle with sexual bondage or desire to learn more about friendships and dating, we recommend *Purity Under Pressure*. To maintain your freedom, we strongly suggest the following as well:

1. Get involved in a loving church youth group or Bible study where you can be open and honest with other believers your age.
2. Study your Bible daily. Many great youth Bibles are available for you to use. Begin to study God's Word and memorize key verses. Remember it is *the truth that sets you free and it is the truth that keeps you free!* You may want to say the Statement of Truth out loud daily and study the verses. In addition, the youth devotionals *Extreme Faith*, *Reality Check* and *Ultimate Love* have been developed especially for you.
3. Learn to take every thought captive to the obedience of Christ. Assume responsibility for your thought life.

Don't let your mind go passive. Reject all lies, choose to focus on the truth and stand firm in your identity in Christ.

4. Don't drift away! It is very easy to become lazy in your thoughts and slip back into old habit patterns of thinking. Share your struggles openly with a trusted friend who will pray for you.

5. Don't expect others to fight your battles for you. They can't and they won't. Others can encourage you, but they can't think, pray, read the Bible or choose the truth for you.

6. Commit yourself to daily prayer. Prayer is dependence upon God. You can pray the following suggested prayers often and with confidence:

Daily Prayer

Dear heavenly Father,

I honor You as my Lord. I know that You are always present with me. You are the only all-powerful and only wise God. You are kind and loving in all Your ways. I love You and I thank You that I am united with Christ and spiritually alive in Him. I choose not to love the world, and I crucify the flesh and all its passions.

I thank You for the life that I now have in Christ, and I ask You to fill me and guide me with Your Holy Spirit so I may live my life free from sin. I declare my dependence upon You and I take my stand against Satan and all his lying ways. I choose to believe the truth and I refuse to be discouraged. You are the God of all hope and I am confident that You will meet my needs as I seek to live according to Your Word. I express with confidence that I can live a responsible life through Christ who strengthens me.

I now take my stand against Satan and command him and all his evil spirits to depart from me. I put on the whole armor of God. I submit my body as a living sacrifice and renew my mind by the living Word of God in order that I may prove that the will of God is good, acceptable and perfect. I ask these things in the powerful and precious name of my Lord and Savior, Jesus Christ. Amen.

Bedtime Prayer

Thank You, Lord, that You have brought me into Your family and have blessed me with every spiritual blessing in the heavenly realms in Christ. Thank You, too, for providing this time of renewal through sleep. I accept it as part of Your perfect plan for Your children and I trust You to guard my mind and my body during sleep. As I have thought about You and Your truth during the day, I choose to let those thoughts continue in my mind while I am asleep. I commit myself to You for Your protection from every attempt of Satan or his demons to attack me during the night. I commit myself to You as my rock, my fortress and my resting place. I pray in the strong name of the Lord Jesus Christ. Amen.

Home/Apartment/Room

After destroying all articles of false worship (crystals, good luck charms, occultic objects, games, etc.) from your room, pray out loud in your sleeping area:

Thank You, heavenly Father, for a place to live and be renewed by sleep. I ask You to set aside my room (or portion of room) as a place of safety for me. I renounce any worship given to false gods or spirits by other occupants, and I renounce any claim to this room (space) by Satan, based on what people have done here or what I have done in the past.

On the basis of my position as a child of God and a joint heir with Christ who has all the authority in heaven and on earth, I command all evil spirits to leave this place and never to return. I ask You, heavenly Father, to appoint guardian angels to protect me while I live here. I pray this in the name of the Lord Jesus Christ. Amen.

Continue to seek your identity and sense of worth through who you are in Christ. Renew your mind with the truth that your *acceptance, security* and *significance* is in Christ alone. Meditate on the following truths daily, reading the entire list out loud, morning and evening, over the next few weeks.

In Christ...
I Am Accepted

John 1:12	I am a child of God.
John 15:15	I am Jesus' chosen friend.
Romans 5:1	I am holy and acceptable to God (justified).
1 Corinthians 3:16	I am united to the Lord and am one spirit with Him.
1 Corinthians 6:19,20	I have been bought with a price. I belong to God.
1 Corinthians 12:27	I am a part of Christ's Body, part of His family.
Ephesians 1:1	I am a saint, a holy one.
Ephesians 1:5	I have been adopted as God's child.
Colossians 1:14	I have been bought back (redeemed) and forgiven of all my sins.
Colossians 2:10	I am complete in Christ.

I Am Secure

Romans 8:1,2	I am free forever from punishment.
Romans 8:28	I am sure all things work together for good.
Romans 8:31f.	I am free from any condemning charges against me.
Romans 8:35f.	I cannot be separated from the love of God.
Colossians 3:3	I am hidden with Christ in God.
Philippians 1:6	I am sure that the good work that God has started in me will be finished.
Ephesians 2:19	I am a citizen of heaven with the rest of God's family.
Hebrews 4:16	I can find grace and mercy in times of need.
1 John 5:18	I am born of God and the evil one cannot touch me.

I Am Significant

Matthew 5:13,14	I am salt and light for everyone around me.
John 15:1,5	I am a part of the true vine, joined to Christ and able to produce lots of fruit.
John 15:16	I am hand-picked by Jesus to bear fruit.
Acts 1:8	I am a Spirit-empowered witness of Christ.
1 Corinthians 3:16; 6:19	I am a temple where the Holy Spirit lives.
2 Corinthians 5:17f.	I am at peace with God and He has given me the work of making peace between Himself and other people.
2 Corinthians 6:1	I am God's coworker.
Ephesians 2:6	I am seated with Christ in heaven.
Ephesians 2:10	I am God's building project, His handiwork, created to do His work.
Philippians 4:13	I am able to do all things through Christ who gives me strength!

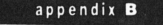

Seeking Forgiveness from Those We Have Hurt

S tep Three in the Steps to Freedom in Christ addresses the issue of how to forgive those who have offended me. Except in cases in which teens have been victimized and are innocent of any wrongdoing, sin usually occurs along a two-way street. In other words, young people need to seek forgiveness from others whom they have offended. The key passage in Scripture that explains this process is found in Matthew 5:23,24:

> "If therefore you are presenting your offering at the altar, and there remember that your brother has something against you, leave your offering there before the altar, and go your way; first be reconciled to your brother, and then come and present your offering."

Several points in these verses bear emphasizing.

First, the worshiper coming before God to offer a gift "remembers" that someone has something against him. The worshiper in this case is the offender. This does not mean the worshiper is to become introspective, probing into his own soul to "dig up dirt" to be confessed. Rather, when young people come before God in worship and prayer, they should ask the Lord to bring to mind anyone they have offended. It is the Lord who brings those incidents to remembrance.

Second, teens are responsible for going to the offended party to seek reconciliation only in cases in which the other person is aware of the offense. If young people have had jealous, lustful or angry thoughts toward another, of which the other is unaware, they are to be confessed to God alone.

An exception to this rule would be in the case where restitution needs to be made (e.g., something stolen to be returned, something broken to be paid for, someone's reputation restored). In those cases, the offended party may be unaware of who did the damage. Teens who are guilty of such offenses need to go to the offended party, seek forgiveness and be prepared to make restitution for the damage done.

Third, Jesus said that as soon as the worshiper remembers his offense, he should go and be reconciled. This is a prerequisite to acceptable worship of God. Apparently, God is not interested in hearing our prayers or receiving our worship until we have been reconciled to our brothers.

So how should teens go about seeking forgiveness and reconciliation with those against whom they have sinned? Here are some basic principles:

1. Regarding people of whom young people need to ask forgiveness, teens should clearly identify the offenses committed. They should write them out, including the wrong attitude behind the wrong action.
2. Teens preparing to seek forgiveness should make sure they have already forgiven the other person for any wrong(s) done to them (if applicable).
3. They should then think through the precise wording of what they will say when they ask forgiveness. They should:
   a. Label their action as "wrong."
   b. Go into only as much detail as is necessary for the offended person to understand what they are confessing.
   c. Make no defenses, alibis or excuses; do not project blame on anyone else.

   d. Not use their confession as a manipulative tool designed to elicit a reciprocal confession.
   e. Finish their confession with the question, "Will you forgive me?" and then wait for the answer.
4. Seek the right place and the right time to approach the offended person. Ask God to give you wisdom here and ask other mature believers if in doubt.
5. Teens should make their quest for forgiveness in person with family members or persons with whom they can talk face-to-face, with the following exception. In cases in which abuse or action of an immoral nature have occurred, young people should NEVER seek to handle this alone and face-to-face. If incest was involved, have a minister or counselor come with them in their face-to-face confession.
6. Except where no other means of communication are possible, DO NOT write a letter.
   a. A letter can easily be misread or misunderstood.
   b. A letter can be read by the wrong people, those having nothing to do with the offense or the confession.
   c. A letter can be kept when it should have been destroyed.
7. Once teens sincerely seek forgiveness, they are free.
8. If forgiveness is refused, and no hope of change on the part of the offended person seems possible, then teens should prayerfully and humbly commit their case to "the Judge" (God, our heavenly Father) and leave it there (see Matt. 5:25; 1 Pet. 2:21-23).
9. After forgiveness, fellowship with God in worship (see Matt. 5:24).

Parental Permission Form

I, _____, the parent, stepparent or legal guardian of _____, a minor child (under the age of 18), do hereby grant my permission for my child to be encouraged in a "freedom appointment." I understand and deem the persons leading this appointment to be encouragers in the Christian faith, who are helping my child to assume his or her responsibilities for finding freedom in Christ. I further understand and agree that my child is going through the "freedom appointment" voluntarily, is under no financial obligation and is free to leave at any time. I understand that no one in this process is functioning in a professional capacity, and I completely release them from all liability.

(Please Print)
Name of Minor Child _____ Sex _____

Name of Parent/Stepparent/Legal Guardian _____

Address _____

City _____ State _____ Zip _____

Phone No. (H) _____ (W) _____

Signed: _____ Date: _____

Statement of Understanding

(For Youth Under Age 18)

I understand that the encourager and prayer partners in this freedom appointment are not professional or licensed counselors, therapists, or medical or psychological practitioners.

I understand that the encourager and prayer partners in this freedom appointment are here to help me assume my responsibilities in finding freedom in Christ. I am also aware that my encourager or prayer partners may need to intervene if he or she suspects that a child (myself or others under the age of 18) or an elder (over age 65) is currently endangered by abuse or if I am a danger to myself or others.

I understand that I am free to leave at any time, that I am here voluntarily, and that I am under no financial obligation.

(Please Print)
Name _____

Address _____

City _____ State _____ Zip _____

Phone No. (H): _____ (W): _____

Signed: _____ Date: _____

Youth Confidential Personal Inventory

(Short Version)

Name_____

Address_____

City_____State_____Zip_____

Telephone ( )_____

Age_____

Sex: Female____ Male____ Highest GradeCompleted_____

Marital Status: Single_____ Married_____

Church Attend or Member_____

1. Do you consider yourself to be a Christian? No Yes Not Sure
2. How did you become a Christian?_____
   _____
   _____

    Never   Once in Awhile   Frequently   All the Time

3. Do you struggle with bad thoughts about God (for example; angry or hateful or cursing thoughts)?
4. Do you have a hard time concentrating when you pray (get distracted easily)?
5. Do you have trouble paying attention during sermons and Bible reading?
6. Do you think that the Christian life works for others, but not for you?

7. Have you struggled with really bad thoughts (lustful, hurtful, angry, etc.) that you just can't seem to get rid of?
8. Have you ever heard "voices" in your head, or have you had persistent negative nagging thoughts in your mind that made you feel bad?
9. Do you have trouble sleeping too little or too much?
10. Do you have nightmares?
11. Have you experienced some supernatural presence in your room (seen, heard or felt) that scared you?
12. Have you had an imaginary friend who talked to you?

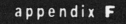

Youth Confidential Personal Inventory

(Long Version)

Personal Information

Name_____

Phone_____

Address_____

Church Affiliation:

Present_____

Past_____

School_____Grade_____

Family History (Religious)

1. Have any of your parents, siblings, grandparents or great grand-parents, to your knowledge, ever been involved in any occultic, cultic or non-Christian religious practices? Which ones?

2. Briefly explain your parents' Christian experience (i.e., are they Christians and do they profess and live their Christianity?).

Family (General)

1. Are your parents presently married or divorced?

2. Who do you currently live with?

3. How many brothers and sisters do you have? What are their ages?

4. How do you feel you get along with your parents?

5. How do you feel you get along with your brothers and sisters?

6. Do both parents work away from home?

7. Is your father clearly the head of the home or are roles reversed where your mother rules the home? Explain.

8. How does your father treat your mother?

9. To your knowledge, has either of your parents ever had an affair?

10. To your knowledge, has there been any sexual abuse within your family?

11. Are you adopted? If yes, how do you feel about being adopted?

Health (Family)
1. Are there any addictive problems in your family history (alcohol, drugs, etc.)?

2. Is there any history of mental illness?

3. Is your family concerned about proper:

Diet

Exercise

Rest

Moral Climate
How would you rate the atmosphere in which you are being raised:

Put an X in the box that best fits your experience

☐ Always Let Me Do What I Want
☐ Usually Let Me Do What I Want
☐ Sometimes Let Me Do What I Want
☐ Hardly Ever Let Me Do What I Want
☐ Never Let Me Do What I Want
☐ Clothing
☐ Dating
☐ Movies/TV
☐ Music
☐ Books
☐ Decision
    Making
☐ Drinking
☐ Smoking
☐ Church
    Attendance
☐ Sex

1. Do you talk with your parents about your friendships?

2. Do you talk to your parents about your relationships with the opposite sex?

3. Have you ever talked to your parents about sex? Do you feel free to discuss the issue of sex with them?

4. How far do you feel an unmarried Christian couple can go physically in a relationship before it is wrong? (Put an X in one box.)
    ☐ Check them out/look
    ☐ Hold hands/hug
    ☐ Kiss
    ☐ Make out
    ☐ Up shirt/light touching

☐ Down pants/major touching
☐ All the way/sexual intercourse

5. What is the farthest that you have gone physically in a relationship with the opposite sex? (Put an X in one box.)
   ☐ Check them out/look
   ☐ Hold hands/hug
   ☐ Kiss
   ☐ Make out
   ☐ Up shirt/light touching
   ☐ Down pants/major touching
   ☐ All the way/sexual intercourse

Physical

1. Describe your eating habits (i.e., are you a junk-food addict, do you eat regularly or sporadically, is your diet balanced, etc.?).

2. Do you have any addiction or cravings you find difficult to control (sweets, drugs, alcohol, food in general, etc.)?

3. Have you ever had a problem with anorexia or bulimia? Explain.

4. Are you presently under any kind of medication for either physical or psychological reasons?

5. Do you have any problems sleeping? Are you having any recurring nightmares or disturbances?

6. Does your present schedule allow for regular periods of rest and relaxation?

7. Have you ever physically been beaten or sexually molested? Explain.

Mental

1. Which of the following have you or are you presently struggling with? (Put an X in as many boxes as apply.)
   ☐ Daydreaming
   ☐ Inferiority
   ☐ Worry
   ☐ Fantasy
   ☐ Insecurity
   ☐ Compulsive thoughts
   ☐ Lying
   ☐ Lustful thoughts
   ☐ Inadequacy
   ☐ Doubts
   ☐ Obsessive thoughts
   ☐ Bad thoughts about God
   ☐ Dizziness
   ☐ Foul language

2. Do you spend much time wishing you were somebody else or fantasizing that you were a different person, or possibly imagining yourself living at a different time, place or under different circumstances? Explain.

3. How many hours of TV do you watch per week?_____ List your three favorite programs:

4. How many hours a week do you spend reading?_____ What do you read primarily?

5. Would you consider yourself to be an optimist or a pessimist (i.e., do you have a tendency to see the good in people and life, or the bad)?

6. Have you ever thought that maybe you were "going crazy" and do you presently fear that possibility? Explain.

7. Do you spend time reading the Bible? When and to what extent?

8. Do you find prayer difficult mentally? Explain.

9. When attending church or other Christian activities, are you plagued with dirty thoughts, jealousies or other mental harassment? Explain.

10. Do you listen to music a lot and what type do you enjoy the most?

11. Have you ever thought about suicide? Explain.

12. Have you ever attempted suicide? If yes, when and why?

13. Do you enjoy school?

14. How do you get along with your teachers and other school authorities?

Emotional
1. Which of the following emotions have you or are you presently having difficulty controlling? (Put an X in as many boxes as apply.)
   - ☐ Frustration
   - ☐ Anger
   - ☐ Anxiety
   - ☐ Loneliness
   - ☐ Worthlessness
   - ☐ Depression
   - ☐ Hatred
   - ☐ Bitterness
   - ☐ Fear of death
   - ☐ Fear of losing your mind
   - ☐ Fear of committing suicide
   - ☐ Fear of hurting loved ones
   - ☐ Fear of terminal illness
   - ☐ Fear of going to hell
   - ☐ Fear of _____
   - ☐ Fear of _____

2. Which of the above listed emotions do you feel are sinful? Why?

3. Concerning your emotions, whether positive or negative, which of the following describes you? (Put an X in the box that best applies to you.)
   - ☐ Freely express them with others
   - ☐ You acknowledge your emotions as being there but are hesitant to share them with others
   - ☐ You tend to hide your emotions
   - ☐ You find it safest not to share how you feel
   - ☐ You tend to ignore your emotions because you cannot trust your feelings to be true
   - ☐ Consciously or subconsciously deny or bury them; it's too painful to deal with them

4. Is there someone in your life whom you know that you could be emotionally honest with right now (i.e., you could tell this person exactly how you feel about yourself, life and other people)?

5. How important is it that we are emotionally honest before God, and do you feel that you are? Explain.

Spiritual History
1. If you were to die tonight, do you know where you would spend eternity?

2. Suppose you did die tonight and appeared before God in heaven, and He were to ask you, "Why should I let you into heaven?" How would you answer Him?

3. First John 5:11,12 says, "God has given us eternal life, and this life is in His Son. He who has the Son has the life; he who does not have the Son of God does not have the life."
   Do you have the Son of God in you?

4. When did you receive Him?
5. How do you know that you have received Him?

6. Do you constantly have doubts concerning your salvation?

7. Are you spending time with other Christians and, if so, where and when?

8. Are you attending a local church where the Bible is taught, and do you contribute to your church through serving?

Non-Christian Spiritual Checklist
(Please check all those that apply to you.)

- ☐ Out of body experience (astral projection)
- ☐ Ouija board
- ☐ Bloody Mary
- ☐ Light as a feather (or other occult games)
- ☐ Table lifting or body lifting
- ☐ Magic Eight Ball
- ☐ Using spells or curses
- ☐ Attempting to control others by putting thoughts into their heads
- ☐ Automatic writing
- ☐ Spirit guides
- ☐ Fortune-telling
- ☐ Tarot cards
- ☐ Palm reading
- ☐ Astrology/horoscopes
- ☐ Hypnosis
- ☐ Seances
- ☐ Black or white magic
- ☐ Dungeons & Dragons (or other fantasy role-playing games)
- ☐ Video or computer games involving occult powers or cruel violence
- ☐ Blood pacts or cutting yourself on purpose
- ☐ Objects of worship/crystals/good luck charms
- ☐ Sexual spirits
- ☐ Martial Arts (involving Eastern mysticism, meditation or devotion to sensei)

- ☐ Buddhism (including Zen)
- ☐ Rosicrucianism
- ☐ Hinduism
- ☐ Mormonism (Latter-Day Saints)
- ☐ Jehovah's Witnesses
- ☐ New Age
- ☐ New Age medicine
- ☐ Masons
- ☐ Christian Science
- ☐ Science of the Mind
- ☐ Science of Creative Intelligence
- ☐ The Way International
- ☐ Unification Church (Moonies)
- ☐ The Forum (EST)
- ☐ Church of the Living Word
- ☐ Children of God (Children of Love)
- ☐ Worldwide Church of God (Armstrong)
- ☐ Scientology
- ☐ Unitarianism
- ☐ Roy Masters
- ☐ Silva Mind Control
- ☐ Transcendental Meditation (TM)
- ☐ Yoga
- ☐ Hare Krishna
- ☐ Bahaism
- ☐ Native American Spirit Worship
- ☐ Idols of rock stars, actors/actresses, sports heroes, etc.
- ☐ Islam
- ☐ Black Muslim

Glossary of Biblical Truth for Teen Struggles

(25 Common Problems)

Anger
   Ephesians 4:26,27; James 1:19,20
Apathy/Laziness
   Proverbs 6:6-11; Romans 12:9-13; Galatians 6:9,10
Assurance of Salvation (lack of)
   John 10:27-30; Hebrews 13:5; 1 John 5:11-13
Broken Relationships
   Psalm 63:1-8; Romans 8:28,29
Busyness
   Psalm 46:10; Matthew 11:28-30; Luke 10:38-42
Critical Spirit/Gossip
   Ephesians 4:29,30; James 4:11,12
Depression
   Psalm 42:11; Romans 15:13; 2 Thessalonians 2:16,17
Drunkenness/Drugs
   Proverbs 23:25-29; Ephesians 5:18
Eating Disorders
   1 Corinthians 6:19,20; 1 Timothy 4:1-5
Fear
   Joshua 1:8,9; Isaiah 41:10; 2 Timothy 1:7
Greed/Materialism
   1 Timothy 6:8-12; Hebrews 13:5
Guilt
   Romans 8:1; 1 John 1:9

Lack of Guidance/Confusion
    Psalm 119:105; Proverbs 3:5-7; James 1:5-8
Loneliness
    Romans 8:38,39; Hebrews 3:12,13
Occult Practices
    Deuteronomy 18:9-13; Isaiah 8:19,20
Peer Pressure
    Proverbs 13:20; Romans 12:1,2; 1 Corinthians 15:33
Perfectionism
    Romans 15:7; Colossians 3:23,24
Poor Self-Image
    1 Samuel 16:7; Psalm 139:13-18
Pride
    Romans 12:3; James 4:6,7; 1 Peter 5:5,6
Rebellion
    Romans 13:1-7; Ephesians 6:1-3; 1 Peter 2:13-15
Selfishness
    Philippians 2:3,4; James 3:13-18; 4:1-4
Sexual Immorality
    1 Corinthians 6:18-20; 1 Thessalonians 4:3-8; 2 Timothy 2:22
Temptation
    Psalm 119:9-11; 1 Corinthians 10:12,13
Unforgiveness/Bitterness
    Ephesians 4:31,32; Hebrews 12:14,15
Worry
    Philippians 4:6,7; 1 Peter 5:6-10

Freedom in Christ Resources

Part One: *Resolving Personal Conflicts*

Victory Over the Darkness
by Neil Anderson

Start here! This best-seller combined with *The Bondage Breaker* will show you how to find your freedom in Christ. Realize the power of your identity in Christ!

Paper $10 • 245 pp. B001
Study Guide • Paper $9 • 139 pp. G001

Living Free in Christ
by Neil Anderson

Based on the inspirational "Who Am I?" list from *Victory Over the Darkness*, here are 36 powerful chapters and prayers that will transform your life and dramatically show how Christ meets all of your deepest needs!

Paper $13 • 310 pp. B008
Free in Christ Audio $10 • A030

Daily in Christ
by Neil and Joanne Anderson

This uplifting 365 day devotional will encourage, motivate and challenge you to live *daily in Christ*. There's a one-page devotional and brief heart-felt prayer for each day. Celebrate and experience your freedom all year.

Hard $17 • 365 pp. B010

Breaking Through to Spiritual Maturity
by Neil Anderson

This is a dynamic Group Study of *Victory Over the Darkness* and *The Bondage Breaker*. Complete with teaching notes for a 13 week (or 26 week) Bible study, with reproducible handouts. Ideal for Sunday school classes, Bible studies, and discipleship groups.

Paper $17 • 151 pp. G003

Resolving Personal Conflicts
by Neil Anderson

This series covers the first half of Dr. Anderson's exciting conference. Learn the truth about who you are in Christ, how to renew your mind, heal damaged emotions and truly forgive others (Part 1 of a 2-part series).

Video Tape Set $95 • 8 lessons V001
Audio Tape Set $40 • 8 lessons A001
Additional workbooks $5 • Paper 32 pp. W001

Resolving Spiritual Conflicts & Cross-Cultural Ministry
by Dr. Timothy Warner

This series has powerful lessons on missions, world view and warfare relationships that are extremely helpful for every Christian. It provides key insights for spiritual growth and ministry.

Video Tape Set $85 • 8 lessons V005
Audio Tape Set $35 • 8 lessons A005
Additional workbooks $8 • paper 47 pp. W005

Part Two: *Resolving Spiritual Conflicts*

The Bondage Breaker
by Neil Anderson

This best-seller shares the definitive process of breaking bond- ages and the *Steps to Freedom in Christ*. Read this with *Victory Over the Darkness* and you will be able to resolve your personal and spiritual conflicts.

Paper $10 • 247 pp. B002
Study Guide • Paper $6 • 121 pp. G002

The Steps to Freedom in Christ
by Neil Anderson

This is a handy version of the *Steps to Freedom in Christ*, the discipleship counseling process from *The Bondage Breaker*. It is ideal for personal use or for helping another person who wants to find his freedom.

Paper $2 • 19 pp. G004

The Steps to Freedom in Christ Video
with Neil Anderson

In this special video experience, Dr. Neil Anderson personally leads you or a loved one through the bondage-breaking Steps to Freedom in Christ in the privacy of your living room. Includes *The Steps to Freedom in Christ* booklet.

Video $20 • 70 minutes • V010

Spiritual Warfare
by Dr. Timothy Warner

This concise book offers balanced, biblical insights on spiritual warfare with practical information and ammunition for winning the spiritual battle. Every reader will benefit by learning from the author's extensive experience.

Paper $9 • 160 pp. B007

Resolving Spiritual Conflicts
by Neil Anderson

This series offers the second half of Dr. Anderson's exciting conference. Every believer needs to fully understand his position, authority and protection in Christ, and the enemy's tactics (Part 2 of a 2-part series).

Video Tape Set $95 • 8 lessons V002
Audio Tape Set $40 • 8 lessons A002
Additional workbooks $6 • Paper 49 pp. W002

Available at your local Christian bookstore or from
Freedom in Christ
491 E. Lambert Road
La Habra, CA 90631-6136

Phone: (562) 691-9128 Fax (562) 691-4035
Internet: www.freedominchrist.com
Email: 73430.2630@compuserve.com

Freedom in Christ Resources

Helping Others Find Freedom in Christ
by Neil Anderson

This book provides comprehensive, hands-on biblical discipleship counseling training for lay leaders, counselors and pastors, equipping them to help others. This resource is Part 3, continuing from the message of Parts 1 and 2.

Hard $17 • 297 pp. B016   Paper $12 • 297 pp. B015

Helping Others Find Freedom in Christ Training Manual and Study Guide
by Neil Anderson and Tom McGee

This companion to *Helping Others Find Freedom in Christ* provides leadership training and a step-by-step plan to establish a freedom ministry (Discipleship Counseling ministry) in your church or organization.

Paper $12 • 229 pp. G015

Helping Others Find Freedom in Christ Video Training Program

This Video Training Program is a complete training kit for churches and groups who want to establish a freedom ministry using the *Steps to Freedom in Christ*. Includes four 45-minute video lessons, a *Helping Others Find Freedom in Christ* book, a *Training Manual/Study Guide* and six *Steps to Freedom in Christ* guidebooks.

Video Training Program $90 • V015
Live Counseling Demonstration Video $25 • V016

Released From Bondage
by Neil Anderson

This book shares true stories of freedom from obsessive thoughts, compulsive behaviors, guilt, satanic ritual abuse, childhood abuse and demonic strongholds, combined with helpful commentary from Dr. Anderson.

Paper $13 • 258 pp. B006

Freedom From Addiction
by Neil Anderson and Mike and Julia Quarles

A book like no other on true recovery! This unique Christ-centered model has helped thousands break free from alcoholism, drug addiction and other addictive behaviors. The Quarles' amazing story will encourage every reader!

Hard $19 • 356 pp. B018   Paper $13 • 356 pp. B019
Video Study $90 • V019

Spiritual Conflicts and Counseling
by Neil Anderson

This series presents advanced counseling insights and practical, biblical answers to help others find their freedom in Christ. It is the full content from Dr. Anderson's advanced seminar of the same name.

Video Tape Set $95 • 8 lessons V003
Audio Tape Set $40 • 8 lessons A003
Additional Workbooks $8 • Paper 53 pp. W003

Setting Your Church Free
by Neil Anderson and Charles Mylander

This powerful book reveals how pastors and church leaders can lead their entire churches to freedom by discovering the key issues of both corporate bondage and corporate freedom. A must-read for every church leader.

Hard $17 • 352 pp. B012   Paper $12 • 352 pp. B013

Setting Your Church Free Video
by Neil Anderson and Charles Mylander

This leadership series presents the powerful principles taught in *Setting Your Church Free*. Ideal for church staffs and boards to study and discuss together. The series ends with the *Steps to Setting Your Church Free*.

Video Tape Set $95 • 8 lessons V006
Audio Tape Set $40 • 8 lessons A006
Additional workbooks $6 • paper 42 pp. W006

Topical Resources

Walking in the Light
by Neil Anderson

Everyone wants to know God's will for their life. Dr. Anderson explains the fascinating spiritual dimensions of divine guidance and how to avoid spiritual counterfeits. Includes a personal application guide for each chapter.

Paper $13 • 234 pp. B011

A Way of Escape
by Neil Anderson

Talking about sex is never easy. This vital book provides real answers for sexual struggles, unwanted thoughts, compulsive habits or a painful past. Don't learn to just cope, learn how to resolve your sexual issues in Christ.

Paper $10 • 238 pp. B014

The Common Made Holy
by Neil Anderson and Robert Saucy

An extraordinary book on how Christ transforms the life of a believer. Dr. Anderson and Dr. Saucy provide answers to help resolve the confusion about our "perfect" identity in Christ in our "imperfect" world.

Hard $17 • 375 pp. B017
Study Guide $8 • G017

The Christ Centered Marriage
by Neil Anderson and Charles Mylander

Husbands and wives, discover and enjoy your freedom in Christ to gether! Break free from old habit patterns and enjoy greater intimacy, joy and fulfillment.

Hard $19 • 300 pp. B020
Marriage Steps $4 • 36 pp. G020
Video Seminar $89.99 • UPC 607135.001218

Freedom in Christ Resources
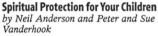

Parenting Resources

Spiritual Protection for Your Children
by Neil Anderson and Peter and Sue Vanderhook

The fascinating true story of an average middle-class American family's spiritual battle on the home front and the lessons we can all learn about protecting our families from the enemy's attacks. Includes helpful prayers for children of various ages.
Hardcover $19 · 300 pp. B021

The Seduction of Our Children
by Neil Anderson and Steve Russo

A battle is raging for the minds of our children. It's a battle parents <u>must</u> win. This timely book will prepare parents to counter the world's assault against their families. Includes helpful prayers for children of various ages.
Paper $9 · 245 pp. B004

The Seduction of Our Children Video
by Neil Anderson

This parenting series will change the way you view the spiritual development of your children. Helpful insights are offered on many parenting issues, such as discipline, communication and spiritual oversight of children. A panel of experts share their advice.

Video Tape Set $85 · 6 lessons V002
Audio Tape Set $35 · 6 lessons A002
Additional workbooks $4 · 49 pp. W002

Youth Resources

Stomping Out the Darkness
by Neil Anderson and Dave Park

This youth version of *Victory Over the Darkness* shows youth how to break free and discover the joy of their identity in Christ (Part 1 of 2).
Paper $9 · 210 pp. B101
Study Guide Paper $8 · 137 pp. G101

The Bondage Breaker Youth Edition
by Neil Anderson and Dave Park

This youth best-seller shares the process of breaking bondages and the *Youth Steps to Freedom in Christ*. Read this with *Stomping Out the Darkness* (Part 2 of 2). Paper $8 · 227 pp. B102
Study Guide Paper $6 · 128 pp. G102

Busting Free!
by Neil Anderson and Dave Park

This is a dynamic Group Study of *Stomping Out the Darkness* and *The Bondage Breaker Youth Edition*. It has complete teaching notes for a 13 week (or 26 week) Bible study, with reproducible hand-outs. Ideal for Sunday school classes, Bible studies, and youth discipleship groups of all kinds. **Paper $17 · 163 pp. G103**

Youth Topics

Helping Young People Find Freedom in Christ
by Neil Anderson and Rich Miller

This youth version provides comprehensive, hands-on biblical discipleship counseling training for parents, youth workers and youth pastors, equipping them to help young people. This resource is Part 3 continuing from the message of Parts 1 and 2.
Paper $13 · 300 pp. B112

Know Light, No Fear
by Neil Anderson and Rich Miller

In this youth version of *Walking in the Light* young people learn how to know God's will for their lives. They will discover key truths about divine guidance and helpful warnings for avoiding spiritual counterfeits.
Paper $10 · 250 pp. B111

Purity Under Pressure
by Neil Anderson and Dave Park

Real answers for real world pressures! Youth will find out the difference between being friends, dating and having a relationship. No hype, no big lectures; just straightforward talk about living free in Christ.
Paper $8 · 200 pp. B104

To My Dear Slimeball
by Rich Miller

In the spirit of C. S. Lewis' *Screwtape Letters*, this humorous story, filled with biblical truth, is an allegory of the spiritual battle every believer faces. Discover how 15-year old David's life is amazingly similar to your own.
Paper $8 each · 250 pp. B103

Youth Devotionals

These four 40-day devotionals help young people understand God's love and their identity in Christ. Teens will learn to establish a positive spiritual habit of getting into God's Word on a daily basis.

Extreme Faith
Paper $8
204 pp. B106

Reality Check
Paper $8
200 pp. B107

Awesome God
Paper $8
200 pp. B108

Ultimate Love
Paper $8
200 pp. B109

How Freedom in Christ Resources Work Together

This chart shows "at a glance" how Freedom in Christ's resources AND conferences interrelate and their correct order of progression from basic to advanced.

Part One

THIS IS FREEDOM IN CHRIST'S CORE MESSAGE OF RESOLVING PERSONAL AND SPIRITUAL CONFLICTS

- *Victory Over the Darkness*
- *Victory Over the Darkness Study Guide*
- *Living Free in Christ*
- *Daily in Christ*

- *Breaking Through to Spiritual Maturity Teaching Guide*
  (Covers parts 1 and 2)

"Resolving Personal Conflicts" and "Resolving Spiritual Conflicts"
Conference and Audios/Videos
(Covers Parts 1 and 2)

"Free in Christ" Audio and "Steps to Freedom in Christ" Video

"Resolving Spiritual Conflicts and Cross-cultural Ministry"
Conference and Audios/Videos
(Covers Parts 1 and 2)

"Shepherd's Time Out" Conference
(Covers Parts 1, 2 and 3)

"If you hold to My teaching, you are really My disciples. Then you will know the truth, and the truth will set you free."

*See separate list for youth or young adult resources!

Part Two

- *The Bondage Breaker*
- *The Bondage Breaker Study Guide*
- *Steps to Freedom in Christ*
- *Spiritual Warfare*

Part Three

PRACTICAL BIBLICAL ANSWERS FOR DISCIPLESHIP COUNSELING

- *Helping Others Find Freedom in Christ*
- *Helping Others Find Freedom in Christ Training Manual and Study Guide*
- *Released From Bondage*
- *Freedom From Addiction*

"Spiritual Conflicts and Counseling" Audios/Videos

"Helping Others Find Freedom in Christ" Video Training Program

"Helping Others Find Freedom in Christ" Counseling Demonstration Video

"Church Leadership and Discipleship Counseling" Conference

"Freedom From Addiction" Conference and Video Study

Part Four

CHURCH LEADERSHIP

- *Setting Your Church Free*
- *Steps to Setting Your Church Free*

"Setting Your Church Free" Conference and Audios/Videos

Topical

- *Walking in the Light*
- *A Way of Escape*
- *The Common Made Holy*
- *The Common Made Holy Study Guide*
- *The Christ-Centered Marriage* (3 versions of the marriage Steps)
- *Spiritual Protection for Your Children*
- *The Seduction of Our Children*
- *Rivers of Revival*

"The Christ-Centered Marriage" Conference and Video Seminar

"The Seduction of Our Children" Conference and Audios/Videos

Contact Freedom in Christ at:

491 E. Lambert Road
La Habra, CA 90631-6136
Phone: (562) 691-9128
Fax (562) 691-4035

World Wide Web:
www.freedominchrist.com

Email:
73430.2630@compuserve.com

Give Youth the Word
YouthBuilders Group Bible Studies

These high-involvement, discussion-oriented, Bible-centered studies work together to give you a comprehensive program, seeing your young people through their high school years–and beyond. From respected youth worker Jim Burns.

The Word on:

The Word on: Sex, Drugs & Rock 'N' Roll
ISBN 08307.16424

Prayer and the Devotional Life
ISBN 08307.16432

Basics of Christianity
ISBN 08307.16440

Being a Leader, Serving Others & Sharing Your Faith
ISBN 08307.16459

Helping Friends in Crisis
ISBN 08307.16467

The Life of Jesus
ISBN 08307.16475

Finding and Using Your Spiritual Gifts
ISBN 08307.17897

The Sermon on the Mount
ISBN 08307.17234

Spiritual Warfare
ISBN 08307.17242

The New Testament
ISBN 08307.17250

The Old Testament
ISBN 08307.17269

Junior High Builders

Each reproducible manual has 13 Bible studies with games, activities and clip art for handouts.

Christian Basics
ISBN 08307.16963

The Life and Times of Jesus Christ
ISBN 08307.16971

The Parables of Jesus
ISBN 08307.16998

Growing as a Christian
ISBN 08307.17005

Christian Relationships
ISBN 08307.17013

Symbols of Christ
ISBN 08307.17021

The Power of God
ISBN 08307.17048

Faith in Action
ISBN 08307.17056

Peace, Love and Truth
ISBN 08307.17064

Great Old Testament Leaders
ISBN 08307.17072

Great Truths from Ephesians
ISBN 08307.17080

Lifestyles of the Not-So-Famous from the Bible
ISBN 08307.17099

Ask for these resources at your local Christian bookstore.

Gospel Light

Resources Youth Can Grow On!

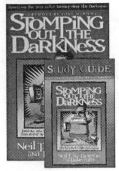

Stomping Out the Darkness
Neil T. Anderson
& Dave Park

Here is the powerful message from **Victory over the Darkness** written especially for young people. Provides youth with keys to their identity, worth, and acceptance as children of God.

Paperback
ISBN 08307.16408
Study Guide
ISBN 08307.17455

Getting Ready for the Guy/Girl Thing
Greg Johnson
& Susie Shellenberger

Wisdom to help 5th to 8th graders form godly relationships.

Paperback
ISBN 08307.14855

Radical Christianity
Jim Burns

Get down to core issues of how teens can make their lives count for Christ. You'll get hands-on, interactive chapters that cover topics like priorities, the cost of discipleship, integrity and more!

Paperback
ISBN 08307.17927
Video Seminar
SPCN 85116.01082

Radical Love
Jim Burns

The very best in life comes by following God's plan. Here's a frank discussion of things that today's youth are facing–like relationships and sex–and how to find God's best.

Paperback
ISBN 08307.17935
Video Seminar
SPCN 85116.00922

What Hollywood Won't Tell You About Sex, Love and Dating
Greg Johnson
& Susie Shellenberger

Youth learn things like how to have a conversation with someone of the opposite sex. It is possible.

Paperback
ISBN 08307.16777

So What's a Christian Anyway?

A fun and simple way to explain the basics of Christianity to youth. It's a 32-page comic-book size evangelism tool.

Paperback
ISBN 08307.13972

90 Days Through the New Testament
Jim Burns

A 90-day growth experience through the New Testament that lays the foundation for developing a daily time with God.

Paperback
ISBN 08307.14561

What the Bible is All About for Young Explorers
Frances Blankenbaker

The basics of *What the Bible Is All About,* in a format designed to make the Bible more approachable for youth.

Hardcover • ISBN
08307.11791